A Theory of Justice for Animals

Animal Rights in a Nonideal World

ROBERT GARNER

OXFORD

UNIVERSITY PRESS

OXFORD
UNIVERSITY PRESS

Oxford University Press is a department of the University of Oxford.
It furthers the University's objective of excellence in research, scholarship,
and education by publishing worldwide.

Oxford   New York
Auckland   Cape Town   Dar es Salaam   Hong Kong   Karachi
Kuala Lumpur   Madrid   Melbourne   Mexico City   Nairobi
New Delhi   Shanghai   Taipei   Toronto

With offices in
Argentina   Austria   Brazil   Chile   Czech Republic   France   Greece
Guatemala   Hungary   Italy   Japan   Poland   Portugal   Singapore
South Korea   Switzerland   Thailand   Turkey   Ukraine   Vietnam

Oxford is a registered trademark of Oxford University Press in the UK and certain other
countries.

Published in the United States of America by
Oxford University Press
198 Madison Avenue, New York, NY 10016

Library of Congress Cataloging-in-Publication Data
Garner, Robert, 1960–
A theory of justice for animals : animal rights in a nonideal world / Robert Garner.
pages cm
ISBN 978-0-19-993631-1 (hbk. : alk. paper) – ISBN 978-0-19-993633-5 (pbk. : alk. paper)
1. Animal rights. I. Title.
HV4708.G387 2013
179'.3–dc23
2012051036

1 3 5 7 9 8 6 4 2
Printed in the United States of America
on acid-free paper

Contents

Acknowledgments

THIS BOOK HAS taken a number of years to research and write. It would have taken me longer had the Leverhulme Trust not awarded me a fellowship that gave me one year free from teaching and administrative responsibilities, and had my institution, the University of Leicester, not granted me a matching period of study leave. Thank you to them both. Chapter 2 of this book began life as two separate articles, and I thank the publishers of the journals concerned for their permission to include substantial parts of them here. These articles are "Rawls, Animals and Justice: New Literature, Same Response," *Res Publica* (2012) 18:159–172 and "Much ado about nothing?: Barry, justice and animals," Critical Review of International Social and Political Philosophy (2012) 15 (3): 363–376.

I have tried out the arguments contained in this book in a variety of forums and I would like to thank the participants of the various seminars, workshops, and conferences I have presented at for their comments and criticisms. Alasdair Cochrane and I have discussed animal ethics on many occasions and I have benefitted enormously from his knowledge and friendship. I would also like to thank Dan Lyons and Angela Roberts for their support and encouragement. Last but not least, Filza Qureshi has been gracefully accepting of the time-consuming nature of preparing an academic research monograph (the REF has a lot to answer for!), and has even made available her own professional expertise to ensure I stayed healthy enough to finish writing it. The book is dedicated to her.

Robert Garner
Leicester
November 2012

I

Introduction: Animals, Justice, and Nonideal Theory

THIS BOOK IS original in two principal ways. Firstly, it attempts to consider our treatment of animals within the prism of justice rather than what I take to be the broader area of ethics or morality (the two latter words are used interchangeably). Secondly, to my knowledge, this is the first work that attempts to apply both ideal and nonideal theory to animal ethics and, in particular, to develop a nonideal theory of justice for animals. In short, the theory of justice for animals developed in this book recognizes the need to reconcile desirable ethical principles concerning the moral status of animals with the constraints that limit what is socially, politically, and economically possible to achieve, at least at the present time.

There are a number of major reasons for considering the moral status of animals through the prism of justice. Firstly, justice is a central concept in political theory, enjoying an extremely high status. Not to be regarded as a recipient of justice, therefore, is apparently a serious obstacle to being regarded as a morally considerable entity deserving of respectful treatment. Despite this, secondly, relatively few political philosophers have tackled the question of what is owed to animals.[1] In addition, thirdly, justice has been ignored, by and large, by many of the key animal ethicists. Many who seek to argue for a considerable moral status for animals have either not used the language of justice, or, by contrast, have merely assumed that animals can be recipients of justice. In the former category, most notably, is Peter Singer. There is no index reference to justice, for instance, in his seminal work *Animal Liberation* (1990). An example of the latter category is Tom Regan (1984), who merely assumes that a rights-based discourse is identical to one founded on justice, and that justice and morality are one and the same thing. As a consequence, for Regan, excluding animals as recipients of justice is equivalent to depriving them of any direct moral worth.

This book asks three interrelated questions. In the first place, it asks whether animals can be worthy recipients of principles of justice. Secondly, it asks whether animals can benefit from being incorporated within a theory of justice, as opposed to being merely beneficiaries of a moral theory, and conversely whether there is a sphere of morality, independently of justice, of sufficient weight within which the interests of animals can be recognized and protected. Thirdly, it asks, insofar as they are worthy recipients of justice, what are animals due as a matter of justice? The expectation is that by the end of the book theorists of social justice will accept that their subject is incomplete without taking seriously the issues raised by our treatment of animals.[2] Equally, it is also hoped that the application of ideas current in political theory to the issue of our treatment of animals will prove valuable, if not indispensible, to those concerned about their well-being.

To sketch out what is to come, I argue in this book—through a critique of two major attempts to deny justice to animals—that animals can be worthy recipients of justice. Moreover, I conclude that animals need justice because of the high status attached to it, and that, as a consequence, a just state of affairs is one that the state ought, and is likely, to seek to enforce. Animal ethicists have spent a considerable amount of time and effort seeking to establish that we have moral obligations to animals, and it clearly makes theoretical sense to suggest that we do have moral obligations independently of justice. However, it is my contention that moral obligations regarded as being outside of the sphere of justice collapse, *in practice*, into the realm of charity and voluntarism precisely because there is no legal compulsion. In other words, I argue that non-justice-based approaches to the protection of animals are weak because they are less likely to justify state enforcement.

What animals are due as a matter of justice, the third question above, is a separate question from merely establishing that animals can, and ought to, be recipients of justice. It is my contention that, in terms of ideal theory, an adequate account of our obligations to animals must go beyond the traditional animal welfare ethic that holds that animals have some moral worth but their interests can be sacrificed in order to promote a significant human interest. A valid ideal theory of justice for animals should also be rights-based, and should reject alternative approaches based on utilitarianism or capabilities. However, I do not endorse an abolitionist animal rights (or species-egalitarian) position that holds that, because animals have rights to life and liberty, it is illegitimate to use them irrespective of how they are used. Such a position is not simply dubious in terms of its validity at the level of ethics, but it also, it seems to me, requires so much of humans and is so far removed from the current moral orthodoxy, that it does not qualify as a valid ideal theory of justice, at least if a particular Rawlsian version of the concept is used.

Rather, at the level of ideal theory, I endorse an alternative animal rights position—what I describe as the *enhanced sentience position*—which recognizes that animals have a right not to suffer but suggests that humans have a greater interest in life and liberty than most species of nonhuman animals. Despite not necessarily ruling out the use of animals, as the abolitionist animal rights position does, it is argued that the enhanced sentience position is still very demanding on us, whilst at the same time rejecting a species egalitarianism that most find intuitively problematic. The enhanced sentience position remains far removed from current practices, however, and therefore animal advocates are in urgent need of a nonideal theory that plots the most appropriate route from where we are now to where ideal theory tells us we ought to be.

This book attempts to suggest such a route. An alternative, *sentience position*, model of animal rights is recommended as the most appropriate nonideal theory of justice for animals. Whilst only requiring that we show that animals have a right not to suffer at the hands of humans, its practical implications are still far-reaching and thereby morally permissible. However, I want to argue that it also provides a reasonable balance between divergent moral positions as well as being more politically acceptable than is perhaps realized.

Contractarianism and Beyond

It is one of my major contentions that the case of the animal advocate would be enhanced if her arguments were couched in the language of justice as opposed to morality. This presupposes, of course, not only that one can distinguish between justice and morality but also that animals can be properly regarded as worthy recipients of justice. It is instructive here to note that most mainstream theorists of justice implicitly assume that justice is anthropocentric, or explicitly rule out animals as potential recipients of justice, or are doubtful whether animals ought to be included. As Vincent (1998: 120) correctly points out, "justice has been, and, by and large, still is, focused on the social, political and economic relations that hold between human beings." For example, as we shall have cause to document in some detail, the most influential contractarian theories of justice at least are quite clear that animals ought to be excluded. Most notably, Rawls's excludes animals because of their lack of moral agency. Barry (1999: 95), similarly, despite superficially being more sympathetic than Rawls to the well-being of animals, still remarks that "it does not seem to me that the concept of justice can be deployed intelligibly outside the context of relations between human beings" because "justice and injustice can be predicated only of relations among creatures who are regarded as moral equals in the sense that they weigh equally in the moral scales." Those who are not advocating a contractarian theory are equally negative about the possibility of animals being recipients of justice. Miller (1999: 1), for instance, regards justice as being about the distribution of goods and bads "among the members of a *human* society" (my italics).

Other political philosophers are lukewarm about the prospect of animals being included within a theory of justice. Campbell (1988: 11), for instance, asserts that justice "does not arise in our treatment of inanimate things, and possibly not in our treatment of animals." Charles Taylor (1985: 36), similarly, comments that: "Our intuitions about distributive justice are continuous with our basic moral intuitions about human beings as beings who demand a certain respect...It is because people ought to be treated in a certain way, and thus enjoy a status not shared by stones and (some think also) animals, that they ought to be treated *equally* in collaborative situations."

What is clear is that the consensus in mainstream Western political thought is that the concept of justice is reserved for humans alone. It is difficult to disagree with Dobson's remark (1998: 174) that "any theory of justice that incorporated justice for even a very restricted set of non-human animals would immediately be regarded as a second division theory." He speculates, rather provocatively, whether this is what happened to Galston's relatively little-known theory of justice (1980) in which animals, as possessors of interests, are entitled to justice, albeit not to the same degree as humans.

Two major objections to the inclusion of animals in a theory of justice are often advanced, and these are considered in chapter 2. The first of these is that justice is not appropriate for animals because it is about distributive questions involving material goods. I would suggest, however, that justice has a wider coverage than this. One possibility is to equate justice with oppression. However, it is sufficient to maintain the distributional paradigm but instead insist that the benefits and burdens to be distributed can be so loosely defined so as to include primary goods such as rights, liberties, self-respect, and a whole host of what Nussbaum (2006) has described as capabilities. These are clearly relevant to animals. In other words, provided that an individual can gain and lose, and (probably) be aware of gaining and losing, from distributive principles she is entitled to be regarded as a beneficiary of justice. All that is required for qualification, therefore, is sentience. Note that we have not, at this stage, decided upon what nonhuman animals, as sentient beings, ought to be due, only that they are entitled to be due something directly as a result of their sentience.

The second major objection to the inclusion of animals within a theory of justice is that animals are not capable of agreeing and upholding principles of justice. They are not moral agents, and they cannot engage in social cooperation. This is a common retort of contractarian theories of justice. In these types of theories, and most notably the theory of justice advanced by Rawls (1971), it may be wrong morally to be cruel to animals, however that is defined, but it cannot be unjust. There are four responses we might make to the exclusion of animals within Rawls's contractarian theory of justice. The first, considered in detail in chapters 2, is to seek to adapt Rawls's contractarian theory to enable animals to be included. Simply rejecting contractarian theories of justice, and taking at face value their exclusion of animals, is unwise, not least because contractarian theories have been perhaps the most popular method of working out principles of justice in the last few decades, mainly due to the influence of Rawls.

As Mark Rowlands (1998) has pointed out, the contractarian approach has certain benefits for those seeking to defend the interests of animals. In the first place, establishing contractual grounds for granting to animals a considerable moral status has the effect, added to well-known rights and utilitarian versions, of covering all the bases.[3] And the added bonus is that contractarian theories of justice have dominated in post-1945 debates about the subject. In addition, the clear and concise and, some would say, objective way in which principles of justice are derived from contractarian theories contrasts with what Rowlands regards as the "mysterious" way in which rights, for humans and for animals, are often justified. Rowlands's target here is the account put forward by Regan (1984), who bases animal rights on what Rowlands (1998: 118) regards as the "controversial metaphysical assumption" that animals, as "subjects-of-a-life," are beings with inherent value. As a result, for Rowlands (1998: 119; 2), we should reject the concept of inherent value as "*mysterious, ad hoc and, ultimately, unnecessary.*" By contrast, "properly understood" contractarianism is the "greatest ally" of animal rights since it "provides the most satisfactory theoretical basis for the attribution of moral rights to non-human and non-rational individuals."

The advantage of the social contract approach, as Will Kymlicka (1993: 186) suggests, is that it seems to provide valid answers to two crucial questions that any moral theory ought to be able to answer: what does morality require of us and why should we be obliged to accept those demands? Contractarian theories answer by declaring that morality requires us to accept only those principles that we have agreed to and we should be obliged to accept them precisely because we have agreed to them. For "Hobbesian" versions of the contract at least, we will agree to enter into a contractual agreement and be bound by the principles agreed upon only when it is in our self-interest to do so. This "Hobbesian morality" may leave a lot to be desired in terms of what we usually take morality to be, but it "may be the best we can hope for in a world without natural duties or objective values" (Kymlicka, 1993: 191).

Most of the work on the role of animals within contractarian thought has focused on Rawls. Some scholars have attempted to adapt Rawls's theory in a way that enables animals to be included within a contractarian theory of justice. One approach has been to challenge his assertion (1971: 4) that only humans are able to contribute toward society. It has been argued by Mark Coeckelbergh (2009), for instance, that animals are not excluded by such a principle because they do, in fact, make a substantial contribution to society. I will argue, however, that much depends upon what counts as a cooperative relationship. If a weak version is adopted, there would not seem to be anything preventing the inclusion of nonsentient entities within a theory of justice, a conclusion that neither Rawls nor Coeckelbergh would be happy with. A stronger version, however, would find it difficult to incorporate animals in a meaningful sense, not least because it would tend to equate cooperation with exploitation. Focusing on a relational position would, in addition, exclude those wild animals that are not in a cooperative relationship with humans and would seem to lead to the distinctly odd conclusion that animals are only due justice whilst they are being exploited by humans.

Most attempts to adapt Rawls achieve the goal of incorporating animals by "thickening" the veil of ignorance so as to allow species membership to be included amongst those things that the participants in the original position are unaware. Whilst logically coherent, this adaptation is problematic. In the first place, it is questionable whether it is possible for participants behind the veil of ignorance to be unaware of their status as human beings. Moreover, as I will argue in chapter 2, whilst Rowlands (2009) is right to claim that employing the Kantian framework of Rawls's theory does provide a justification for including animals as beneficiaries of justice, the effect of this is to devalue the force of the contractual element to the point where it might be dispensed with entirely.

The second response to Rawls's exclusion of animals, also considered in chapter 2, is to look for an alternative contractarian account that might allow us to include them. One possibility is Brian Barry's approach (1995), justice as impartiality, which is influenced by the work of Thomas Scanlon (1982;

1988; 1998). Nothing much has been written on the role of animals in Barry's version of contractarianism. This represents a gap in the literature in the sense that, superficially at least, Barry would appear to be more sympathetic to the interests of animals than is Rawls. In particular, Barry hints that animal protection can be incorporated within a theory of justice as impartiality, and, even if this is not in fact the case, he is prepared to contemplate a procedural device whereby the state intervenes to uphold one conception of the good over another. This leaves open the possibility that a conception of the good that promotes animal protection might be translated into public policy.

Despite the optimism that Barry might offer a theory of justice that can provide substantial protection for the interests of animals—promoted, in part, by his critique of Rawls—it is argued that he is unable ultimately to break the shackles of his contractarian framework. Not even the device of including species membership as another unknown characteristic behind the veil of ignorance, used by those who seek to adapt Rawls, is open to Barry because his version of the contract, derived from Scanlon, insists that the parties to the contract are aware of their positions within society. Insofar as animals can be protected within Barry's theory of justice as impartiality, they are not being protected as a result of their intrinsic value, but merely as one, nonvital, *human* set of beliefs included within a conception of the good. Such a conception ultimately rules out the inclusion of anything but the most gratuitous cruelty to animals as a principle of justice.

Barry does offer the possibility of adjudicating between competing conceptions of the good according to principles laid down by justice as impartiality. This does offer the prospect of political decisions increasing protection afforded to animals. However, these decisions (as opposed to the procedure by which they are made) are not themselves substantive principles of justice and are therefore contingent upon enough humans regarding them as important, and are open to repeal at any point in the future. Moreover, it is unlikely that many issues involving animals will be subject to the justice as impartiality procedure anyway since Barry is committed to the liberal position that, as far as possible, individuals should be left alone to pursue their own conceptions of the good.

Dispensing with Justice?

As a result of this critique, those concerned about the well-being of animals need to either go beyond contractarianism, and look for alternative theories of justice that are more amenable to the inclusion of animals, or to consider the strength of those direct duties that can be owed to animals within a moral realm independently of justice. The former task is the major aim of chapters 5 through 9. The latter task provides the subject matter of chapters 3 and 4. To reiterate, it has been assumed that it is beneficial to attempt to incorporate animals as recipients of justice. But how far is this necessary? Should we, that is, accept the contractarian claim that animals cannot be recipients of justice and instead consider the degree of protection that can be achieved for them within a moral realm independently of justice? This question derives from the fact that Rawls, for one, argues that his theory of justice is not a comprehensive moral theory, and the treatment of animals should be part of such a moral theory, and not a more narrow theory of justice.

The question of the value of justice to animals is examined in chapter 3. It is argued that it is possible to conceive of a moral realm independently of justice, and that its existence is consistent with a contractarian theory of justice, as opposed to a contractarian theory of morality. In this sense, critics of Rawls from both sides of the debate about animals have mistakenly suggested that he automatically excludes animals, and marginal humans, as beneficiaries of direct duties. This is not the case. As far as it is possible to tell, Rawls thinks that we have direct duties to animals, only that these duties are not based on justice.

However, a critical analysis of a number of attempts to explicate this moral realm independently of justice (including a care ethic) reveals that it is doubtful if any direct moral duties to animals, equivalent to or greater in weight than those attached to justice claims, can in practice be established. Animal ethicists have spent a considerable amount of time and effort seeking to establish that we have moral obligations to animals, and it clearly makes theoretical sense to suggest that we do have moral obligations independently of justice. However, it is my contention that moral obligations regarded as being outside of the sphere of justice collapse, *in practice*, into the realm of charity and voluntarism precisely because there is a much weaker link with legal compulsion. In short, I argue that non-justice-based approaches to the protection of animals are weak because they are less likely to justify state enforcement. In practice, then, excluding animals from a theory of justice amounts, at best, to the claim that we have very limited direct duties to some animals, and, at worst, that we only have indirect duties to them.

The task of deciding whether animals need justice is not complete until we have examined the case for indirect duty views toward animals. This is carried out in chapter 4. According to the indirect duty view, the protection of animals does not come about because they are regarded as having intrinsic value, but because animal and human interests converge. Thus, whereas a direct moral object is "something *to* which moral consideration is paid," an indirect moral object is "something *about* or *concerning* which moral consideration is paid." As a result "not everything of moral *value* has moral *standing*" (Morris, 1998: 191).

There are clear political benefits in attempting to develop a credible indirect duty approach to animals. We saw that contractarian theories of justice have been particularly influential partly, at least, because they enable us to explain *why* people should behave justly. Indirect duty views, similarly, are based on the idea that we should seek to behave respectfully toward animals because it is in our (human) interests to do so. This, of course, provides a political model for how animal interests are represented in practice. It is humans who put animal issues on to the political agenda, and it is humans who decide whether or not animals should be treated well. An indirect duty approach is a theoretical model of that political reality.

It is undoubtedly true that indirect duty views have offered very little for animals in the way they have been usually framed, since it is often in our narrow economic interests to exploit them rather than protect them. However, it is argued in chapter 4 that indirect duty views about animals do not have to be presaged merely on narrow self interest. The degree to which interests, on the one hand, and values and norms, on the other, are logically distinct can be exaggerated. It could be in our interests, then, to protect animals not just, if at all, because it serves our narrow—economic or environmental—interests, but because it is in our (wider) interests to behave altruistically. Seeking to relate the interests of animals to a flourishing human life clearly allows us to explore the role that virtue ethics can play in animal ethics. In part, therefore, chapter 4 assesses the claims of the virtue ethics approach to offer a non-justice-based account of our moral obligations to animals.

It is argued that, despite the potential offered by virtue ethics, it is doubtful if a credible indirect duty approach to animals can be developed. For one thing, an approach based on the virtues is vulnerable to conflicts between virtues, and these, as it will be shown, are particularly prevalent in the case of human/animal relationships. Moreover, conceived in relation to the indirect duty approach, virtue ethics depends upon the validity of the claim that behaving virtuously toward animals ultimately benefits the virtuous person. Such a claim is, at the very least, doubtful. Finally, virtuous behavior as regards animals is surely predicated on the duties we owe to them directly as a result of their capacity to be harmed. If so, then there would seem to be no obstacle to the recognition of the intrinsic value of animals, a position that is now widely accepted in theory and practice. The question then remains whether it is intellectually and practically credible to run a direct and indirect approach to animals simultaneously.

Ideal and Nonideal Theory

The third, and by far the most significant—and difficult—question this book seeks to answer is what are animals due as a matter of justice? This book seeks to recommend one particular ideal theory of justice for animals. The evaluation of competing ideal theories, however, only takes us so far. Ideal theories focus on the validity of a theory of justice or morality in relation to how far it is considered to approximate the truth, in as far as normative arguments can arrive at such a determinate answer. This is the line traditionally taken by animal ethicists. But this is not the only criterion of adequacy it is possible to adopt. A theory of justice must also be judged in relation to its feasibility, how far it is practically possible to achieve at any point. Moreover, a valid theory of justice must also consider how we get from where we are now to where we want to be. I have often made the point that an animal rights ethic—or at least a particular version of it—is, in the present climate, not a realistic proposition (Francione and Garner, 2010). As a result, I have been an exponent of a position that my critics have described as "New Welfarism" (Francione, 1996). This position holds that, whilst recognizing the ethical limitations of animal welfare, animal welfare-based reforms are the best that the animal protection movement are going to get, at least for now, and that these are not likely to be a hindrance to future, more extensive, measures.

Such a position might, or might not, be regarded as politically astute. It is always, however, presented as a position centered on political pragmatism rather than ideals. As such, it is vulnerable to the charge that it erroneously seeks to defend the status quo, and is a moral "sellout." A key question, then, is whether there is a way of converting what is regarded as political pragmatism, in the face of clear ethical demands, into a principled position. I believe there is. This can be achieved, I argue, through the application of the debate about ideal and nonideal theory current in the political philosophy literature. In contemporary political discourse, this debate emerged as a result of increasing frustration by many at the discrepancy perceived between the abstract normative work of political philosophers, in which ideal political and moral principles are advocated, and the difficulty of applying such principles in the nonideal real world. Rawls's theory of justice is often taken to be the classical example of an ideal theory. As he writes (1971: 9), "the nature and aims of a perfectly just society is the fundamental part of the theory of justice."

The starting point for much of the contemporary discussion is Rawls who, as we shall see below, identifies ideal and nonideal components of a theory of justice. However, use of the distinction goes back as far as Plato (Ypi, 2010: 537–8). It was commented on too by Kant (1970), as long ago as 1793. Kant was highly critical of those who sought to demean ethical arguments on the grounds that they appeared to be unrealistic, and sought to distinguish between what he saw as the essential task of developing general rules of right conduct and their application in practice. There is certainly an ever-present danger of a counsel of despair, in which the force of a moral clarion call is blunted because its advocates are convinced that not enough people can be persuaded to overcome their selfish desires. It should be pointed out that this book seeks explicitly to avoid such an outcome. What it does seek to do, however, is to recognize, and deal with, the constraints that inevitably confront all radical social movements.

As indicated, Rawls himself recognized the importance of the distinction between ideal and nonideal theory, and, although it is not compulsory to adopt his version, he does offer us a very useful framework that can be utilized in this book to consider ideal and nonideal theories relating to animals. Ideal theory, for Rawls (1971: 246), "presents a conception of a just society that we are to achieve if we can." It is important to note, though, that ideal theory, for Rawls, should not be regarded as the same as utopianism in the sense that it would be impossible to achieve. Even ideal theory must take into account the constraints afforded by human nature so that it probes "the limits of practicable political possibility" and "depicts an achievable social world" (Rawls, 2001: 4; 6). Ideal theory, then, is equivalent to what Rawls (1999: 7) describes as a "realistic utopia" that involves "taking men as they are and laws as they might be." In this sense, David Miller (2008: 31) is correct when he writes that "even the basic concepts and principles of political theory are fact-dependent: their validity depends on the truth of some general empirical propositions about human being and human societies." Here, we need to distinguish between "universal features of the human condition," which are unalterable, and "facts about particular societies, or types of society, and their inhabitants," which may not be (Miller, 2008: 39). Determining whether a particular set of principles represents a realistic utopia involves, to some extent, relying "on conjecture and speculation" where we have to argue "as best we can that the social world we envision is feasible and might actually exist, if not now then at some future time under happier circumstances" (Rawls, 1999: 12).

Any theory that contains principles contrary to such "universal features of the human condition" would constitute a utopian, rather than an ideal, theory. What ideal theory does assume, for Rawls, however, is "strict compliance," in the sense that it is assumed that not only are the laws of a society just but also that "(nearly) everyone strictly complies with, and so abides by, the principles of justice" (Rawls, 2001: 13).

By contrast, nonideal theory, for Rawls (1971: 246), considers how the long-term goal of ideal theory "might be achieved, or worked toward, usually in gradual steps." Insofar as nonideal theory refers to how we get from where we are now to where we want to be, it is a process rather than an end-point. What it does recognize is that, at present, we are unable to achieve our ideal goal. For Rawls, nonideal theory should be very much a secondary concern of political philosophers who ought to focus on developing ideal theories. Others argue that Rawls's ideal theory, and that of many other political and moral philosophers, is so far removed from reality that ideal theories of justice ought to be given a much reduced status, if not dispensed with entirely. Farrelly (2007: 860), for instance, argues that taking into account the political, social, and economic realities within which ideal theory has to operate, "will mean that there is less room for armchair theorizing and that the primary focus will not be on winning a philosophical debate among first-order theories of justice." Amartya Sen (2009: 15), likewise, argues that: "If a theory of justice is to guide reasoned choice of policies, strategies or institutions, then the identification of fully just social arrangements is neither necessary nor sufficient." Those who advocate this strong version of nonideal theory are not then claiming simply that political pragmatism should prevail over normative political philosophy, but rather that any political or moral philosophy that does not take account of the nonideal world in which it is attempting to influence and address is *normatively* deficient (Dunn, 1990; Carens, 2000; Farrelly, 2007, 2007a; Sher, 1997).

I do not share this hostility toward ideal theory, at least if we adopt Rawls's version of it. For Rawls, as I indicated above, an ideal theory that is impossible of realization because it conflicts, say, with a universal nonalterable trait of human nature is not, in any case, a valid ideal theory and can be labeled as utopian. Seen in this sense, it seems to me that, despite the fact that an ideal theory is not concerned with offering any desirable and achievable recommendations that are possible immediately, we still need an ideal theory as a guide to the validity of any particular nonideal theory. As Stemplowska (2008: 230) rightly points out, "identifying the full extent of actual injustice requires knowledge of all that is wrong with the society in question, and this, in turn, requires knowledge of what a society in which no such wrongs were present would be like." It is not being denied, then, that the distinction between a sociological account of justice and morality, on the one hand, and a normative account, on the other, is an important one. An inquiry into what moral beliefs people have, why they have them, and what, in practice, this permits them to do, is very different from an account of what moral beliefs people ought to have. It is not being claimed here, as Miller (1976: 253–335) seems to do, that political theorists cannot favor one account of justice over another but simply have to accept the relativist position that certain societies give rise to particular principles of justice.

What *is* being claimed here, then, is that a valid analysis of a particular theory of justice must take into account the degree to which it is realizable in practice now, or in the medium or long-term. It must not, that is, be divorced from questions relating to nonideal constraints, whether they concern unsympathetic social, economic, or historical circumstances, moral disagreement, or human nature. This boils down to the well-known moral principle that "ought implies can." As Farrelly (2007: 845) points out, "there is some conceptual incoherence involved in saying 'This is what justice involves, but there is no way it could be implemented.'"

A valid analysis of a theory of justice must also consider what is the most effective route to the establishment of the principles enshrined in the ideal theory. It must, that is, include nonideal theory. Rawls, again, provides some guidance here. He argues that, to some extent, what constitutes valid nonideal theory must be a matter of intuition but, in addition, nonideal theory "looks for courses of action that are morally permissible and politically possible as well as likely to be effective" (Rawls: 1999: 89). The meaning of the second of these is well understood, albeit perhaps difficult to determine. The moral permissibility of a course of action, for Rawls, is a function of the degree to which it removes the most grievous or most urgent injustice, the one that departs the most from the ideal theory (Rawls, 1971: 246). Finally, Rawls holds to the view that the effectiveness of a nonideal theory can be judged by the degree to which it moves society toward the ideal position.

Rawls provides little guidance on how we are to weigh these three features. Clearly, they might conflict. For example, a course of action that is politically achievable might not be morally permissible or effective, whereas one that is morally permissible might not be politically possible or effective. Not all advocates of nonideal theory do emphasize the importance of effectiveness (see, for example, Murphy, 200), but it is clear that this is one way in which nonideal theory can be distinguished from the commonsense, "second best," position that if we cannot achieve all that justice demands we should, instead, get what we can (Simmons, 2010: 25). Rather, Rawls insists that only those courses of action that are functional for the achievement of the ideal theory are permissible. Thus, he is committed to the position that even where it is politically possible and morally permissible to remove an injustice, we should only do so if it does not impede the process whereby our ideally just end-point is achieved.

Animal Rights, Abolitionism, and Nonideal Theory

A major part of this book is concerned with assessing the major positions developed by animal ethicists in terms of both ideal and nonideal theory. An appropriate starting point is one strand of animal rights thinking, the self-styled abolitionist position that, more accurately, might be described as the species-egalitarian version of animal rights. For most animal rights philosophers, animal rights activists, and, indeed, their opponents too, animal rights and abolitionism is synonymous. The abolitionist position draws its inspiration from the work of Tom Regan (1984) and its best-known contemporary advocate is probably Gary Francione, who has written extensively on the subject (2006, 2008) and runs a popular website called "Animal Rights: The Abolitionist Approach" (http://www.abolitionistapproach. com/). Abolitionism seeks, on the grounds that animals have a right to life and liberty, a prohibition on the use of animals by humans *irrespective of the ways in which they are treated*. Thus, for Regan, the animal rights movement "is abolitionist in its aspirations. It seeks not to reform how animals are exploited...but to abolish their exploitation. To end it. Completely" (Cohen and Regan, 2001: 127). Moreover, for many animal rights thinkers of this ilk, once this exploitation of domesticated animals is abolished, the very notion of domesticating animals, of, in other words, humans having close relationships with animals, ends too.

It is a major claim of this book that it is mistaken to regard the abolitionist, or species-egalitarian, animal rights position as an ideal theory, the end-point to which the animal rights movement should aspire. It ought to be rejected as an appropriate ideal theory, firstly since it is mistaken on the grounds of ethical principle. This is because, as will be argued in chapter 8, it fails to take into account the moral significance of those interests—in liberty and in life—associated with persons and the fact that persons have a greater interest in life and liberty than nonpersons. In other words, the abolitionist, or species-egalitarian, strand of animal rights, which rules out using animals irrespective of what is done to them whilst they are being used, is not justified because it is difficult to argue against the claim that the differences between "normal" adult humans and adult animals *are* substantial and *are* morally significant. In short, the level of complexity of an individual affects what can be a harm for that individual.

Without an additional argument, then, the different characteristics and capabilities of humans and animals would appear to justify differential treatment. The species egalitarianism argued for in the abolitionist animal rights position can only be justified if the so-called argument from marginal cases is employed. The use of this device is considered in chapter 9. It is revisited in this book partly in order to demonstrate how central it is to the argument of those who advocate the abolitionist position. Much of the force of the argument from marginal cases is based on the assumption that marginal humans are regarded, in practice, as having a moral status on a par with other humans, and ought to be treated accordingly. This chapter is devoted, in part, to an examination of that claim. This is designed partly to put the ethical force of the argument from marginal cases to the test, and partly to examine the degree to which the moral status attached to marginal humans can provide us with a model of a just way to treat animals.

Another central claim of this book is that rejecting moral egalitarianism, the view that humans and animals are of equal moral value, is not equivalent to rejecting an animal rights-based position. The constituent parts of an alternative animal rights position, described in chapter 6, consist of a capacity-oriented approach, an interest-based theory of rights, and the equal consideration of interests principle. I will argue in chapter 7 that a rights-based ethic grounded in these constituent elements is preferable not only to the species-egalitarian version of animal rights but also, ethically, to a rights-based theory's two major rivals. In the animal's debate, at least, these two rivals are the utilitarian position associated with Singer (1990) and the capabilities approach associated with Martha Nussbaum (2004; 2006).

The constituent elements of an alternative rights-based position are then utilized, in chapter 8, to develop a strand of animal rights that I label the *enhanced sentience position*. According to this position, which constitutes my preferred ideal theory of justice for animals, animals have a right not to have suffering inflicted upon them but not a right to life, since humans, all things being equal, have a greater interest in life. This does not mean, however, that animals have *no* interest in life. Consequently, most animal lives are of some moral importance, although less than those of most humans. This position would be exceedingly restrictive in the sense that very significant human benefits (such as the protection of human lives) would have to accrue from the loss of animal lives at human hands.

It is also argued that the abolitionist strand of animal rights should be rejected as an ideal theory because its species egalitarianism means that it ought to be regarded as closer to what Rawls deemed as a utopian, rather than an ideal, theory. It is not, then, equivalent to what Rawls defines as a "realistic utopia." This is because its insistence that, to all intents and purposes, animals and humans are of equal moral value—in the sense, most notably, that animal lives are of equal value to those of humans—seems to demand too much of human beings in a qualitatively different way from radical social movements of the past. That is, it requires us to engage in a paradigmatic leap across the species divide jettisoning the anthropocentric culture that has dominated human social and political life. At the same time, animal rights abolitionism does not take enough account of the relationships that humans do have with animals, which are either prohibited or neglected by at least some animal rights thinkers.

The ideal theory of animal rights promoted in this book, the enhanced sentience position, is very demanding in terms of its implications for humans. From an ideal theoretic perspective, however, it does have the advantage of accepting that the moral status of humans is greater than that of animals, a value that is held intuitively by most people, in addition to accepting that, in certain circumstances, humans may still use animals. Nevertheless, it is sufficiently at odds with current practices to warrant a debate about the route that can be profitably taken in the short and medium term. That is, there is a role for nonideal theory.

A number of characteristics of an effective nonideal theory can be identified. One such characteristic is the notion of finding a reasonable balance between morally divergent positions. A non-ideal theory would, in Farrelly's words (2007: 859), attempt to determine "what would constitute a *reasonable balance* between conflicting fundamental values." In this regard, a useful model of a nonideal theory is provided by George Sher (1997: ch. 11) in his discussion of abortion. Sher wonders (155), how should society "respond to the deep moral disagreement about abortion that divides its constituent groups"? He also notes that abortion is a complex and uncertain subject where both sides adopt moral principles backed by "plausible-sounding arguments." In such a situation, "only a dogmatist will deny that he may well be mistaken, and his adversary correct." As a result, Sher (161) recommends adopting a "higher order moral principle that moderates what one is required to do when one's efforts to act morally conflict with the similarly motivated efforts of others."

The compromise Sher (162) recommends in terms of the abortion debate centers on a recognition that it would be legitimate to expect liberals to accept measures—such as greater emphasis on family planning and an end to government funding for elective abortions—that might decrease the number of abortions but without undue government interference. On the antiabortion side, in return, there would be an expectation that extreme direct action tactics would stop, as would the use of language—for instance, that abortion is murder—that inflames the debate. The exact details of Sher's recommendations on abortion are not important here. What is important is the model adopted that would seem to be equally applicable to the debate about the treatment of animals, one with strongly held moral positions on either side, accompanied by inflamed language and sometimes extreme action. This is an issue that is not going to be resolved any time soon.

One of the problems with this approach to nonideal theory is that it appears to assume that the "reasonable balance" is an end-point, that the inevitability of moral pluralism will prevent the eventual achievement of the chosen ideal theory. This is close to being a counsel of despair, albeit one that is perhaps politically realistic. By contrast, Rawls himself is very clear that nonideal theory should be judged by the degree to which it can facilitate, or is not inconsistent with, the ideal theory end-point. As we saw above, this "effectiveness" characteristic coexists in Rawls's theory with an insistence that nonideal theory is also morally permissible and politically achievable. The starting point for Rawls is to identify the most grievous examples of injustice. That is, Rawls argues that it is only morally permissible to prioritize the most urgent cases of injustice, the cases that diverge furthest from our ideal theory. Rawls's lexical ordering of his major principles of justice makes it easy for him to specify what constitutes the most serious cases of injustice. Thus, violations of his liberty principle (requiring extensive and equal basic liberties) are more serious than infringements of the "equal opportunity principle" or the "difference principle."

What is interesting here is that Rawls assumes, correctly of course, that humans are granted bodily integrity, and thus it would be unjust to kill or maim members of our own species, a position accepted universally in the case of the developed countries his theory of justice is meant to apply to. No such protection is granted to animals, who, of course, regularly suffer at the hands of humans and are killed by them for a variety of reasons. The enhanced sentience position, the goal to which it is argued we should be heading, does not stipulate that animals have a right to life or liberty, although it does place some value on animal lives. What it does insist upon, however, is that animals have a right not to suffer, irrespective of the benefits that might accrue to humans as a result. It would seem appropriate, therefore, to regard eliminating suffering as the most urgent injustice in the case of animals.

In the context of nonideal theory, therefore, the position described in this book as the *sentience position* reflects most accurately the urgent need to eliminate animal suffering at the hands of humans. This position, developed in chapter 8 in particular, does clearly prohibit morally the infliction of suffering on animals for human benefits, but at the same time accepts that humans can still, under certain circumstances, use them. Because it does not engage at all with the question of the value of animal lives, sacrificing animal lives for human benefit is not regarded as problematic ethically. This theory is far from being a defense of the status quo. Indeed, as will be shown in chapter 8, it is very demanding on human beings. On the other hand, it is more realistic than a theory based on denying the ethical validity of using animals as, for example, sources of food and as experimental subjects irrespective of what is done to them whilst they are being used (the abolitionist position). Likewise, it is more realistic than the enhanced sentience position, which accepts that animals do have an interest in continued life, albeit not as great an interest as possessed by humans.

Despite conforming to one of Rawls's major conditions for effective nonideal theory, it is clear that there is a potential conflict between the sentience position and one of his other conditions. The political possibility of securing the sentience position as the dominant principle of justice governing our treatment of animals would seem to be relatively low in comparison to other ethical positions because it would have the effect of prohibiting many of the ways in which animals are currently treated. Less demanding is the indirect duty position and the animal welfare ethic, and it is for this reason that animal rights advocates have tended to utilize these as their preferred "stepping stone" to an animal rights end-point.

A viable indirect duty approach to animals eliminates completely the conflict between human and animal interests because it is only ethically valid to protect animals when it is in our interests to do so. As I will show in chapter 4, however, it is unlikely that an indirect duty approach constitutes a valid nonideal theory of justice for animals. Whilst it is politically acceptable, the indirect duty position is not morally permissible, nor effective as a transitional mechanism because it does not recognize the intrinsic value of animals and therefore will only eliminate suffering when it is in human interests to do so.

The contribution that animal welfare can make to the question of animal justice is considered in chapter 5. An animal welfare ethic is modeled by reference to what it is not. It is not equivalent to what contributes to the welfare of animals as determined by animal welfare scientists. Similarly, it is not equivalent to the utilitarianism associated, above all, with Peter Singer. Armed with this conceptual clarity, one may explain that animal welfare can be consistent with an ideal theory of justice if it can be shown that animals are morally inferior to humans in a way that prescribes only protection from unnecessary suffering as something to which animals are due. The fact that this is not the case means that it must be rejected as an ideal theory of justice for animals. The starting point here is a recognition that the animal welfare ethic is flawed ethically because it accords too much moral weight to the fact that humans are persons and most animals are not. The characteristics of personhood may justify the argument that humans have a greater interest than most animals in life and liberty, but it does not justify the claim that an animal's interest in avoiding suffering is any less important to it than a human's. As a result, if humans have an interest in not having suffering inflicted on them by others, then, all things being equal, so do animals.

Even as a nonideal theory, however, animal welfare leaves something to be desired. In the first place, it is a possibility that the degree to which popular opinion is prepared to recognize a higher moral status for animals than the animal welfare ethic allows for can be underestimated, not least because, in the public mind, the animal welfare ethic is often conflated with the conclusions of animal welfare science. Moreover, although animal welfare clearly is a principle that is widely accepted, and is sufficiently flexible to justify, in theory at least, the alleviation of a great deal of animal suffering, it is shown in chapter 5 how the moral inferiority of animals postulated can justify a great deal of animal exploitation. Such a position, therefore, is not, in practice, a reasonable balance between divergent moral positions. In addition, I do not think that the animal welfare ethic is morally permissible in the sense that it justifies inflicting suffering on animals provided that a significant benefit to humans accrues. This is to visit on animals a clear and fundamental injustice, thereby infringing Rawls's principle that a nonideal theory should focus on the most urgent injustices. It is a central claim of this book that the sentience position achieves this goal more effectively than an animal welfare ethic can, whilst at the same time offering a politically achievable program.

2

Contractarianism, Animals, and Justice

THE FIRST QUESTION this book seeks to answer is whether animals can be recipients of justice. This chapter proceeds to answer that question by considering two major objections to the claim that it is appropriate to apply principles of justice to animals. The first objection—that justice is inappropriate for animals because it is a distributive concept involving, typically, material goods—is quickly dispensed with. Justice, it is argued, can be equated with oppression, which allows for animals to be included. Moreover, the distributional paradigm can be extended to include primary goods that clearly apply to animals. The bulk of this chapter deals with the second objection, that animals, not being moral agents, are incapable of agreeing and upholding principles of justice. For this reason, animals are excluded as recipients of justice in contractarian theories.

Contractarianism represents an appropriate starting point for this book because it has been an extremely influential theory of justice in recent decades. An adequate response from those who entertain the idea of including animals as recipients of justice is therefore essential. The most important contemporary contractarian theory of justice has been provided by John Rawls, and much of the debate about animals within contractarian thought has centered on his work. Rawls's exclusion of animals has led a number of scholars to challenge his position. This literature is reviewed in the first part of the chapter. Much less, if anything, has been written about Brian Barry's contractarian theory and, particularly given that he appears to be more sympathetic to the claims of animals than other contractarians such as Rawls, his version is worth examining. This is undertaken in the second part of the chapter.

Justice as a Distributive Concept

There is a consensus that justice is essentially about giving "to each his due" (Raphael, 2001: 183). In its formal sense, justice refers to treating like cases alike, or treating individuals fairly. In this sense, there would seem to be little problem in applying the concept of justice to animals, as individuals whose lives can go well or badly as a result of other people's actions. Indeed, much of the extentionist animal ethics literature, which seeks to extend moral consideration beyond the human species, is predicated on the claim that we ought not to make different moral judgments about identical cases, thereby considering the interests of animals and humans equally. This would seem to be another way of saying we should not act unjustly.

The lack of compatibility between animals and justice might be said to arise when the latter is constituted in a distributive sense and therefore is concerned with "how the good and bad things in life should be distributed" (Miller, 1999: 1). Here, it is true that, conventionally, justice has been concerned primarily about the distribution of economic resources and the principle—whether equality, merit, or need—by which this distribution is to be effected. In other words, justice is about what economic resources individuals are due. As Miller (1976: 22) confirms, "most people would consider" this "the most important concern of social justice." Clearly, if this is all there is to justice, then animals cannot really be included, or at least only partially so. Animals can clearly benefit from material goods in the same way as humans can, in terms of food and shelter, and a distribution based on need would seem highly appropriate (see Benton, 1993: 212). But applying this principle to animals would seem highly conservative given that it does not say anything about whether it is just to continue using them as, for instance, sources of food or as experimental subjects.

Intuitively, being just, for both humans and animals, however, requires much more than ensuring that material goods are distributed according to some agreed principle. Some political thinkers seek to equate injustice with oppression. Iris Marion Young (1990: 3) argues, for instance, that "instead of focusing on distribution, a conception of justice should begin with the concepts of domination and oppression." For her, social justice must focus "on the social structures and processes that produce distributions rather than on the distributions" themselves (Young, 1990: 18). The aim of justice, for Young, should be to combat five faces of oppression based on class, exclusion from the workforce, lack of autonomy and powerlessness in the workplace, cultural imperialism, and violence by the majority.

A number of these categories, defined in a broad sense, might apply to animals as well as humans. Animals, it can be argued, are regularly deprived of their autonomy, for instance, as when they are confined for human purposes. A feeling of powerlessness might be applicable here, too. Likewise, violence toward animals is a central part of their exploitation by humans. Equating justice with the ending of oppression, however, is problematic for both humans and animals. Young is right to point out that distributive outcomes are often a product of wider societal forces, but this is not to undermine the distributive paradigm rather than to recognize the factors determining a particular distribution, and what needs to be done in order to achieve a preferred one. Young's analysis, in her own words, "confuses the empirical issue of what causes a particular distribution with the normative issue of whether the distribution is just" (Young, 1990: 29).

Young raises this objection in order to reject it, but this rejection only holds if one accepts her critical social theory perspective, which does not accept the division between empirical and normative social theory. Thus, she argues (29) that, "Inquiry about social justice must consider the context and causes of actual distributions in order to make normative judgements about institutional rules and relations." I would agree with this but add that without some idea of what a "just" distribution looks like, there can be no worthwhile evaluation of the processes that prevent it from being a reality. In this sense, Miller (1976: 22) is right to claim that questions of power are not questions of social justice per se but concern the causes of justice and injustice. In other words, patterns of distribution can be evaluated independently of their causes.

More to the point, here, the effective incorporation of animals into a theory of justice does not require that we dispense with the distributional approach, for justice need not be concerned merely with the distribution of economic goods. Instead, the goods and bads, or benefits and burdens, to be distributed can be "loosely defined so as to cover any desirable or undesirable thing or experience" (Campbell, 1988: 19). Thus, for Rawls (1971), distributive justice regulates the allocation of primary goods—rights and liberties, powers and opportunities, self respect—as well as income and wealth. Likewise, the capabilities approach to justice, developed by Amartya Sen and applied to animals by Martha Nussbaum (see chapter 7), argues that the state should distribute goods and bads so that humans and, according to Nussbaum, animals, can flourish by having the freedom to pursue their essential selves. For Dworkin (1977: 199), justice is concerned with the distribution of rights, since "the institution of rights rests on the conviction that the invasion of a relatively important right...is a grave injustice." Therefore, justice is ultimately about *"rightful possession,"* about the "appropriate assignment of entities to individuals" (Galston, 1980) and, defined in such a way, it does not seem to exclude animals given that they have interests and, it is commonly believed, can be harmed directly.

Rawls, Animals, and Justice

In the two decades or so after the publication of John Rawls's *A Theory of Justice* (1971), a considerable amount of literature appeared designed to assess the degree to which Rawls's contractarian political theory could be utilized by those concerned about protecting the interests of animals. Despite Rawls's own reluctance to include animals as recipients of justice, many argued that his theory was still useful for the animal advocate (Richards, 1971; Rowlands, 1997, 1998; Van De Veer, 1979a). My initial contribution to this debate, published a decade ago, answered in the negative. Those interested in theorizing the protection of animals, I suggested, ought to look beyond contractarianism (Garner, 2003). Since then, a number of scholars have sought to renew interest in Rawls as a source of resources for animal protection (Abbey, 2007; Coeckelbergh, 2009; Filice, 2006) and Mark Rowlands (2009: chapter 6) has, in a second edition of a book originally published in the 1990s, (1998) repeated the claim that a revised version of Rawls's contractarianism represents the most promising means of theorizing the protection of animals.

The aim in this chapter is to revisit the relationship between Rawls's contractarianism and the moral status of animals, paying particular attention to the recent literature, in order to assess the degree to which my original dismissal of Rawls's position can still be maintained. The discussion is structured around the two major responses to Rawls's insistence that animals are not recipients of justice. The first takes him at face value but argues that animals can still be protected, either within a moral realm he identifies independently of justice, or as a result of their interests being represented by those who are participants in the contractual arrangement. The second seeks to adapt Rawls's theory in a way that enables animals to be included as recipients of justice, either through amending the veil of ignorance so as to make species, along with gender, race, and social situation, as an unknown, or through denying that animals do not contribute to society's cooperative relationship, thereby challenging Rawls's assertion that justice is only due to those who add to the collective welfare.

Rawls's Position on Animals

Contractarian theories have provided one arena for those seeking to theorize animal protection, existing alongside more traditional rights and utilitarian approaches (Regan, 1984; Singer, 1990). The key characteristic of the contractarian approach is the postulating of an arena whereby rational individuals decide which principles of justice or morality they can accept. In other words, contractarian theories are committed to the idea that legitimate principles (of justice and morality) are those that are, or would be, agreed upon by rational individuals in appropriate circumstances. That is, legitimate principles are the outcome of an agreement. It is widely assumed by contractarian theorists that animals, because they are unable to be parties to the agreement, cannot be protected directly from within it (Carruthers, 1992: 98–9; Sandoe and Christiansen, 2008: 19). Rawls appears to confirm this since he excludes animals from his theory of justice on two related grounds. The first is that, since society is regarded as "a cooperative venture for mutual advantage," (Rawls, 1971: 4) to benefit from society's collective endeavors requires an ability to be able to provide something in return. Since animals do not contribute to society, at least in conventional ways such as earning money, they are not entitled to be recipients of justice. Secondly, Rawls argues that only "moral persons" are entitled to be beneficiaries of justice (1971: 504–5). Moral personhood, for Rawls (1971: 505), has two features. First, moral persons "are capable of having…a conception of their good (as expressed by a rational plan of life); and second they are capable of having…a sense of justice, a normally effective desire to apply and to act upon the principles of justice, at least to a certain minimum degree."

Rawls does not rule out protecting animals from cruel treatment, but, for him—as for many liberal political theorists—this concern belongs to a broader moral arena that is not part of the realm of justice. "It does not follow from a person's not being owed the duty of justice," Rawls (1963: 302) writes, "that he may be treated in any way that one pleases. We do not normally think of ourselves as owing the duty of justice to animals, but it is certainly wrong to be cruel to them." In *A Theory of Justice* (1971: 512) he makes a very similar claim, writing that "it is wrong to be cruel to animals…The capacity for feelings of pleasure and pain and for the forms of life of which animals are capable clearly impose duties of compassion and humanity in their care." What these "duties of compassion" are we are not told. What we do know is that, as a result of the structure of Rawls's contract, there is a disincentive for participants to accord any consideration to the well-being of animals since they know they will be human once the veil of ignorance is lifted.

Accepting Rawls at Face Value

Two general types of arguments have been made in response to Rawls's reluctance to include animals as beneficiaries of justice. The first response is that we can accept his insistence that those not represented in the original position cannot be beneficiaries of the principles of justice there decided. We can then either explore what Rawls might have meant by including animals as part of a wider moral realm or look elsewhere for a more convivial theory of justice.

An example of the first response is provided by Ruth Abbey (2007), who argues that we should accept Rawls's exclusion of animals from a theory of justice, but take at face value his argument that we still have moral duties to them. There are, Abbey argues, more non-justice-based normative resources for animals in Rawls's work than has been recognized previously, particularly in *A Theory of Justice* (1971) as opposed to *Political Liberalism* (1993). For Abbey (2007: 6), then, Rawls is suggesting that "humans have duties to animals that derive not from the considerations of justice, but from those of morality." Since Rawls refers to our "duties" to animals, we should regard him as serious about the moral claims of animals, despite the fact that he does not provide any detail. Abbey (2007: 9) infers that "Rawls is seeking to limit the hegemony of rights discourse by recognising that not all issues of ethical concern can be appropriately dealt with via this discourse" with the implication that "morality with its duties, requirements and obligations, is greater than, and different from, justice and its rights."

It is certainly the case, as we have seen, that Rawls recognizes that we have duties to animals, and he seems to be saying that we owe these duties directly to them.[1] This is consistent with his claim that justice is a much narrower area of inquiry than morality, and the treatment of animals is an issue that is incorporated within the latter and not the former. Rawls touches upon this in *A Theory of Justice*, where he remarks (1971: 512) that "a conception of justice is but one part of a moral view," but a more detailed account can be found in his book *Political Liberalism*. Here (1993: 12–13) he suggests that a "political" conception of justice is narrower than a comprehensive view in that it only concerns the basic political structure and not "all kinds of subjects ranging from the conduct of individuals and personal relations to the organization of society as a whole." As a result, "the status of the natural world and our proper relation to it is not a constitutional essential or a basic question of justice," and therefore that "our conduct towards animals is not regulated by" the principles of justice (1993: 246; 1971: 504).

The question of whether there is a viable moral realm independently of justice within which the interests of animals can be protected is discussed further in chapter 3. For now, it should be noted that the problem with Abbey's position is that Rawls does not attempt to answer it, so that her interpretation of Rawls represents supposition. We cannot know that Rawls did take the moral worth of animals seriously, and we cannot know that he regarded the duties of morality as "greater than, and different from" those of justice. It seems just as likely that Rawls was putting forward the conventional animal welfare position that holds that the rights of humans trump the interests of animals, or "Kantianism for humans and utilitarianism for animals" as Nozick (1974: 35–42) puts it (see chapter 5). The problem is that in the form understood by Rawls, cruelty to animals probably means very little, since, according to one interpretation of the animal welfare position, the treatment of animals only becomes cruel when it ceases to have any useful human benefit. It is difficult to see how gratuitous cruelty, such as inflicting suffering on an animal for the fun of it, could be objected to on the grounds that it is an interference with a conception of the good. But the problem is that most suffering on animals, by contrast, is inflicted for a reason, whether it be on religious grounds (as in ritual slaughter) or in the pursuit of cheap food or public health.

More significantly, Abbey does not take enough account of what Rawls actually does say, and in particular the primary importance that he attaches to his principles of justice. Crucially, any suggested moral duties to animals are likely to conflict with these principles. In particular, Rawls's liberty principle, designed to allow individuals to pursue their own conceptions of the good without interference from the state, are always likely to trump attempts to protect the interests of animals, where such attempts conflict with the liberty of humans. Thus, the problem for animals within Rawls's theory of justice is that central to it is the common liberal assertion that it is no part of the state to intervene in competing conceptions of the good. Since the treatment of animals is regarded as a conception of the good for Rawls, the logical con-clusion is that the state should not intervene to regulate the treatment of animals. Whatever is done to animals, therefore, is entirely legitimate, and the state has no justification in intervening to prohibit it. I would argue that this paradigmatic liberal principle, of moral pluralism, has had a consider-able practical impact on the way animals are treated in practice, particu-larly in relation to the issues of hunting and ritual slaughter (Garner, 2005a: 66–81)—see below.

Abbey suggests two possible responses to this negative impact that Rawls's principle of moral pluralism seems to have for animals. First, she asks (2007: 11) whether the cruel treatment of animals might be regarded by Rawls as a type of "unreasonable" pluralism in the moral sphere, in the sense that it would be prohibited precisely on the grounds that it harms animals unjus-tifiably. The problem here is that, for Rawls, what counts as "unreasonable" is defined by what would be allowed by principles of justice. That is, Rawls wants to rule out those doctrines and conceptions of the good life that are "in direct conflict with the principles of justice" and, in particular, those "requiring the repression or degradation of certain persons on, say, racial, or ethnic, or perfectionist grounds" (Rawls, 1993: 195–6). On these grounds, Rawls rules out human slavery as unacceptable (1993: 151–52, 161). By contrast, since animals are not included in his theory of justice, what is done to them cannot be constrained by rules of unreasonable pluralism.

It is true, as Abbey points out in her second response to the problem for animals of moral pluralism, that Rawls's commitment to moral pluralism was more pronounced in his later *Political Liberalism* than in *A Theory of Justice*. Nevertheless, it is consistent with the structure set up in *A Theory of Justice*, whereby justice, and therefore the state, is clearly to be kept out of morality. Thus, it is in *A Theory of Justice* that Rawls (1971: 446) writes that "each person is free to plan his life as he pleases (so long as his intentions are consistent with the principles of justice)." It is in *A Theory of Justice*, too, as I pointed out above, that Rawls sets out the lexical priority of liberty, and this was designed precisely so as to allow the pursuit of various conceptions of the good once the veil is lifted. As Rawls confirms (1971: 450; 447), "To have a complaint against the conduct and belief of others we must show that their actions injure us," since "it is, in general, a good thing that individuals' conceptions of the good should differ in significant ways."

As a result, the question here must be that if Rawls thinks animals are significant enough morally, then why did he not include them as recipients of justice? This is not to say that Abbey (2007: 14–15) is necessarily wrong when she emphasizes the potential usefulness of non-rights and justice-based animal protection discourses (although, as chapter 3 will reveal, I think she is). It is only to say, at this point, that the Rawlsian version offers nothing much to animals if they cannot be incorporated into *his* theory of justice.

Another example of the first response to Rawls—that we should accept his conclusion that animals cannot be direct beneficiaries of justice—is to allow individuals within the original position to protect nonhuman animals, not because they calculate they might end up being nonhuman animals, but because of some other motivational device. Such an approach does not dispense with moral agency as the crucial qualification for being considered a beneficiary of justice. Rather, it sees the moral agents in the original position acting on behalf of, in this case, animals. Clearly, the motivational device cannot be based on altruism, since Rawls's contract is predicated on the self-interest of the participants in the original position. However, it could be based on a calculation that, once out from behind the veil of ignorance, the participants in the original position might discover that they do care about animals and the ability to do so is important to them.

Interestingly, Rawls (1971: 128) himself does use such a motivational device to accord justice to future generations. Thus, he argues that "we may think of the parties as heads of families, and therefore as having a desire to further the welfare of their nearest descendants." Participants in the original position still pursue their own interests, but these interests are expanded so as to include the welfare of (at least some) future generations. The mantle for animals is taken by David Richards, a PhD student of Rawls's, who incorporates animals into his theory in the same way that Rawls incorporates future generations (1971: 207). Participants in the original position are aware "that persons generally have certain basic sympathies with animals and animal life," and, to add an anthropocentric element, they "will understand cruelty to animals as an extension of a personality orientation which is prone to cruelty to persons" (182).

However, there are problems with this move. In the first place, as Brian Barry (1989: 192) points out in the context of future generations, obligations are "dependent purely upon the actual goodwill of contemporaries towards their descendants" and the same would apply to the goodwill of humans towards animals. Therefore, "the demands of justice thus depend on the contingent facts about the extent to which people care about the welfare of (at least some) future people" (Barry, 1989: 192). This move is necessary because future generations (and animals) "would not have any just claims in their own right, but would simply have indirect claims by virtue of the sentiments of the principal parties to the social contract" (Barry, 1989: 245). Here, we can speculate that humans are likely to care more about what happens to future humans than they are to contemporary animals. There must be a significant doubt whether the contractors would know that people are generally sympathetic to animals, since it is far from being a universal human trait and, insofar as it does exist, tends to be reserved for companion animals and not those used to produce food or as scientific subjects.

Contributing Animals?

The second response to Rawls's exclusion of animals from his theory of justice is to seek to adapt his theory in a way that enables animals to be included. Two main adaptations are possible. The first, considered in this section, is to deny that animals do not contribute to society's cooperative relationship, thereby challenging Rawls's assertion that this characteristic excludes them from being owed duties of justice. The second, considered in the next section, is to amend the veil of ignorance so as to make species, along with gender, race, and social situation, as an unknown. Since participants in the original position will then not know whether they will end up being humans or animals, they will protect themselves against the latter eventuality by making sure that animals are owed duties of justice.

Rawls asserts (1971: 4) that only humans are able to contribute toward society. "We are not to gain from the cooperative labors of others without doing our fair share," Rawls (1971: 82) writes, and it is clear that he only has humans in mind here. It has been argued by Mark Coeckelbergh (2009) that animals are not excluded by such a principle because they do, in fact, make a substantial contribution to society. He therefore argues that a moral evaluation of animals should move away from a focus on "what non-humans are" (in terms of their intrinsic value or capacity to suffer) "towards what 'we'...*do together*" (69. Italics original). Animals are therefore morally considerable because of their relations with us. Thus, animals are a source of food for human and other animals, they contribute toward medical research and toxicity testing, and they provide entertainment for us. In return, animals (or at least domesticated animals) depend on us for their lives. In this way, it might be argued that we enter into some form of social contract with animals and animals, implicitly, sign up to it, too.

Rawls chooses to ignore the contribution animals make, writing as if they are outside of society. "A correct conception of our relations to animals and to nature," he writes "would seem to depend upon a theory of the natural order and our place in it" (Rawls, 1971: 511). Wild animals might come into this category, although even wild animals provide plenty of benefits for humans, but countless numbers of animals are domesticated and are therefore very much part of society. As Siobhan O'Sullivan (2007: 8) points out:

> Almost all the animals whose interests are addressed by animal welfare legislation exist explicitly because humans chose to bring them into the world. Indeed, from the moment the animal is bred, until he or she is killed, humans manipulate every aspect of the lives of most captive animals.

As a result, animals are part of a larger co-operative scheme.

There are a number of problems, however, with Coeckelbergh's analysis. Social cooperation is clearly a key feature of Rawls's contractarianism, but incorporating animals on the same grounds as humans, as cooperating beings, is difficult. Much depends on what cooperation means, and what we regard as, in Donaldson and Kymlicka's (2011: 88) words, "fair terms of interaction." In its strongest sense, cooperation would be active and voluntary. This, however, would exclude nonhuman animals and some humans, too. On the other hand, if it is established that all contributions to society count, and we ignore whether this contribution is voluntarily given or whether those who do contribute get anything themselves out of the arrangement, there would seem little to prevent the inclusion in a theory of justice of those objects, such as rivers, trees, and mountains, which contribute to the sum of benefits in society. Of course, there is an argument, put forward by some environmental ethicists, that nonsentient parts of nature *ought* to be recipients of justice. However, it is not in the remit of this book to consider this large ethical issue. What can be pointed out, however, is that neither Rawls nor Coecklelbergh would accept this outcome.

We could avoid this outcome, of including the whole of nature within the ambit of justice, by limiting cooperation to contributions that are voluntarily given. However, this would also produce results undesirable to both Rawls and Coeckelbergh. In the case of Rawls, it would have the effect of denying justice to those humans, such as slaves, whose contribution is not voluntarily given (Baxter, 2005: 79). For Coeckelbergh, it would deny the force of his argument that animals contribute to society, since it is stretching credulity somewhat to claim that they volunteer to be raised and killed for food or to be the subjects of scientific experiments.

We could also, as Baxter (2005: 84) does, make the claim, in the context of a theory of ecological justice, that "something making a contribution to the sum of environmental benefits is a necessary, but not sufficient, condition of its being an appropriate recipient of ecological justice." What is missing here, though, is a theory of moral considerability possessed by those due justice and not by those denied it. The problem here, of course, is that Rawls would insist upon personhood as the necessary criterion, which rather takes us back to square one because this would exclude most, if not all, nonhuman animals and therefore deny the force of Coeckelbergh's argument about the importance of cooperation and the contribution animals make to society.

A further objection to Coeckelbergh's approach, as he himself recognizes, is that it only obviously applies to domesticated animals. It is true that, as indicated above, wild animals may contribute to human society (in the sense that they provide aesthetic pleasure for humans or income as in the case of ecotourism). However, the interests of wild animals also often conflict with those of humans. Insofar as they do, they are excluded from a theory of justice dependent upon social cooperation. We could, of course, ask what is wrong with excluding those animals that are not domesticated. One persuasive response, in my view, is that if wild animals are excluded from a theory of justice, and if, as this book suggests, the claims of justice are greater than those of morality, then our obligations to wild animals will be much less onerous than those we owe to domesticated animals, and perhaps nonexistent. This is an outcome that is, I believe, morally problematic, if not counterintuitive.

This critique of relational theories will be revisited in a number of places in this book, particularly in chapter 6. For now, it should be noted that, according to Coeckelberg, animals will only be owed duties of justice whilst they are in a cooperative relationship with humans. But, in order to include the bulk of domesticated animals—those in laboratories and factory farms—as cooperators this means equating cooperation with exploitation. This amounts to the rather odd position that animals are only due justice whilst they are being exploited. In practical terms, it means, for instance, that it is just for humans to eat animals because in this way they contribute to human society, but, since vegetarians are no longer in a cooperative relationship with food animals, desisting from eating animals is neither a just nor an unjust act.

Rowlands, Rawls, and Animals

In terms of the second type of adaptation, it is, of course, the case that amending the veil of ignorance to incorporate animals challenges Rawls's assertion that only moral agents can be recipients of justice.[2] One difficulty for Rawls here (and for contractarianism in general) is that insisting upon moral agency as an entry qualification for justice also has the effect of excluding some humans, such as the very young and the severely mentally disabled, so-called "marginal" humans. As will be noted in chapter 9, this term might be regarded as offensive by some. I appreciate these points, but agree with Dombrowski (1997: 2) that the term "marginal" remains useful, not least because it enables the reader to follow the extensive debate where marginal is the usual label and because it encompasses all of the humans we want to consider, including the congenitally mentally disabled, those who have acquired mental deficiencies, and infants.

Rawls's justification for including so-called "marginal" humans is that infants will eventually become persons and marginal adults have been persons in the past. Of course, some "marginal" humans have never been persons and never will be, but Rawls still includes them within his theory of justice on the grounds partly that to fail to do so is "a risk to just institutions," and partly because these individuals would have been parties to the contract but for their unfortunate circumstances (1971: 509). He does not, however, explain further what this "risk" might be, although others, such as Carruthers (1992: 114–18), have opined that excluding marginal humans from an entitlement to justice would lead to a slippery slope whereby the boundary line for inclusion and exclusion would become blurred (see chapter 9). In addition, Rawls's second reason for including marginal humans—that those humans born as nonpersons were unfortunate and should not be penalized for their bad luck—is open to the response that being born as an animal is similarly a matter of chance.

Recognizing, no doubt, the potential inconsistency of his position, Rawls does, at one point, cast doubt on the strength of his commitment to the importance of moral agency, arguing that he is unsure whether it is a necessary condition for being a recipient of justice (Rawls, 1971: 505). Barry (1989: 211) is right to suggest that this doubt is because Rawls recognizes the inconsistency of not including animals but including those humans who have not yet gained moral agency or who will never possess it. His initial assumption, that animals are not to be included as recipients of justice is, though, confirmed.

The reality is that Rawls's contractarian political thought finds it difficult to include those entities who are not moral agents, whether they are marginal humans or animals. The claim that it is counterintuitive to exclude the former as recipients of justice does not by itself, of course, validate amending Rawls's contract to include both marginal humans and animals. What it might do is to persuade us that we have to look elsewhere for a theory that can do this work, or, alternatively, we could reject arguments based on intuition and argue that neither marginal humans nor animals are the kind of beings who can be recipients of justice. This position might be made more palatable if we expand the duties owed within the moral realm identified by Rawls to marginal humans as well as animals.

In order to justify amending the terms of the contract to include animals (and marginal humans), we need a further argument. The most sustained attempt has been provided by Rowlands (1997, 1998, 2009). To get to grips with Rowlands's argument, it is necessary to see, initially, why it is that Rawls (and contractarian theories in general) finds it difficult to incorporate animals as well as marginal humans. When one thinks of a contract designed to come up with principles of justice, one envisages a situation where self-interested individuals meet to decide upon principles under which they are to live. In this type of contract, "consisting of mutually advantageous rules of conduct"

(Rowlands, 2009: 123), the principles of justice adopted are constituted by the contract, and their authority derives from the fact that those in the contractual situation have agreed to them because they are perceived to be in the self-interest of the participants. In this scenario, the only justification for seeking to agree principles with others is if they can help or hinder us in some way. Since animals do not come into this category, they must be excluded from the contractual situation.

For Rowlands, this type of contract is a Hobbesian version. But there is another version of the contract, a Kantian version, and Rowlands argues not only that this version enables us to include animals, but also that this is the version that Rawls, in the main, adopts. So, for Rowlands, only a Hobbesian type of contract, where the self-interest of the participants is the sole concern, is consistent with the exclusion of animals.[3] In a Kantian-type of contract, on the other hand, the principles of justice adopted are not merely constituted by the participants. Rather, the principles arrived at through the contract have to be continually checked against preexisting moral values that exist independently of the contract and the contractors. Thus, "Contained in the idea of Kantian contractarianism ... is an at least minimal conception of moral *objectivity* that is independent of the contract and the agreements reached by contractors" (Rowlands, 2009: 126). Rowlands argues that the key "moral law" that Rawls advocates is "equal consideration," or what Rowlands calls the "intuitive equality argument" (IEA). This is the argument that individuals should not benefit from the possession of characteristics, such as ability or rationality, for which they are not responsible. The principles of justice emanating from the contract, then, must, for Rowlands, be consistent with the IEA.

If we adopt this principle, Rowlands suggests, there is nothing to stop us from including nonmoral agents, such as animals and marginal humans, as beneficiaries of principles of justice. Rawls's failure to see this, according to Rowlands (2009: 153), was because of the "unexpurgated and unnecessary elements of Hobbesianism" in his theory. For Rowlands, the IEA insists that we do include animals (and marginal humans) because rationality itself is not a characteristic that we have earned. Rather, we just have it as a matter of luck. Thus, just as specific human abilities, and more general characteristics such as age, gender, race, and class, are hidden behind the veil of ignorance, rationality is an equally undeserved natural advantage that also ought to be hidden. Indeed, a failure to include species as a hidden characteristic, it is argued, would be tantamount to speciesism in the same way that to allow knowledge of race or gender in the original position would be racist and sexist (Van De Veer, 1979a: 374).

Including species as an unknown characteristic behind the veil of ignorance means, then, that the participants in the original position do not now
know if they are going to turn out to be moral agents, or nonrational entities
such as animals or marginal humans. This would then allow Rawls's principles of justice to apply to animals. Thus, the "difference principle," that social
and economic inequalities are to be arranged so that they are to the greatest
benefit of the least advantaged, would now benefit all those sentient beings,
including animals and the most vulnerable humans, as the least able to defend
their interests. In practice, this "would entail that many widespread standard
ways that animals are treated are grossly unjust" (Van De Veer, 1979a: 373). As
Rowlands (2009: 166) concurs:

> Once it is allowed that knowledge of one's species should be one of
> those things excluded by the veil of ignorance, it would be just as irra-
> tional to opt for a system that permitted harmful or injurious treat-
> ment of non-humans as it would be to opt for a system that permitted
> the same sort of treatment for humans.

Three major criticisms can be made of Rowlands's attempt to amend
Rawls. I will deal with the two relatively minor ones before outlining what
I see as the major problem. The first is raised by Brian Baxter (2005: 95–6),
who questions, with some justification, whether it is possible for participants
behind the veil of ignorance to be ignorant of their status as human beings.
Rawls imputes to the contractors a number of intellectual capacities, and not
least the capacity to understand the "maximin" principle (the risk-averse strategy Rawls claim contractors in the original position will adopt). Given this,
Baxter argues, "there is no room for the idea that they could also be ignorant
of their species, for they would know for certain that they would be members
of species which possess at least these minimal attributes."

Of course, Rowlands and others would respond by saying that this does
not preclude the possibility of the human contractors *imagining* that they
may still turn out to be nonhumans once the veil is lifted. We might say,
for instance, that the contractors possess the characteristics of personhood
only for the duration of the debates in the original position, and once the
veil is lifted these characteristics no longer necessarily apply. Baxter (2005:
96) claims this move is "impossible to make sense of" because the resulting change would be too drastic. Now, whilst Baxter is right to claim that it
would be difficult, if not impossible, for the rational contractors in the original position to imagine turning out to be a bacterium—indeed it is surely

inconceivable—it is not so difficult for a human person to imagine being a sentient mammal. Indeed, there is a case for saying it is no more difficult for a human person to imagine being a mammal than it is for her to imagine being a severely mentally disabled human.

It should be noted that we can accept that the interests of animals can be incorporated into Rawls's theory of justice and still dispute Rowlands's assertion that this would produce principles of justice that would sanction abolitionist objectives such as a prohibition on the eating of animals. There is a great deal of literature on Rawls that questions whether his contractors would adopt the maximin strategy (Wolff, 1996: 177–86). In the case of animals, it might be the case that contractors would risk turning out to be nonhuman. This likelihood is enhanced if they rationalize that, as animals, they would not be autonomous agents and therefore had less to lose by death (see chapter 8). Of course, the exploitation of animals in factory farms involves the infliction of a great deal of suffering. However, prohibiting intensive animal agriculture is not the same as prohibiting the eating of animals. It is least a possibility, then, that the contractors behind Rawls's veil of ignorance might choose to prohibit the infliction of suffering on animals—on the grounds that they might turn out to be animals—whilst still sanctioning the eating of animals—on the grounds that this pleasure would not be denied to them if they turned out to be humans.[4]

The biggest problem with the approach suggested by Rowlands relates to his Kantian interpretation of the contract. We can readily accept that this is closer to Rawls's own position than the Hobbesian version. Crucial here is Rawls's reliance upon a process of "reflective equilibrium" whereby his principles of justice are measured against widely accepted moral intuitions (1971: 48–52). However, the problem with accepting that there are moral principles we value independently of what is decided by the participants in the contractual situation is that it reduces the importance of the contract device. It amounts to saying that the contract must be so organized as to reflect these important preexisting moral principles, or at least to consider them seriously. Rawls's exclusion of animals is arguably, therefore, made prior to his use of the contractual device. That is, by concluding that only moral agents should be beneficiaries of justice, Rawls has already made the decision that animals ought to be excluded from his theory of justice. Principles emanating from the contract are, therefore, not the result of an objective account of what participants in the original position would choose, but reflect preexisting normative judgments, one of which is that justice only applies to persons.

What I am arguing here, then, is that a "pure" form of the contract does make it difficult to include animals as beneficiaries of a contractarian theory of justice. Rawls does not, however, offer such a "pure" version of contractarianism in which the principles of justice adopted are constituted by the contract, and where their authority derives from the fact that those in the contractual situation have agreed to them. Therefore, there is a strong case for saying that Rawls does offer resources for the protection of animals. That is, Rowlands may well be right to say that what he describes as the "intuitive equality argument" does, in fact, despite Rawls's denial, allow for the inclusion of animals and marginal humans.

What should be recognized, however, is that the principle that allows for the inclusion of animals as beneficiaries of justice, for both Rawls and Rowlands, derives from outside the confines of the contractual arrangement. Indeed, Rowlands (2009, 127–8) admits that the "contract does not determine who does and who does not count morally." The question to ask, therefore, is what is the value-added of persevering with a contractarian approach for those interested in the protection of animals? And if the answer, as it must be, is that it adds very little, then there is a compelling case for saying that we would be better off invoking the intuitive equality argument as a free-standing principle from which the justice claims of animals and marginal humans can be derived independently of the contract. That is, the use of the contract device, which is the most distinctive element of Rawls's thought, is not necessary to establish the validity of the intuitive equality principle and the inclusion of animals as beneficiaries of justice.

Justice as Impartiality

One way of rescuing the type of position Rowlands adopts is to consider the contractarian account—justice as impartiality—put forward by the British political philosopher Brian Barry (1995). Nothing much has been written on the role of animals in Brian Barry's version of contractarianism. This represents a gap in the literature because, superficially at least, Barry would appear to be more sympathetic than Rawls to the interests of animals. In particular, Barry hints that animal protection can be incorporated within a theory of justice as impartiality, and, even if this is not in fact the case, he is prepared to contemplate a procedural device whereby the state intervenes to uphold one conception of the good over another.

Barry's contractarian theory of justice—justice as impartiality—starts by arguing that Rawls's original position is inadequate, and therefore ought to be replaced with an alternative, derived from Scanlon (1982; 1988, 1998). This Scanlonian approach, originally devised as a vehicle for moral arguments rather than those concerned with justice, "takes the fundamental question to be whether a principle could reasonably be rejected by parties who, in addition to their own personal aims, were moved by a desire to find principles that others similarly motivated could also accept" (Scanlon, 1988: 137–8). The Scanlonian contract differs from Rawls's version in two crucial ways. In the first place, it dispenses with the veil of ignorance. In other words, parties in the original position are aware of their identities and their interests. Secondly, the parties are not merely self-interested, as in the Hobbesian version of the contract, but are motivated by "the desire for reasonable agreement" (Barry, 1995: 67). Individuals, therefore, have a "desire to behave fairly" (52). Principles of justice, for Barry, therefore, will come about as a result of bargaining and negotiation within the original position. It is thus impartial because it "entails that people should not look at things from their own point of view alone but seek to find a basis for agreement that is acceptable from all points of view" (Barry, 1989: 8). Only those principles that cannot be reasonably rejected by others pass the test and can be included as principles of justice. To this end, Barry envisages a veto power for each person "on all proposed principles for regulating social life" (Barry, 1995: 69).

Where does Barry's version of the contract leave animals? According to him, the inclusion of animal protection principles within justice as impartiality would require that they be principles that cannot be reasonably rejected. Unlike Rawls and consistently with Rowlands, Barry can include the interests of animals within a theory of justice because he adopts a broad notion of interests. That is, for Barry, the term "interests" can also include altruistic wants such as a desire to see animals well-protected. Thus, Barry's original position contains "people who are well informed, concerned to further their own interest and conceptions of the good, but capable of recognizing reasonable objections on the part of others" (Barry, 1995 99). This approach can be contrasted with what he calls justice as mutual advantage, associated with Hobbes and, more recently, Gauthier (1986), which is the approach that Rowlands seeks to expunge from Rawls's contractarian theory. As we saw, justice as mutual advantage is clearly inadequate for a theory that seeks to protect the interests of animals, and indeed nonrational humans too, since, as Buchanan (1990: 227) points out, it is "founded solely on mutual gain and...for this reason animals, as beings from whom one can benefit without reciprocating, are not within the scope of justice." Thus, as we saw, both Hobbes and Gauthier do exclude animals as beneficiaries of contractual agreements.

Despite the positive noises Barry makes about the moral status of animals, however, there is every reason to think that all but the most basic animal protection principles would fail to achieve reasonable agreement, and thus be excluded from a theory of justice. In the first place, note that, according to the terms of the Scanlonian contract, a principle of justice involving animals would not be owed directly to animals, since principles of justice can only apply to those moral agents who are capable of negotiating the contract. The interests of animals can only be considered indirectly by those humans who regard it as a good they wish to promote. In Barry's Scanlonian version of the contract, the participants know they are humans and know what their particular, narrow, self-interests are. This can be contrasted with Rawls's theory of justice whereby it is open to us to argue, as Rowlands does, that participants in the original position ought to seek the direct protection of animals just in case any of them turn out to be animals.

It is easy to see why the protection of animals—conceived as a good—is likely to be rejected in a Scanlonian contract. Consider an interest directly impinging on (human) participants in the original position such as an interest in not being harmed. Now, a principle protecting humans from harm is unlikely to be rejected since to do so would sacrifice a fundamental interest, one that is necessary for the pursuit of any conception of the good. In a similar vein, as Barry (1995: 8) points out, although you would benefit from privileged treatment being given to your skin color or gender, you cannot reasonably expect this to be acceptable to those (with a different skin color or gender) who would lose out. However, this is a very different category from the upholding of a particular conception of the good, such as the protection of animals. In this latter category, it might not be reasonable to reject a principle that prohibits gratuitous cruelty, defined as cruelty that does not serve any nontrivial human purpose. Many would object, however, to a principle of justice aimed at protecting animals precisely on the grounds that it impacts negatively upon their alternative conception of the good such as one involving a fundamental economic interest.

This conclusion is heightened by the fact that all that is required for a proposed principle of justice to be rejected is an individual veto. As Kelly (1998: 57) points out, Barry's contract "seems to weight the argument too much in favour of an individual's own self-interest." This resort to (usually economic) self-interest is exactly, of course, how the exploitation of animals is usually justified. In fact, the position of animals may well be worse under Barry's justice as impartiality than it would under the current animal welfare orthodoxy (see chapter 5). For example, the economic interests of agribusiness or pharmaceutical companies are likely, if the Scanlonian model is applied, to act as a veto upon measures to improve the welfare of animals, and this veto would override public opinion. It is difficult to see how measures, say, to eliminate the worst excesses of factory farming—which are beginning to happen in practice—would be justified by justice as impartiality.

Barry (1995: 172) is, in fact, clear that "no conception of the good should be built into the constitution or the principles of justice." Only if animals themselves are regarded as being direct beneficiaries of justice, as opposed to being part of a human's conception of the good, would substantial animal welfare measures be acceptable according to justice as impartiality. This is consistent with Barry's statement that "it does not seem to me that the concept of justice can be deployed intelligibly outside the context of relations between human beings" precisely because "justice and injustice can be predicated only of relations among creatures who are regarded as moral equals" (Barry, 1999: 95).

One option that is open to Barry, although he does not take this up, is to imagine that the interests of animals could be represented by a trustee or surrogate. This would ensure that the interests of animals could be considered directly in the original position. Some, such as Martha Nussbaum (2004: 335), regard this as a weak form of moral entitlement in that, in Andrew Cohen's words, "it denies them their independent standing by filtering their interests through the interests of trustees" (Cohen, 2007: 195–96). I am inclined to agree with Cohen (2007: 195–96) that this is a criticism of "irresponsible or sloppy" trusteeship rather than a criticism of trusteeship in general. In other words, if it is accepted that animals can be represented by trustees under the terms of the contract, then their interests can be considered directly, and all that is left is the, by no means easy, task of deciding the practicalities of representing animals in this way.

A more significant question for our purposes is to ask whether there are grounds for including animals as worthy recipients of trustee representation within Barry's contractarian theory. Cohen (2007) thinks so. He distinguishes between what he calls primary and secondary moral standing within a contractarian framework. Primary moral standing is attached to those (normal rational adult humans) who are part of the "circumstances of justice" in the sense that they are able to participate in the making of agreements. Secondary moral standing is attached to those unable to participate in the making of agreements (nonhuman animals and marginal humans). This latter form of moral standing applies when enough rational agents (the advocates) insist upon other contractors regarding animals and marginal humans as beings with moral standing in return for their (the advocates') cooperation.

Christopher Morris (1998: 191) adopts essentially the same position in defense of contractarianism. Thus, he argues that, "No normal human being would interact cooperatively with someone who was not ready to accord genuine moral standing to one's children," and by extrapolation animals.

It is acceptable, as a matter of practice, for the interests of animals to be represented directly by a trustee. What is much harder to accept is the position that secondary moral standing, as described by Cohen, provides grounds for the effective representation of animal interests. The problem is, as with our discussion of Barry's contract in general, that justice (secondary moral standing for Cohen) is owed to animals insofar as other humans regard it as a good worth having. As a result, the extent to which animals are accorded moral standing will be dependent upon enough humans wanting this outcome, plus their ability to persuade others that it is worthwhile. It is, in other words, contingent. Cohen (2007: 196) admits this when he writes that the awarding of secondary moral standing to animals "would depend on empirical considerations: how many people insist on direct moral regard, and for which animals?"

What I have said so far, in this consideration of Barry's contractarianism, suggests that it is unlikely, by utilizing justice as impartiality, that substantial animal welfare measures would be adopted as principles of justice. Nevertheless, he also raises the possibility that the state does not have to remain neutral about competing conceptions of the good but might intervene to promote one at the expense of another (Barry, 1995: 77). The outcomes would not be regarded as principles of justice but are part of justice as impartiality in the sense that decisions are taken in accordance with procedural justice. This is promising, from an animal protection perspective, because Barry is right to say that the preclusion principle—issues raising moral controversy should always be settled by leaving the decision to the individual, at least where to do so does not cause harm to others—is used "by defenders of the continued legality of barbarous sports such as fox hunting, stag hunting, and hare coursing, and could, presumably, be used with equal force for the restoration of legality to such things as cock fighting, dog fighting, and bear baiting" (Barry, 1995: 91). In this context, for instance, it is no accident that the defenders of fox hunting in Britain campaigned against the proposal to ban the practice primarily on libertarian grounds, that it was a matter of individual conscience and liberty.[5]

Barry, therefore, appears to offer a way out of the difficulty of reconciling moral pluralism with a moral imperative to treat animals humanely, since it would seem justifiable for the good of animal protection to be pursued by the state through the mechanism of a democratic procedure, even though by so doing competing conceptions of the good might be damaged in the process. For those concerned about the welfare of animals, however, Barry's acceptance that a theory of justice must have a procedure to adjudicate between competing conceptions of the good does not seem to offer much. Even though majority decisions—accompanied by a full, free, and well-informed debate—are acceptable, so there is no veto, it is a hit and miss affair with no guarantee that decisions would be made protecting animals. As Richard Arneson (1998: 66) points out, the claim that "'we are following fair procedures' cannot be an adequate answer to someone who complains that she is unfairly disadvantaged by sectarian state policy." Moreover, Barry's liberal focus means that he is still committed to the distinction between the right and the good. Therefore, because he thinks that competing conceptions of the good "cannot be resolved by rational argument," (Barry, 1995: 30) he is clear that the state should remain neutral about them. That is, because disputes about the good are irresolvable, neutrality is "the only fair, and thus generally acceptable, way of dealing with this fact" (Barry, 1995: 13).

Barry (1995: 171) himself, for example, admits to being an admirer of a conception of the good that seeks to attach intrinsic value to nature, including animals, living but nonsentient entities, and wholes such as ecosystems and species. "But I do not see," he confesses, "how its claims can be presented in such a way as to show that it would be unreasonable to adopt a different view, and I take it that any other conception of the good is subject to the same liability." This is why, for Barry, a communitarian attempt to derive a theory of justice from a particular conception of the good is doomed to failure. Thus, in a comment with obvious relevance to the topic of this book, Barry (1995: 171) argues that "I shall be surprised" if (MacIntyre's) *Whose Justice? Which Rationality?* "makes as many converts to Thomism as Peter Singer's *Animal Liberation* has to vegetarianism."

Justice as impartiality, then, is not in itself a comprehensive moral system but instead sets "the legitimate limits to the pursuit of any particular moral system's precepts" (Barry, 1995: 77). These limits are set by the prevention of harm which is the fundamental principle of justice as impartiality because "what is harmful is deleterious to the furtherance of virtually any conception of the good" (143). All of this would seem to suggest that only when it is absolutely necessary for the state to adjudicate actively between competing conceptions of the good should it do so. Thus, putting competing conceptions of the good to the vote must surely be a last resort for liberals such as Barry since to do so offends against moral pluralism.

Clearly, in some cases a decision has to be taken one way or the other. Where such a decision can be avoided, though, a commitment to moral pluralism surely necessitates inaction. Barry accepts that many different conceptions of the good pursued by individuals and groups do not conflict. I, for instance, may abstain from pork on religious grounds whereas you do not. Even if I think that your moral view is misguided, Barry (1995: 80) argues, "we may still agree that each of us has a perfect right... to do either x or y." This, as a matter of fact, is the way that the treatment of animals tends to be framed in liberal societies. Thus, I may choose to abstain from eating meat whereas you do not and I may choose to buy "cruelty free" cosmetics whereas you do not. Both of our conceptions of the good are thereby accommodated in a liberal polity.

The problem with this from an animal protection perspective, however, is obvious. As long as the interests of animals within a liberal framework are framed in terms of a human conception of the good—that is, a conception of the good that is thought of by humans—their protection is likely to be limited, if not nonexistent. Protecting animals in most cases is, as we have seen, unlikely to receive the reasonable agreement that Barry demands to be incorporated as a principle of justice. Moreover, the neutrality principle is always likely to be an obstacle to putting animal protection issues through the just decision procedure that Barry recommends, and even if an issue involving animal protection is decided in a way that benefits animals, its existence is fragile.

Conclusion

This chapter focused on two objections to the inclusion of animals as recipients of justice. We gave short shrift to the distributive objection. The contractarian objection is more difficult to answer. The main conclusion of this chapter is that attempts to find support in Rawls's political theory for the protection of animals generally fail. It is wishful thinking to suppose that animals would receive indirect protection as a result of contractors in the original position coming to the conclusion that they might care about them once out from behind the veil of ignorance. Secondly, the tactic of "thickening" the veil of ignorance so as to include species as an unknown characteristic is only justified if one imports principles from outside of the contractual agreement. These principles can be found in Rawls's work but they are not dependent on his distinctive contract device. Similarly, placing emphasis on social cooperation as a means of incorporating animals into a theory of justice may, counterintuitively, exclude some humans as beneficiaries of justice, requires that cooperation is voluntary given, in order to exclude inanimate objects, and equates justice with exploitation and therefore "liberation" as an unjust act.

Similarly, it is unlikely that participants in Barry's Scanlonian original position would opt for principles of justice that involved considerable protection for animals. To propose such principles would invariably fail to get reasonable agreement since they would be vetoed—as conceptions of the good that do not serve the vital interest of their advocates—by those with a fundamental interest in continuing to exploit animals. To avoid this conclusion from within a contractarian framework requires either that species membership is included as an unknown behind a veil of ignorance, or that some justification is found for representing the direct interests of animals within Barry's version of the original position. The former option is unavailable to Barry and the latter, as we have seen, is a doubtful prospect. Barry does offer the possibility of adjudicating between competing conceptions of the good according to principles laid down by justice as impartiality. However, the decisions (as opposed to the procedure by which they are made) emanating from Barry's procedural device are not themselves substantive principles of justice, to be constitutionally entrenched, and are open to repeal at any point in the future. Moreover, it is unlikely that many issues involving animals will be subject to the justice as impartiality procedure anyway since Barry is committed to the liberal position that, as far as possible, individuals should be left alone to pursue their own conceptions of the good.

It is understandable why attempts have been made to utilize contractarianism in general, and Rawls's version in particular, on behalf of animals. Not only is contractarianism in general able, apparently, to answer key questions about moral obligation, but, in addition, Rawls's version of it has, of course, taken a central place in Western political thought. It is possible that alternative versions of a contractarian position might be able to incorporate animals, although it is not the purpose of this book to attempt to develop such an alternative. Such a task might be necessary if contractarianism were the only way animals could be incorporated as recipients of justice. However, this is not the case. Indeed, two separate moves are suggested by this chapter. The first is to look for an alternative theory of justice, based, for example, on a free-standing equal consideration of interests principle. The second is to consider whether the moral realm independently of justice, suggested by both Rawls and Barry, is sufficiently robust to merit jettisoning the attempt to incorporate animals within a theory of justice. The former option is explored in chapters 5 through 9, the latter is the subject matter of the following two chapters.

3

Why Animals Need Justice

WE HAVE ESTABLISHED that major objections to the inclusion of animals within a theory of justice fail. In particular, I argued that we can either successfully incorporate animals within a contractarian theory, a task that I suggested was difficult, or we can look elsewhere to find more fertile territory. This chapter examines one possible response to the exclusion of animals from the contractarian theories developed by political philosophers such as Rawls and Barry. The reader will remember that three major responses to this claim are possible. In chapter 2, the first possible response—to try to adapt Rawls so as to include animals as recipients of justice or to find an alternative contractarian theory that enables us to do so—was considered and rejected. Subsequent chapters will explore the possibility of finding an alternative theory of justice that fares better, the second response. Before I do that, however, it is worthwhile to stand back for a moment and consider a third response. This is the possibility that animals do not, in fact, need justice. The idea that they do not derives from the assumption of contractarians such as Rawls and Barry that there is a moral realm operating independently of justice. In this chapter and the next I will ask, what is the character of this moral realm and what degree of protection can animals receive within it?

The analysis in this chapter should begin by reminding ourselves of three important observations. Firstly, it has been noted that animals have very rarely been regarded by political and moral philosophers as the kind of beings who are entitled to justice. Secondly, most theories of justice mention animals in passing, as an afterthought, without explaining why it is that they should be excluded. Rawls is the exception here. As we saw, he excludes animals explicitly from his theory of justice mainly on the basis that they are not moral agents. Finally, despite excluding them from his theory of justice, Rawls does not rule out protecting animals from cruel treatment, but for him this concern belongs to a broader moral arena that is not part of the realm of justice. Barry (1995: 77) concurs with Rawls here. "It is...a great mistake," he writes, "to suppose that justice as impartiality is intended to constitute a complete, self-sufficient moral system."

We also saw in chapter 2 that Ruth Abbey (2007) takes Rawls at face value, arguing that the task of the moral philosopher is to "examine what sort of moral relationship humans might have to animals" that is not dependent on arguments relating to justice. Abbey devotes the majority of her article to establishing that it was Rawls's *real* intention to attach considerable importance to a moral realm independently of justice within which duties to animals could exist. She concludes that the implication of Rawls's approach is that "morality with its duties, requirements, and obligations, is greater than, and different from, justice and its rights" (Abbey, 2007: 9). Abbey spends less time examining the character of this moral realm, something that this chapter seeks to do.

The Arenas of Justice and Morality

The starting point here is to try to tease out the differences between the concepts of justice and morality. Clearly, if justice is regarded as part, but not the whole part, of the moral realm, then logically there *is* a moral realm independently of justice that might offer an arena where some protection for animals might occur. On the other hand, if, as some animal ethicists do, we conflate justice with morality, then it is difficult to see how we can owe any direct duties to animals if animals are excluded, as they are in most contractarian theories, as recipients of justice. What is open to us, then, is to claim that our duties to animals are indirect, in the sense that the protection of animals is dependent upon the degree to which it benefits us. Chapter 4 is devoted to a consideration of such indirect duty views.

Liberal political theorists such as Rawls and Barry are very clear that their theories of justice are not comprehensive moral theories, and that, in Rawls's case at least, although animals cannot be recipients of justice, we still have direct duties toward them. For Rawls, then, not being included in a theory of justice does not mean that animals have no intrinsic value, nor does it mean that the duties we owe to them are indirect. This leaves open the possibility of a realm of morality wider than justice in which animals could prosper. It is clear that Rawls's position has been misinterpreted by those with diametrically opposed positions on the moral status of animals. The confusion has been occasioned by the conflating of a contractarian theory of justice with a contractarian theory of morality. Rawls argues that animals' lack of moral agency prevents them from benefitting from principles of justice. It does not, however, mean that they cannot benefit directly from principles of morality. We *could* adopt a contractarian theory of morality, but this is not what Rawls is proposing.

Both Tom Regan and Gary Steiner, from an animal rights perspective, and Peter Carruthers, who seeks to deny the moral standing of animals, are guilty of the same error here. Regan, for instance, remarks (1985: 17) that Rawls's contractarianism "systematically denies that we have direct duties to those human beings who do not have a sense of justice—young children, for instance, and many mentally retarded humans," as well as animals. In a more recent work, Regan repeats the claim that Rawls's "moral outlook prejudicially excludes nonhuman animals from direct moral concern" (Cohen and Regan, 2001: 171). For Steiner (2008: 119), similarly "Rawls…like Kant, takes it for granted that only rational agents can be owed direct duties." From the other end of the moral continuum, Carruthers (1992: 99) makes the same mistake, incorrectly stating that, "Animals will…have no moral standing under Rawlsian contractualism, in so far as they do not count as rational agents." Carruthers does go on to develop a contractarian theory of morality and, having done so, concludes there is no question of animals being owed direct duties within a moral realm independently of justice. But such a theory is not as Rawlsian as he seems to suggest. Alison Hills (2005: 93) recognizes this distinction. As she points out, it is only if "the *whole* of ethics is defined by a contract," as it is for Carruthers, that animals might be deemed to have no moral standing so that we have no direct duties to them. Rawls, by contrast, wants to distinguish between ethics and justice, with animals excluded only from the latter.

Animal ethicists have, of course, expended a great deal of effort seeking to establish what moral obligations we have to animals, and, particularly in the case of advocates of animal rights, have concluded that our moral obligations to nonhuman animals are considerable and ought to be enforced by the state and adhered to by individuals whether or not the state enforces them. What animal ethicists do not focus on is the relative importance that might be attached to their moral principles vis-a-vis the concept of justice. An answer to this question should allow us to suggest what it means for animals if they are excluded from a theory of justice. Moreover, establishing a moral realm independently of justice, but not necessarily inferior to it, would allow a solution to a much-noted problem with contractarian theories: that excluding nonrational moral agents as recipients not only excludes animals but also nonrational humans as recipients of justice. Many who do not find it troubling that animals are excluded as morally considerable *are* uncomfortable with the notion that nonrational, or "marginal," humans—such as infants, and severely cognitively impaired adults—are excluded too. If there is a moral realm of substantial weight within which direct duties to such humans can be justified, then their exclusion from contractarian theories of justice is less troubling.

The first step in an attempt to determine what importance can be attached to animals within a moral realm independently of justice is to try to delineate the differences between justice and morality, not an easy task given the elusive character of both concepts. For some thinkers, justice is regarded as synonymous with morality, so that what is unjust is roughly equivalent to what is morally wrong. Others seem to regard justice as a specific form of morality. In my view, morality is clearly a broader concept than justice, and I fully concur with John Passmore's observation (1979: 47) that those who adopt a broader concept of justice are "trying to pack too much into the concept... The question of whether it is *wrong* to act in certain ways is not the same question as whether it is *unjust* so to act."

For one thing, not all moral arguments necessarily result in corresponding obligations. It is clearly possible, for instance, to claim that a particular action or way of behaving is immoral without insisting that those behaving in such a way have an obligation to desist or that the state intervene to prohibit it (Scanlon, 1998: 6). Actions that Mill describes as self-regarding obviously fit into this category. For example, I might decry morally the promiscuous behavior of many within modern society, and yet this does not automatically mean that those engaging in such behavior have an obligation to desist from it or that the state should intervene to force them to behave differently, although a case can be made that this should be the outcome perhaps on the grounds of paternalism. Most moral philosophers, therefore, would want to make a distinction between ought and duty such that "one ought to do that which one has a duty to do but one does not always have a duty to do that which one ought" (Raz, 1986: 195). In other words, what we believe we ought to do can be separated from what others can justly demand that we do.

A further distinction that is crucial here is between justice, on the one hand, and charity or compassion on the other. Justice differs from charity and compassion in the sense that the former is associated with corresponding obligations. Justice therefore involves an element of compulsion. To behave justly is "a requirement rather than an optional extra" (Campbell, 1988: 20). Charity or compassion, by contrast, is regarded as a voluntary act, one which, whilst a good thing to do, is not a wrong thing not to do. As Nussbaum (2004: 302) points out: "What we most typically mean when we call a bad act unjust is that the creature injured by that act has an entitlement not to be treated in that way, and an entitlement of a particularly urgent or basic type."

Of course, *moral* entitlements, with corresponding obligations, can exist independently of charity. There are, however, two further distinguishing characteristics of justice that follow from the assertion that it is a concept associated with entitlements and obligations. The first is that because action against injustice is regarded as so pressing, the political status of justice is extremely high. It is common for political philosophers to recognize it as such. A few examples will suffice. Vincent (2004: 110) sets the scene when he describes justice as the "major preoccupation of the history of political theory from the Greeks to the present." Tom Campbell (1974: 5) acknowledges that the word "justice" has strong emotive meaning such "that to describe one's policies as just can be rhetorically efficacious" and that it "tends to be assumed that showing a course of action to be a just one is equivalent to ensuring its definitive vindication." Christopher Morris (2008: 75), likewise, describes justice as an "imperial" concept and "its partisans often seek to secure its dominance, sometimes even by banishing other virtues from the realm of ethics and morality." Iris Marion Young (1990: 75) concurs with this when she writes that, "Appeals to justice still have the power to awaken a moral imagination and motivate people to look at their society critically, and ask how it can be made more liberating and enabling." This is echoed by Michael Sandel (1998: 2), who insists that "Justice is not merely one value among others, to be weighed and considered as the occasion arises, but the highest of all social virtues, the one that must be met before others can make their claims." This, in turn, mimics Mill's claim (2002: 59) that justice is "the chief part, and incomparably the most sacred and binding part, of all morality."

The second distinguishing characteristic of justice is that, because the claims of justice are regarded as so pressing, the obligation to act so as to avoid injustice falls most often on the state or other political authority (O'Neill: 2001). As Antony Flew (1985: 199) pointed out, "the claims of justice, unlike some other moral claims, may properly be enforced by the public power." This is not to say that acts of injustice cannot be perpetrated by individuals or by collective entities such as corporations, but that it is political institutions that are best placed to alter these injustices. As Barry (2005: 25) states, "If things are better now, it is not on the whole because those with economic power are nicer people, but because they are forced by law to behave better." Focusing on *justice* in the context of the moral status of animals, then, directs attention away from how we, as individuals, ought to regard the treatment of animals (whether, for instance, we ought to be vegetarians), and toward the way in which the state ought to regard their treatment. Moreover, it is common to hear that principles of justice should be entrenched in constitutional provisions that are out of the reach of majorities.

To reiterate, it is not being claimed here that the moral realm independent of justice is equivalent, in theory, to the voluntary character of charity. Moral obligations, whether we owe them to animals or other humans, *are* obligations in the sense that we ought to abide by them. However, given the status accorded to justice, the benefits to animals of being incorporated within a theory of justice would seem to be considerable, and, conversely, little would seem to be gained by their inclusion in a moral realm independently of justice. The requirement to be just to animals means, in practice, that it is regarded as a pressing matter, one that should be considered compulsory and not left to individuals to decide if they want to abide by obligations. Moreover, it is incumbent on the state, above all, to ensure that animals are treated justly. Insofar as there are direct *duties* owed to animals within a moral realm independent of justice, they cannot be based on the principles of charity or compassion, since the decision to act so as to benefit animals according to these principles is entirely voluntary. No duties, in other words, are invoked. But in order to avoid moral obligations to animals being regarded, in practice, as equivalent to charity, the case for deeming them as principles of justice is overwhelming. Only then is legal compulsion likely to become a reality.

Rawls and Moral Pluralism

The difficulty of seeking to demonstrate that a valid, duty-producing, notion of morality can, in practice, carry the same kind of weight as claims made by invoking the concept of justice can be illustrated by considering a number of separate attempts to achieve it. Firstly, as we saw in chapter 2, Rawls provides such an attempt when he argues that, whereas only moral agents are entitled to justice, animals, lacking this characteristic, are excluded. For Rawls, however, this does not mean that we have no moral duties to animals.

The problem for Rawls, however, is that the importance he attaches to justice implies, at the very least, that he is prioritizing it over other values, and this lexical prioritizing of justice over morality, without any further argument, condemns animals to an inferior moral position. In other words, the implication is that what is left is the claim that direct duties can be owed to those excluded as recipients of justice but only at an inferior level. Indeed, Rawls probably has in mind for animals something close to the moral orthodoxy that argues animals are to be protected because of their capacity to suffer, but that this can be overridden if human interests are served by so doing (see chapter 5).

In fact, for Rawls and other liberal thinkers, even this inferior moral status for those excluded as recipients of justice is not guaranteed. This is because, as we noted in chapter 2, a central feature of liberal theories of justice is the assertion that the state should resist interfering with different conceptions of the good held by citizens. This moral pluralism would presumably include different attitudes toward the treatment of animals. Thus, Rawls's liberty principle, designed to allow individuals to pursue their own conceptions of the good without interference from the state, is always likely to trump attempts to protect the interests of animals where such attempts conflict with the liberty of humans. Whatever is done to animals, therefore, is entirely legitimate, and the state has no justification in intervening to prohibit it. The only way of avoiding this conclusion is to include animals as recipients of justice so that, as with humans, moral pluralism is constrained at the point that it harms animals.

Ruth Abbey's responses to this interpretation of Rawls's thought, as we also saw in chapter 2, fail. The claim that allowing a free-for-all in our treatment of animals might be regarded by Rawls as a type of unreasonable pluralism fails because what he regards as unreasonable pluralism is defined by his theory of justice. That is, Rawls makes it clear that only behavior that harms humans directly can be considered as behavior worthy of constraining. As he points out, "each person is free to plan his life as he pleases (so long as his intentions are consistent with the principles of justice)" (Rawls, 1971: 446). Moreover, the emphasis on moral pluralism is not, as Abbey claims, limited to his later work but rather is a central feature of his mature theory of justice. In particular, moral pluralism is enshrined in the priority Rawls accords to the liberty principle.

Justice and Humanitarianism

The distinction between humanity and justice in terms of the question of world poverty provides the second attempt to locate a realm of duty-producing moral obligations independently of justice. Brian Barry, for one, insists that the two are distinct, that aiding the world's poor as a matter of humanitarian aid is different from behaving in a just way toward them (Barry, 1991). The obvious way to differentiate the two, consistent with our distinction between justice and charity, is to say that humanitarian aid is laudable but not compulsory, whereas justice requires compulsory action so as to reduce inequality. As we saw, however, moral obligations are of a different category from the voluntary requirements of charity. Thus, Barry, as he must do, rejects this distinction. Both humanity and justice are morally obligatory and should be regarded as of equal weight.

Barry, however, finds it difficult to explain how the concepts of humanity, as he defines it, and justice differ and why, in particular, the distribution of humanitarian aid, if morally obligatory, is not to be regarded as a just act. "I have no way of proving," he writes, "that it is a mistake to use the term 'just' to mark out the line between, on the one hand, what is morally required and, on the other, what is praiseworthy to do but not wrong to omit doing" (Barry, 1991: 188). One way of making a distinction between justice and morality is to say that justice is a distributive question. The problem for Barry here, though, is that humanitarian aid, of course, *is* a matter of distribution and therefore, if obligatory, complies with what it means to be just.

Campbell (2006: 165) suggests that one alternative means of distinguishing justice from humanity in this context is to say that the former is based on the duties of those who have brought about the poverty in question, whereas the latter refers to duties of those who are not responsible but are able to help without sacrificing their own standard of living. Campbell (2006: 167) recognizes, however, that attaching responsibility is difficult to say the least and reverts to the claim that we can still justify imposing duties on the grounds of humanity with corresponding entitlements of those who require the humanitarian assistance. He also accepts that by making this move the distinction between justice and humanity disappears. That is, it becomes an "injustice if these humanitarian obligations are not fulfilled." Thus, it is difficult to see how a valid principle of duty-producing morality can be developed that does not suffer from being contrasted with justice and that, in practice, does not collapse into the category of charity from which we cannot derive obligations to act.

A similar distinction, between humanitarian aid and justice, is made in response to Peter Singer's well-known call for those in the developed world to distribute a (substantial) proportion of their wealth to the poorest in the world (Singer, 1972). Critics such as Andrew Kuper (2002) and Anthony Langlois (2008) argue that Singer's approach is inadequate because he is operating with an individualistic theory of charity rather than justice. Singer, it is true, does not, at least in his initial article on the subject, mention the word justice. However, he is quite clear that there is nothing voluntary about the moral obligation he advocates. Indeed, he explicitly notes that whilst giving money to help the poorest in the world is usually regarded as an act of charity, this is mistaken. He is quite clear, that is, that such giving is not a supererogatory act—one which it would be good to do, but not wrong not to do. "On the contrary, we ought to give the money away, and it is wrong not to do so" (Singer, 1972: 235).

The point, then, is that if this moral obligation is to be distinguished from a voluntaristic charitable act, then the redistribution of resources has to be compulsory, one that is insisted on by the state as an agent of justice. If that occurs, Singer's call becomes indistinguishable from justice. That is, if we have a moral obligation to help the world's poor, then is it not *just* to help the world's poor, and should not the state step in and ensure Singer's moral obligation is met? And if it is not *just* to help the world's poor, but merely praiseworthy, then does this not amount to an act of charity, which, in Barry's words, is "not wrong to omit doing"? Singer does not explicitly insist that the state should act in such a way, but there is nothing in his account that would preclude it. Indeed, he does not dispute the fact that governments in the developed world ought to be giving more aid, irrespective of whether individuals give to private charities (Singer, 1972: 240).

Campbell, Justice, and the Welfare State

One way around this apparent impasse is to adopt the approach suggested by Tom Campbell (1974), which is the third attempt I will discuss to distinguish between justice and a weighty, duty-producing, notion of morality. Campbell recognizes that the welfare state is usually validated by reference to social justice but argues that this is conceptually mistaken since, whilst there is a close logical association between justice and desert or merit, there is no similar relationship between justice and need. Distributing scarce resources according to need is, for Campbell, a matter of beneficence or humanity rather than justice. As a result of separating justice from humanitarianism, Campbell (1974: 4) is able to claim that "Justice as one amongst other moral values may quite properly be required to give way to other considerations." In the case of the welfare state, Campbell suggests, this is precisely what has happened with a humane justification preferred to a just one based on merit.

Campbell, therefore, provides us with a conceptual space, between justice and charity, which is occupied by the duty to be humane. For him, this "duty of humanity...is not only distinct from the duty to be just but may properly be regarded as at least on an equal footing with (and perhaps as overriding) justice in the determination of our moral priorities for the distribution of benefits and burdens" (Campbell, 1974: 6). The development of a welfare state based on need is, according to Campbell, a classic example of a situation where justice is overridden by humane considerations.

In response to Campbell, it is extremely contentious to define justice in terms of a distribution based on merit but not on need. To distinguish between needs and desert in the way that Campbell does is to suggest that needs are a consequence of failure or a lack of merit or desert. Indeed, he recognizes that it is necessary to distinguish between needs that come about as a result of personal failure (which are subject to the duty of humanity) and those that arise as the result of maltreatment at the hands of others (to be remedied by justice) (Campbell, 1974: 12).[1] By arguing, therefore, that only certain needs are worthy of inclusion in a just distribution, Campbell is suggesting that it is not required by justice to remedy those needs that are not worthy of remedy, although it may be humanitarian to do so.

The problem here, of course, is that equating justice with merit (or lack of blame for one's predicament) is to imply that justice is somehow a morally more important—or worthwhile—entity. Campbell's interpretation certainly does not lead one to think that we should sacrifice a just distribution for one based on the value of humanity. That is, linking justice with merit, and humanitarianism with dealing with the problems caused by an individual's failings, strongly suggests, contrary to Campbell's assertions, that we should prefer the former. It is very noticeable, in fact, that justice theorists have tended both to ignore or downplay the distinction between deserved and undeserved need, and to reject desert as a distinguishing feature of justice. Rawls, for one, organizes his original position in such a way that the participants do not know whether they will have particular talents or not, including the capacity to work hard, precisely because he does not think they are deserved as opposed to being innate. In other words, for Rawls, meeting needs, however they come about, is a fundamental feature of justice. At the very least, then, Campbell is guilty of excluding need from the domain of justice on purely conceptual grounds. As Miller (1976: 126) points out, though: "People who use need claims to ground their judgements of justice mean what they say. To show that they are misguided one must engage in substantive moral argument, not rely on conceptual analysis alone."

Care Ethics and Justice

Our fourth example of an attempt to locate a moral duty-producing realm independently of justice is provided by feminist advocates of a care ethic. The care ethic approach has been set up by some as an alternative to an ethic of justice in moral philosophy in general, and in the animal rights debate in particular. Indeed, Abbey (2007) regards the care ethic as a potentially fruitful arena of inquiry for a moral theory, independently of justice, within which animals can be protected. This emphasis on care derives from the work of Carol Gilligan (1983), who posits a dualism, based on gender, between a masculine focus on rights, justice, and autonomy and a feminine tendency to focus on caring, responsibility, and interaction with others. For Gilligan, then, an ethic of care and an ethic of justice are "fundamentally incompatible." Care ethicists have argued, therefore, that we should value emotion and sentiment over reason, and that our moral obligations should derive from the relationships we develop and not as a result of impartial rules. Applied to animals, then, our duties to them are based not on the grounds of impartial and abstract principles but on our duty to care about those animals we forge relationships with (see Donovan and Adams, 2007). Moreover, at an empirical level, it has been suggested that it is an awareness of, and sympathy for, animal suffering that draws people toward animal rights and not an acceptance of abstract moral principles that seek to show the inconsistency of protecting humans but not animals (Luke, 2007).

Of course, those who advocate an ethic based on justice regard the care ethic as inferior. Barry (1995: 234–57), for instance, suggests that there need not be a conflict between justice and care because the proper position for the latter is as a supplement to the former, so that it is employed to inform people how to use the discretion left open to them by an ethic of justice. In terms of the debate about animals, as Todd Lekan (2004: 187) points out, justice theorists can allow that sympathetic feelings might play a purely motivational role in that "sympathy may motivate people to seriously consider, and perhaps even to act upon, principle-based arguments." In addition, some feminists regard the alleged differences in moral thinking between men and women suggested by Gilligan as a myth that serves to devalue women's status even further. As Marilyn Friedman (1987: 96) complains, "*whatever* moral matters men concern themselves with are categorized, estimably, as matters of 'justice and rights,' whereas the moral concerns of women are assigned to the devalued categories of 'care and personal relationships.'"

The status of justice is no doubt part of the reason why the care ethic is often now presented not as an alternative to justice but as a *different* form of justice. That is, care ethics is not meant to run alongside a liberal theory of justice but to replace it. In other words, the status claims of justice are not challenged, only the particular rights-based conception of it put forward in liberal political thought. Diemut Bubeck (1998: 163) claims, for instance, that an ethic based on care "does represent a genuine new ethical epistemology with which to reconceive the moral realm, including justice." Daniel Engster (2007: 5), likewise, looks to "outline a theory of justice based upon the practice of caring" whereby "the aims and virtues of caring may be said to precede and underlie all other theories of justice." Similarly, Michael Slote (2007) argues that it is possible to develop a theory of justice predicated upon a virtue-based account of caring.

Those who seek to conceptualize care theory as an alternative theory of justice do so at least partly, no doubt, because the effect is to elevate it. Most care ethicists, though, probably still regard their moral theory as a valid alternative to a theory of justice, and not its inferior. They would make the point that the conventional liberal theory of justice and rights—the kind that is usually advanced by extentionist animal ethicists—occupies such an exalted position merely as a reflection of patriarchal dominance. Its exalted position is, therefore, undeserved, and cannot be used as an intellectual argument *in favor* of liberal theories of rights and justice and against the care ethic. Thus, Bubeck (1998: 155) asserts that "no care theorist would be prepared to accept" the lexical priority of liberal theories of justice over care and the inferior position of an ethic based on the latter.

There is, nevertheless, a strong case for saying that the care ethic *does* suffer in comparison with justice. This is primarily because it emphasizes the importance of partial relationships and not impartial rules typical of theories of justice. As Lawrence Blum (1988: 476–7) points out, "morality is founded in a series of concrete connection between persons, a direct sense of connection which exists prior to moral beliefs about what is right and wrong." However, if we adopt a theory that grounds moral duties, in this case of care, in the relationships we forge, it is difficult to see how moral duties can be applied to those with whom we do not forge a relationship. As Regan (1991: 95) asks, "What are the resources within the ethic of care that can move people to consider the ethics of their dealings with individuals who *stand outside* the existing circle of their valued interpersonal relationships?" This limitation appears most notably in Nel Noddings's (1984) groundbreaking account of care ethics. Thus, Barry (1995: 252) argues forcefully that Noddings's case for prioritizing personal relationships leads to "nothing less than a call for a moral revolution of a far-reaching and potentially catastrophic nature," since "whenever a choice has to be made between adherence to principle and doing a favour for somebody with whom they have a pre-existing relation, they would sacrifice the principle."

Care ethics divorced from principles of justice, then, is likely to lead to an illegitimate prioritization of our particular relationships. Applied to our treatment of animals, this model of the care ethic does not offer very much for those interested in their protection. Noddings (1984: 154) recognizes this. She argues that we are only obligated to care for those species of animals—pets, it seems—that we have had a particular relationship with. Thus, there is no moral obligation to care, for instance, for farm animals and therefore no obligation to be a vegetarian. Indeed, it could be argued that the protection of animals is *less* likely to be ensured by an ethic that focuses on partial relationships, since our relationships with members of our own species are apt to be stronger than the ones we develop with nonhumans (Becker, 1983).

The care ethic appears, therefore, to be of only limited use to those concerned about the protection of animals, and, in addition, it would seem intuitively wrong to base moral consideration on the relationships we forge as opposed to some less random characteristic. A number of care ethicists, though, have sought to challenge Noddings's restricted scope of caring. In the case of animals, Josephine Donovan (2007: 185) argues that, in practice, we do, or potentially could, extend care more widely to include strangers, and that it is therefore appropriate to apply the care ethic to all animals and not just to members of those species with whom we forge relationships. There are at least two problems with this. In the first place, insofar as an ethic of care can be universalized, it is in danger of collapsing into the very ethic of justice that it seeks to condemn. Joan Tronto, for instance, recognizes that ensuring that care relationships are "spun widely enough so that some are not beyond its reach remains a central question." But answering this question requires accepting a central feature of justice. Thus, Tronto (1987: 660–1) continues: "Whatever the weaknesses of Kantian universalism, its premise of the equal moral worth and dignity of all humans is attractive because it avoids this problem."

The second issue with the claim that an ethic of care can be universalized beyond those with whom we develop a particular relationship is a doubt about its viability. It is surely an exaggeration to suggest that such care is expressed now for human strangers, let alone animal strangers. It is no doubt true that there is social, political, and economic pressure that serves to shape our attitudes toward animals, but it is contentious, to say the least, to claim, as Donovan (2007: 181) does, that "sympathy for animals is…a deep, primary disposition." Moreover, the further claim that this "natural" sympathy "is only obscured and repressed by a process of intense social conditioning" is, as a counterfactual, extremely difficult to establish.

The approach of care ethicists such as Donovan, then, does not provide a strong enough basis upon which to build a theory of morality that can challenge universalist principles typically associated with justice, since it remains dependent on the extent to which we actually do care. As a result, we are left with the conclusion that in order to ensure universal moral obligations to animals, it is necessary to invoke the impartial language that is a characteristic of justice. This is not to say that values such as caring and compassion should not be a component of justice. Indeed, as Susan Moller Okin (1989: 230; 247) pointed out, one can exaggerate the distinction between an ethic of care and an ethic of justice. At the center of Rawls's theory of justice, for instance, "is a voice of responsibility, care, and concern for others." How else can one interpret the idea of the veil of ignorance that forces us to think what it would be like to be other people in a variety of circumstances? However, there is no question, for Moller Okin, of justice being replaced by "contextual caring thinking."

Care Ethics and Nonideal Theory

It has been argued that the focus on partiality central to care ethics does not provide us with a valid ideal theory of justice for animals. It might, however, be effective as a nonideal theory. As Rollin (2005) has noted, partiality to those we are close to is a principle that meets with wide public support. As a result, Rollin argues that animal advocates should, initially at least, focus on the better treatment of companion animals, those with whom we have close ties of love, friendship, and affection, since it is more likely to be a strategy that will meet with public approval than the "harder" cases of farm and laboratory animals. Moreover, he argues that companion animals are the only animals that we currently treat as moral persons, as ends in themselves. Establishing this principle for companion animals can then be used as a starting point for similar treatment of other animals that are currently treated as means to our ends.

To a certain extent, many animal advocates do already operate with such a priority. Whether it constitutes the basis of a valid nonideal theory is a different question. Utilizing Rawls's framework, it can be seen that whilst prioritizing companion animals, or more generally those animals with whom we have a particular relationship, is clearly politically possible, it is by no means clear that it is morally permissible or effective in the Rawlsian sense. In the case of the former, focusing on companion animals cannot be regarded as a move that will eliminate the most grievous of injustices. Whilst there are numerous problems with the way in which animals destined to be our companions are treated, these pale into insignificance, in terms of both the number of animals involved and the suffering endured, as compared to farm and laboratory animals.

In terms of effectiveness, too, I would dispute Rollin's assertion that the treatment of companion animals necessarily reflects the fact that they are regarded primarily as moral persons or ends in themselves. If this were the case, then focusing on the treatment of companion animals might be said to be a useful device in furthering the progress of our ideal theory of justice. This is because regarding other animals—the ones we use for food and for scientific research—as not merely means to our ends is the objective of our ideal theory based on rights. It is at least as possible, however, that companion animals are regarded by many as means to our ends as much as other animals we use are. The difference is that no purpose is served by inflicting suffering on, or killing, our companion animals. Indeed, the purpose of keeping companion animals is precisely not to inflict suffering on them. Rather, the purpose is to provide us with company that aids our psychological and physical well-being. Furthering the protection of companion animals, then, does not necessarily serve to move society toward the ideal theory of justice that recognizes their right not to suffer. The fact that most people seem comfortable with lavishing affections on their companion animals whilst at the same time tucking into their ham sandwiches, without considering how the meat arrives on their plate, does not suggest that prioritizing the protection of companion animals is going to result in a moral shift in the way that other animals are treated.

It is worthwhile here as well to consider Luke's assertion that people are attracted to the animal protection movement not because of the abstract theorizing associated with justice but because of their empathy and sympathy with the suffering of animals (Luke, 2007). If correct, this would be a useful ingredient of a nonideal theory, since it is building on what is already present. I do support the emphasis on suffering, and my preferred nonideal theory, described in detail in chapter 8, is based on prohibiting the infliction of suffering on animals. However, Luke's position is dependent on an empirical claim that, as has been pointed out, he provides little evidence for. (Cochrane, 2010: 133; Lekan, 2004: 187). It is at least as possible that one of the reasons the modern animal rights movement has prospered is precisely because it can now call upon a great deal of rational philosophical justifications for its claims, thus ridding itself of the previously common charge that it consists of people who are well meaning but misguidedly sentimental.

Moreover, focusing on aversion to suffering and care alone is surely inadequate from a strategic point of view without reasons explaining *why* the infliction of suffering in any particular case is morally wrong and who we should be caring about. For one thing, care can work both ways in the debate about our moral obligations to animals. For instance, as defenders of animal experimentation have been increasingly vocally pointing out, the *care* of humans—men and women, adults and children—is, they argue, dependent on animal research. In such a conflict of caring, whose interests should we choose to uphold? Whilst an approach based on principles of justice has a clear answer to this question, an ethic of care does not tell us that we should necessarily side with the animals.

Conclusion: Indirect Duties, Morality, and Justice

A critical examination of the four attempts cited illustrate that it is doubtful that a duty-producing moral theory independently of justice can, in practice, achieve an equivalent or even greater weighting to one based on justice itself. The status attached to the concept of justice means that it is a prime candidate for state enforcement. Because of this, the fact that animal ethicists and advocates have spoken, largely, in the language of morality is, it seems to me, a mistake. If we think that animals have moral standing, that we have direct duties to them (a relatively uncontroversial claim), then it is appropriate to frame these obligations in the language of justice, because justice entails legal compulsion. To frame our obligations to animals in the language of morality is to fall foul of the, probably correct, assertion that there are no duty-producing moral obligations that are not, in practice, either overridden by the liberal emphasis on moral pluralism, or which do not collapse into the category of charity from which we cannot derive obligations to act. Subsuming our obligations to animals in the language of justice avoids this outcome.

Before we focus on seeking to identify an appropriate theory of *justice* for animals, one more step is necessary. The conclusion we have reached is that if animals are excluded from a theory of justice, then, in practice, their protection can only come about either as the result of charitable action, to which no moral obligations are attached, or because it benefits humans to protect them. In other words, insofar as we have duties to animals independently of justice, these duties are indirect ones. According to the indirect duty view, the protection of animals does not come about because they are regarded as having intrinsic value, but because (some) humans regard the protection of animals as being part of a good (human) life. Thus, whereas a direct moral object is "something *to* which moral consideration is paid" an indirect moral object is "something *about* or *concerning* which moral consideration is paid." As a result "not everything of moral *value* has moral *standing*" (Morris, 1998: 191). Given that indirect duty views dispense with any potential conflict between human and animal interests, because animals will only be protected if it is in our interests to do so, it is worthwhile exploring it as a possible nonideal theory. This is attempted in the next chapter.

4

Indirect Duties, Virtue Ethics, and Animals

IN CHAPTER 3, the character of a moral realm independent of justice was explored, in order to test Rawls's claim, embellished by Abbey, that whilst animals are not recipients of justice, their interests can still be protected. It was argued that such a project is largely a failure because, whilst moral obligations outside of the sphere of justice clearly do exist in theory, in practice they are unlikely to be backed up by legal enforcement unless couched in the language of justice. In particular, moral obligations to protect animals are unlikely to be subject to state enforcement when they clash with human justice claims—for example, for freedom of action and expression. In such a context, the moral obligations to animals identified by animal ethicists take a backseat to justice claims, and, in practice, collapse into the realm of charity.

If this analysis is accepted, then two options are open to us. We could, firstly, seek to enshrine animal protection within an amenable theory of justice, or we could focus on demonstrating that we have indirect duties to animals, that the protection of animal interests might be beneficial for at least some humans. The former option is explored in subsequent chapters of this book. The latter option is explored in this chapter. Here, it is asked whether an indirect duty view and, in particular, one based on virtue ethics, can provide an acceptable degree of protection for animals.

The Advantages of Indirect Duties

I noted earlier in this book that one advantage of contractarian theory is that it helps to explain *why* we ought to behave morally or behave justly. That is, we ought to behave morally or justly because it is in our interests to do so, or, if one wants to insist upon a strict demarcation between interests and aims, because it is something we want to happen. As Morris (1998: 188) has emphasized, then, contractarianism is "not merely a method for determining the nature and content of the requirements of justice; it may also give us a way of providing reasons for accepting and complying with justice." Morris is referring here to a theory of justice as mutual advantage in which self-interest is a condition upon agreeing to abide by principles of justice. As he writes, "the fact that certain principles or practices are determined by rational agreement is a reason for accepting and abiding by them" (Morris, 1996: 218). As we have seen, such a theory explicitly excludes animals. Invoking a theory of justice or morality based on self-interest, however, may help to explain a contemporary reality about animal protection politics. For why is it that, despite the work of many animal ethicists, and the strength of their arguments that animals deserve to be regarded as morally considerable, the message has tended to have so little influence? Animals are exploited mercilessly and made to suffer in innumerable ways and not, in short, treated as if they *are* morally considerable.

The answer might lie in the fact that it is not enough to simply state in dry philosophical language that animals have intrinsic value, because of the characteristics—sentience or autonomy—they possess, and therefore ought to be treated in a certain way. Many accept the logic of this position, however imperfectly, but still ignore and tacitly accept the exploitation of animals. One conclusion to this paradox relates to Morris's (2008: 16) claim that because of its "other-directed" character—the fact that it benefits others—"sometimes we do not have reason to be just" or, to put it in a stronger way, "sometimes it pays not to be just." As Donaldson and Kymlicka (2011: 252) suggest: "Moral arguments are notoriously ineffective when they run so fully against the grain of self-interest and inherited expectations." As a result, it might be argued that what is needed, as well as—or instead of—a case for the moral considerability of animals, is a focus on how the protection of animals benefits us.

The advantage of an indirect duty approach to animal ethics is precisely that it does focus on how the protection of animals benefits us. Indeed, it holds that we should only protect animals insofar as it serves a human interest to do so. Given that it removes the conflict between protecting the interests of animals and forwarding our interests, an indirect duty approach to animal ethics does seem to be a viable candidate for a nonideal theory. Whilst we may regard this anthropocentric position as counter-intuitive, an indirect duty approach to our treatment of animals does have the advantage that it reflects the political reality that it is humans who do the valuing of animal interests and it is humans who put animal interests onto the political agenda. This is an important insight that is politically significant. Indeed, the indirect duty approach provides a political model for how animal interests are represented in practice. As Baxter (2000: 49) points out, "whether or not any component of non-human nature is saved depends on whether or not enough people can be persuaded" that they ought to be. In the context of environmentalism, Rawls and Barry's liberalism is, in Bell's words (2002: 721), a "'contingently green liberalism' rather than an 'intrinsically green liberalism'" and it is "up to the environmentalist to persuade enough of their fellow citizens of the value of their 'green ideals.'" In the same way, then, Barry offers us contingent support for the protection of animals.

Indirect Duty in Practice

It is undoubtedly true that indirect duty views have offered very little for animals in the way they have been usually framed. The contractarian account of our duties to animals by Carruthers (1992: 105–10), for instance, is very limited. Animals could be protected as a result of their human owners upholding their rights as owners. Thus, "I am morally obliged not to kill your dog, just as I am obliged not to set light to your car" (106). Invoking property rights, however, only takes us so far because there is then no limitation to what the owners may do to the animals they own. In addition, animals in the wild have no owners and therefore cannot be protected by property rights.

An additional factor, introduced by Carruthers, is that the protection of animals could be regarded as "a matter of legitimate public interest" since many people care about animals. This concern could then override the owner's right to do what she likes with her animals. However, the problem here is that the concerns of "animal lovers" are no match for what many would regard as more fundamental human interests involving economic benefits, or, indeed, those relating to physical well-being or even life itself. This is, of course, because we are here weighing human benefits from animal exploitation not against animal suffering but against the concerns of animal lovers. Carruthers (1992: 107) further limits the effectiveness of the concern of "animal lovers" by adding the rider that "the constraints would only apply to suffering that occurs in a manner that is unavoidably public." Animal suffering that occurs in private, on this view, would remain legitimate on the grounds that "animal lovers" will only be affected by those activities they can see. Since the vast majority of animal exploitation takes place in windowless factory farms and laboratories, not much animal suffering is left for public gaze (although this principle does provide great incentives for animal rights activists to get, by one means or another, detailed information on what happens to animals away from the public gaze).

Carruthers (1992: 108) ties himself in knots trying to reconcile this position—that only the public suffering of animals is wrong—with common sense beliefs about animals, at one point suggesting that torturing an animal in private might be wrong because of the possibility that the animal might escape and come into public view. Carruthers is forced into this move because, as he recognizes, it does not really make sense to regard, say, the beating of a dog in the street as more morally reprehensible than doing so in private. But our intuition that it does not matter *where* the dog is beaten derives from a strong suspicion that what we are doing to the dog matters to the dog directly and not just, if at all, to the sensitivities of those who might be offended by it. And if we accept this intuition, then this, of course, means that we are not reliant on indirect duty views to justify the moral condemnation of inflicting suffering on animals.

Indirect duties are more far-reaching, however, than Carruthers suggests. In the first place, the benefits of protecting animals may not be restricted to so-called "animal lovers." It is possible to show that, in some situations at least, it *is* in our collective narrow interest to promote actions that have the effect of protecting at least some animals. For example, a common indirect reason for justifying the protection of animals, held by Locke and Kant among the key figures in the history of moral thought, is that those who are cruel to animals are likely to be inclined to treat humans in the same way. This alleged link, it has been suggested, was the rationale for much of the early nineteenth-century animal protection law. Cruel practices such as bear baiting, for instance, were prohibited, not only because of the suffering inflicted on the animal, but primarily because it despoiled the moral character of the working classes, encouraging cruelty as well as gambling, drunkenness, and absence from work (Ritvo, 1987).

Although there are some dissenting voices (see Piper, 2003), the research consensus is that those who are violent toward animals are more likely to be violent toward their partners and children, and that abused children are more likely to abuse animals (Bell: 2001). Identifying a link between animal and human abuse, however, is not the same as demonstrating that the former causes the latter. Carruthers (1992: 153–4), for one, adopts the former position when he writes that being cruel to animals betrays "an indifference to suffering that may manifest itself...in that person's dealings with other rational agents." The phrase "may manifest" here would not seem to mean that cruelty to animals *causes* cruelty to humans. An indirect duty to protect animals would only be justified if it was found that stopping someone being cruel to animals also stopped them being violent toward other humans. If it was the case that those who are cruel to animals are also likely to be violent toward humans (the more likely scenario), then no such duty follows. Indeed, in this eventuality, there would be a case for doing nothing to prevent cruelty to animals but to merely monitor those who engage in it in order to identify those most likely to be violent to other humans. Alternatively, as Devine (1978: 503) points out, "it would be equally plausible to maintain that animals should serve as punching bags—as outlets, that is, for aggressive and sadistic impulses which might otherwise find their target in human beings."

In the examples we have cited so far, the only possible prohibition on humans' treatment of animals is to avoid being cruel to them. Cruelty in this sense can be defined as the infliction of suffering that serves no useful human purpose. These justifications for indirect duties to animals would not seemingly apply to institutional uses of animals, as sources of food and as subjects of scientific experiments. There are other sources of indirect duty, however, that have a better chance of prohibiting the infliction of suffering on such animals. For example, part of the case against industrialized animal agriculture (or "factory" farming) is that it has severe health and environmental consequences affecting many people (Garrett, 2007; Mason and Singer, 1990). In this sense, Pluhar (2010: 458) is right to say that "it is difficult to imagine a moral theory that would sanction the continuation of factory farming." In addition, there is a strong case for saying that vegetarianism serves human interests given the claim that the raising and killing of animals for food is an extremely inefficient form of food production (Mason and Singer, 1990: 74).[1]

It is also the case that many human lives are enriched by the presence and well-being of companion animals. In the case of wild animals, likewise, much of the practical case for conservation is based on the benefits to humans of the continued existence of species of animals. These benefits, for example, might be aesthetic (we get pleasure out of seeing majestic creatures such as elephants and whales), economic, or medicinal. The problem in this latter case, however, is that such benefits do not depend upon the protection of individual animals as opposed to the maintenance of the species. The conservation of a species, furthermore, is not inconsistent with the dismissal of the interests of individual animals.

Even more significantly, indirect duty views about animals do not have to be presaged merely on narrow self-interest. Barry, as we saw, does not adopt such a narrow version, thus allowing a desire to see animals well protected to be a valid objective of those in the original position. The degree to which interests, on the one hand, and values and norms, on the other, are logically

distinct can, then, be exaggerated. The common, very narrow, interpretation of interests regards them as equivalent to self-interest, so that it is only
in someone's interests to act to protect animals if they stand to gain in the
short-, medium-, or long-term through an improvement in health or their
environment. This might, following Swanton (1980: 86), be described as a
"self-regarding" want. Interests, then, can be defined as wants or objectives
that benefit, often in an economic sense, a particular individual or a group
of people. Values or norms, on the other hand, are wants or objectives that
are not conceived in terms of the self-interest of an individual or a group.
It is often thought that interests and norms are opposites. Moreover, it is
sometimes said that, although norms are extremely commendable, they often
lose out to narrow self-interest. Thus, it might be argued, the norm of animal
protection loses out to the human self-interest that is served by continuing
to exploit them.

The gap between norms and interests, however, is not as clear-cut as this
dichotomy makes out. In the first place, norms may benefit certain interests
and it may be thought *just* that they do so. As Henry Shue (1995: 454–6) has
pointed out, a norm of entitlement reflects the interests of those to whom the
entitlement is granted. For example, the successful entrenchment of the right
to development of poorer countries is both an interest and a norm. In terms of
the norm of animal protection, of course, the interests being served are those
of animals themselves. Shue is making the point that "Ethics rests upon taking
the interests of others seriously" (1995: 457). It can be argued, though, that we
may go further than this by considering the claim that those who seek to promote the interests of others are not necessarily acting against their own interests. Such a claim cannot be justified if interests are always to be conceived
in terms of narrow self-interest. But why should this be the case? For it may
be that interests can include altruistic wants as well as self-interested ones.
This might be described as an "other-regarding" want, which Swanton (1980,
86) labels as including "any wants for *another* to do, have or be certain things."
It follows, therefore, that "it is possible that satisfaction of an other-regarding
want increases A's opportunities to satisfy wants for himself to do, have, or be
certain things. Therefore actions satisfying an other-regarding want can be in
A's interests" (87).

The implications of this analysis for animal protection should be clear. We
could say that it is in the self-interest of a person to advocate protecting animals, even if it does not benefit them economically or environmentally. This
is, for example, because acting in such a way might give a person a great deal
of pleasure, or might be character-forming in some way. Of course, there are

political limits to focusing on indirect duty views, not least, as we have seen, because a conception of the good that includes animal protection will be challenged by other conceptions of the good that include an interest in exploiting them. Nevertheless, the widening of the notion of an interest does not rule out the advocacy of pretty radical abolitionist goals—such as the moral prohibition of meat eating and/or scientific experimentation on animals—on the grounds that it is desired by some humans. Moreover, changing the focus of animal protection from intrinsic value to a preoccupation with the contribution animal protection can make to human flourishing also avoids the problem of the "exacting metaphysical demands" (O'Neil, 1997: 128) of an intrinsic value approach.

Indirect Duties and Virtue Ethics

Including concern for the interests of animals within the ambit of a flourishing human life clearly offers an opportunity to apply virtue ethics to our treatment of animals. Virtue ethics, which has undergone something of a revival since the 1970s, is a term used "to distinguish an approach in normative ethics which emphasizes the virtues, or moral character, in contrast to an approach which emphasizes duties or rules (deontology) or one which emphasizes the consequences of actions (utilitarianism)" (Hursthouse, 1999: 1). According to the virtue ethics approach, then, what is wrong, say, with killing is "not so much that it is unjust…but that it is callous and contrary to the virtue of charity" (Hursthouse, 1999: 6). A virtue, then, is a "good, or admirable, or praiseworthy character trait" (Hursthouse, 2000: 147).

Virtue ethics are consistent with applying direct duties to animals, and indeed a number of virtue ethicists, including Slote (2001) and Swanton (2003), reject versions that seek to focus on the claim that the virtuous benefit from their virtue. As Rosalind Hursthouse (2007: 159) remarks: "If cruelty is a vice, then to recognise an act as one of cruelty to animals is thereby to recognise it as wrong, and no further account of wherein its wrongness consists is called for." Indeed, it makes little sense to applaud virtues such as kindness, caring, compassion, or charity in our dealings with animals, and condemn vices such as cruelty or a lack of compassion, unless animals can be harmed by not behaving in a virtuous way. We would not, by contrast, seek to claim that it is possible to behave compassionately toward, say, a work of art or a historical monument. Virtuous behavior as regards animals, therefore, is predicated on the duties we owe to them directly as a result of their capacity to be harmed. Insofar as virtuous behavior benefits the virtuous does not mean, then, that it is the only, or even the main, reason for such behavior (Hursthouse, 2007: 159).

As a non-justice-based theory of morality, however, virtue ethics is likely to fall foul of the lexical priority of justice. One can imagine in such a scenario how to behave compassionately, or kindly, or charitably toward animals would be regarded as traits that should be applied *after* the demands of justice have been met. Indeed, this is how the notion of cruelty to animals tends to be applied in modern societies. The fact that behaving virtuously toward animals can also be regarded as beneficial to those humans behaving in such a way may, then, be the best use of the virtue ethics position. This indirect duty version of virtue ethics is derived from Aristotle, for whom behaving virtuously is connected with *eudaimonia*, translated as happiness or flourishing. Thus, for Aristotle, a fully virtuous person does not just act virtuously because she knows what she should do, irrespective of whether or not it is contrary to her desires, but acts virtuously because she desires to act in such a way. Thus "she does what she desires to do, and reaps the reward of satisfied desire" (Hursthouse, 1999: 9–10; 92). Virtue ethics, therefore, or at least one version of it, "offers a distinctively unfamiliar version of the view that morality is a form of enlightened self-interest" (Hursthouse, 1999: 190).

Applied to animals, we might want to say that a concern for animals is part of living a full and flourishing, and rounded and satisfying, human life involving the use of such faculties as imagination, openness, responsibility, and empathy (Hursthouse, 2000). Cooper (1995: 147) sets out well the potential benefits of adopting this approach, and rejecting the moral extensionism that is prevalent in the animal ethics literature, when he writes that:

> Reasons for doing or feeling are reasons for us. To serve as such, they must be capable of motivating us; and to do that, they must engage with what we want. Claims about the "inherent value" of nature, made in an anti-anthropocentric spirit, could never provide us with reasons to care about nature, unless it could also be shown that such caring is implied by, or answers to, the ways in which we care about our own lives.

Cooper is well aware that these reasons for treating animals well are not based on justice. All the better for this, he suggests, since it means that "the vocabulary of justice is not the most felicitous one in which to express a concern for other species" (Cooper, 1995: 148). The care ethic, too, although it is primarily regarded as a direct duty view when applied to humans and animals, can be interpreted as an indirect duty view when caring is regarded as a virtue. As Engster (2007: 18, 19) points out, "caring is not only morally obligatory but is also one key to a happy life" because "caring for others is not all drudgery and toil but is often a joyous and deeply meaningful experience."

Virtue Ethics Assessed

The strength of this revised indirect duty approach is to a considerable degree dependent on its virtue ethics element. There are, however, a number of general problems with the virtue ethics approach. In the first place, whilst it is possible to identify virtues and vices in the abstract, it is difficult to judge particular actions without some prior ethical theory. As Koller (2007: 192) points out, "it is impossible to reduce a sound conception of morality completely to the idea of virtue, as some advocates of virtue ethics believe, since, without any prior moral standards, we could neither identify moral virtues nor determine their content." For instance, the notion of being "cruel" to animals is defined, in the law of most developed countries, in terms of an ethical theory that regards the exploitation of animals for human benefit as acceptable. It seems to be the case, therefore, that "a conception of moral virtues can never provide a complete account of morality, since it presupposes further normative standards that cannot be reduced to virtues" (Koller, 2007: 193).

Secondly, it is clear that virtue ethics, like care ethics, does not always provide a clear guide to action or moral judgment (Walker and Ivanhoe, 2007: 7). In the case of animals, for instance, Hursthouse (2007: 156) argues that cruelty and a lack of compassion can be used as vices to justify "change in the many ways in which we use animals, particularly for food." What this does not tell us, however, is whether or not it is therefore virtuous to be a vegetarian or merely desist from eating animals raised in factory farms. In the context of virtue ethics as an indirect duty view, we can ask, Is a flourishing life to be had by being vegetarian or by merely ensuring that we do not eat the products of industrialized animal agriculture?

Indeed, there are some doubts about whether it is always the case that avoiding the use of animals and treating them well is an example of virtue. This is particularly the case where virtues conflict. An illustration of this is the debate between Hursthouse (2000: 157–64) and Roger Scruton (1996) on blood sports. Both invoke virtue ethics in the case of blood sports, the former arguing that it is illegitimate because those engaging in it are behaving callously, the latter contending that those participating in it are behaving courageously. Here we have, then, a conflict between the vice of callousness and the virtue of courage. Again, in the context of virtue ethics as an indirect duty view, if we choose to hunt, are we behaving courageously, in which case our lives flourish, or are we behaving callously, in which case they do not?

Resolving this dispute, and being able to make a moral judgment on virtue ethic grounds, is not easy. We could examine the empirical validity of the claims. Thus, it might be argued that to label hunting as courageous is factually incorrect, although much will depend on what is meant by courage in this context (Rowlands, 2009: 108–10). Rowlands (2009: 112) is probably correct to say that "Scruton does not have a moral leg to stand on," as least as far as fox hunting is concerned, because it is possible to "replicate the conditions under which the virtue is exercised whilst eliminating the exercise of the vice." Thus, the courage of riding at speed and jumping across obstacles (which might be regarded as an example of courageous behavior) can still be practiced through replacing the hunting of the fox with drag hunting. The putting forward of a replacement, however, is not always possible. In the case of bull-fighting, for instance, the courage exhibited by matadors is intrinsic to the suffering inflicted on the animals.

Rowlands (2009: 113–115) suggests an ingenious way of avoiding this problem of conflicting virtues, by invoking the importance of the virtue of mercy. The advantage of mercy is that it is required for the possession of many of the other moral virtues. We cannot be regarded as kind, for instance, if we only exhibit this virtue to the powerful and not the powerless, since to do so might be branded as self-interest. The "possession of the virtue of mercy," therefore, "is a necessary condition of the possession of the virtue of kindness." The same might be said of the virtues of compassion, generosity, and benevolence. Rowlands (2009: 113) quotes the writer Milan Kundera to illustrate the obvious relevance of this to animals. "True human goodness," Kundera writes, "can manifest itself, in all its purity and liberty, only in regard to those who have no power. The true moral test of humanity...lies in its relations to those who are at its mercy: the animals." In the context of virtue ethics as an indirect duty view, then, only when our actions are driven by mercy can we flourish as individuals.

This emphasis on mercy, however, is less decisive than it sounds as a means of establishing that it is always virtuous to treat animals well and not exploit them. For it is not only animals who are powerless, not only animals who require our mercy. As an example, imagine a poor community who depend upon catching and killing animals for food. Are we not then faced by a conflict between exhibiting mercy toward the needy humans and exhibiting mercy toward the animals who desire our protection? Similarly, imagine a situation—often presented by those defending scientific research on animals—whereby we are faced with a choice between being merciful toward the animals that are assigned to be used in scientific research and being merciful toward the sick children who might benefit from such research. Conflicts are still likely in the application of virtue ethics. Other moral theories, by contrast, seem to offer much more decisive guidance.

For our purposes here, the most important empirical claim is that being virtuous in our treatment of animals is actually beneficial to the person being virtuous. If it is not, of course, then it is no longer an indirect duty view, since it is not in my interests to behave virtuously. The debate over the extent to which it is beneficial to the agent to behave morally or virtuously is a long-standing one in the ethics literature. The modern debate can be traced back to an article by Harold Prichard (1949) in which it was famously argued that philosophers such as Plato had been wrong to claim that it is in our interests to behave morally. Others, such as Philippa Foot, have argued, conversely, that not only can the virtuous benefit but that this is the very point of behaving virtuously. As she comments, following Plato, unless it can be shown that the just person benefits from being just, "justice can no longer be recommended as a virtue" (Foot, 1978: 125).

One initial issue ought to be addressed here. One might argue that behaving virtuously must be independent of the benefits one receives from it. That is, to act virtuously because of the benefits one is likely to derive from it is, it might be argued, not actually to behave virtuously. Thus, Slote (1997: 209), who adopts an "agent-based" virtue ethics that does not require any derivative justification, remarks that "making virtue status depend on what benefits just the possessor of a trait seems an overly egoistic view of what is required of a trait or general motive in order for it to count as a virtue." In the words of Phillips (1964–5: 48), "the relevance of morality does not depend on whether it pays or not" and therefore Foot is guilty of trying to "find a non-moral justification for moral beliefs."

We can tackle this issue by distinguishing between the motive for acting virtuously and the benefits gained from it. Thus, for Hursthouse (1999: 180), "one can...be adequately motivated to perform virtuous action for the right reasons and, as a quite separate issue, give justifying grounds for one's belief that the virtues...benefit their possessor." In other words, it is possible to distinguish between whether virtuous behavior, in itself, benefits the virtuous and whether the actor behaves in such a way merely in order to gain those benefits. Indeed, Aristotle would argue that one's life can only flourish if one behaves genuinely virtuously, which excludes acting in such a way because of an expectation of benefit. We are entitled, then, to encourage individuals to behave virtuously in their treatment of animals, and, if virtue ethicists are right, to expect those individuals who do behave in such a way to flourish.

A more substantive question is the issue of whether behaving virtuously does, in fact, benefit the possessor. For some, the assumption that justice pays is "murky mythology" (Phillips, 1964–5: 50). Clearly, being virtuous on a particular occasion does not always benefit the person being virtuous. This would be a ridiculously high standard to maintain. As R. M. Hare (1981: 191) rightly asserts, "it is not the case, and it is hard to see why anybody should have ever thought that it was the case, that to do what we morally ought to do is always in our prudential interest." Instead, the claim to defend here, as Hursthouse (1999: 171–2) points out, is that being virtuous benefits the person being virtuous in general terms. Certainly, behaving virtuously is no guarantee of happiness or a flourishing life. A virtuous person living in poverty, for example, may well not lead a flourishing life. The question then is whether behaving virtuously is necessary, rather than sufficient, for a flourishing life. But, clearly, happiness or flourishing can be achieved without behaving virtuously.

If we accept this, we are left with a much weaker claim that boils down to saying that following the virtues is *one* way in which we can flourish, provided that the other circumstances of our lives are amenable. But is this view credible? Hooker (1996), for instance, invokes the "argument from lack of sympathy" to cast doubt on even this weaker interpretation of the utility of virtue. Thus, consider two people, the "Unscrupulous" one and the "Upright" one, both of whom have lived "sad and wretched lives." Hooker claims that we would not "feel sorrier" for the former and "one possible explanation of this is that we do not really believe Unscrupulous's life has gone worse in self-interested terms than Upright's" (Hooker, 1996: 154). One objection to this denial of the instrumental value of virtue, however, is the argument that such a popular sentiment is inadequate as evidence for the conclusion reached. The general public may be misguided. It may be the case that only those who have been virtuous are entitled to judge on the state of mind of another virtuous person.

In defense of the claim that behaving virtuously is prudential, it is often asked whether we would bring up our children to be virtuous. Given that we presumably have our children's interests at heart, an answer in the affirmative would appear to demonstrate a link between virtue and self-interest. And it is probably the case that, on balance, most parents do teach their children to be virtuous. Are they irrational to do so? Arguably not. As Hare (1981: 195) points out, it is hard work to live the life of the "immoral egoist" and only some have the "talent" to behave in such a way, not least because to be self-centered requires that one not be affected negatively by remorse or guilt. Moreover, an immoral egoist, unless he can hide it (Sayre-McCord, 1989), is likely to find it very difficult to develop mutually beneficial relationships with others. By contrast, a virtuous person is more apt to be liked, or even loved, by others.

Conclusion: A Defense of Indirect Duties?

A viable indirect duty approach to animals would be hugely advantageous to those concerned about the protection of animals because it removes the conflict that is endemic in human/animal relations. Animals are only protected if at least some human interests are served by so doing. This may help to overcome the motivational deficit apparent in the fulfillment of justice claims in general and particularly acute in the case of animals where traditional extensionist moral arguments ask us to accept moral principles that will not obviously benefit members of our own species. Of course, this is not to say that such a link exists. It has been argued in this chapter that an indirect duty approach toward animals offers more to those concerned about their protection than has, perhaps, been previously recognized. This is primarily because such an approach need not be based on narrow self-interest, but rather associated with an interest humans have in behaving altruistically. In particular, from the perspective of virtue ethics, behaving in a virtuous fashion toward animals can be related to leading a flourishing human life.

Here, it was argued that defending the interests of animals indirectly through the contribution it can make to human flourishing offers a politically astute way of providing a justification for action to improve the treatment of animals. The focus here is on the benefits to humans that derive from living in a society that treats animals with respect. Gandhi's famous line, that "The greatness of a nation and its moral progress can be judged by the way its animals are treated" expresses this view succinctly. Attention is directed away from characteristics of animals that make them worthy of moral consideration, to the impact on humans of what we do to animals. Defined in a wide sense, human interests can be enhanced hugely by treating animals well.

However, as we saw, despite the potential offered by virtue ethics, an indirect duty approach to animal ethics is problematic. An approach based on the virtues does not provide clear guidance on how we should act toward animals, and therefore, in the context of indirect duty views, does not tell us how to live flourishing lives. Moreover, the claim that being virtuous in our treatment of animals actually does benefit the virtuous is, at the very least, open to doubt. Last, but far from least, is the point that virtuous behavior as regards animals is surely predicated on the duties we owe to them directly as a result of their capacity to be harmed. If so, then there would seem to be little in the way of recognizing the intrinsic value of animals, and condemning an indirect duty approach as illegitimate ethically. That is, animals have value that is noninstrumental—they are an end in themselves rather than merely a means to some other, human, end.

Indeed, the major problem with indirect duty views in general is that their anthropocentric flavor leaves a bad taste. Cohen (2007: 196–7) outlines accurately the cost to animals of its anthropocentric character. "The theory," he writes, "is committed to holding that torturing horses is permissible if nobody believes it is impermissible. But there is an unanswerable case for arguing that torturing horses is wrong. Not only is it wrong, it is wrong *to the horses*," and "it remains wrong even if no one believes it is." An indirect duty approach to animal ethics would, therefore, seem to represent a backward step in the sense that most moral philosophers now accept that we have direct duties to animals, that they can be harmed directly as a result of their capacity to suffer. Thus, it is widely held that because animals are sentient, and have varying degrees of cognitive ability, what we do to them matters to them, and would continue to do so even if no human was prepared to act as though it did. Animals therefore have moral standing and should be regarded as a direct moral object, "something *to* which moral consideration is paid" in Morris's words (1998: 191).

As a result of the anthropocentric character of the indirect duty position, it would seem to be a deficient nonideal theory. Its goal—protecting the interests of animals when there is a human benefit in so doing—is eminently politically achievable. Indeed, the indirect duty view is valuable in the political arena since it is humans who raise concern about the treatment of animals and it is humans who uphold or reject measures to improve the treatment of animals. The likelihood of a positive view of animal well-being is enhanced if it is associated with human flourishing. However, the indirect duty position struggles to be morally permissible and effective, in the Rawlsian sense. Pursuing a strategy based on indirect duties would not ensure that the most grievous injustices are removed. Moreover, seeking to ignore the moral standing of animals completely could well hinder the eventual acceptance of an ideal theory centering on the according of rights to animals.

The conclusion must be, then, that only a theory of justice that accords moral standing to animals—so that it is recognized that at least some harm inflicted on them ought to be prohibited, not because it benefits at least some humans, but because it is of direct benefit to the animals themselves—is valid. Clearly, the claim that animals lack moral standing is incompatible with our "commonsense" view of animals. For about two hundred years, in Britain at least, the moral orthodoxy has been that inflicting unnecessary suffering on animals is a wrong done *to the animal* and not to those humans who might be affected negatively by it.[2] This commonsense view of animals, moreover, has a great deal of intellectual support.[3]

If we accept that animals do have intrinsic value—so that what happens to them matters to them directly—and are regarded as morally considerable, and that there is, in practice, no viable moral realm independently of justice within which animal interests can be protected directly, then what follows is clear. The case for including animals as worthy recipients of justice would seem to be unanswerable. Of course, all of this leaves out of consideration exactly what is due to animals as a matter of justice, but it does make embarking on such a task a morally valid exercise. The rest of this book is concerned with this task.

5

The Animal Welfare Ethic

ANIMAL WELFARE AS an ethic has tended to be neglected in much of the animal ethics literature. It stands condemned by those advocating an animal rights position and also by Singer's utilitarian approach. It is defended, almost begrudgingly, by those who seek to critique animal rights, and is often associated in this literature with the much more ethically dubious notion of indirect duties to animals. And yet, animal welfare represents what might be described as the moral orthodoxy, at least in the developed world. This suggests, it seems to me, that it deserves more attention. This chapter seeks to give the animal welfare ethic the attention it deserves. I will start by outlining the principles behind the ethic, thereby distinguishing it from what it is often mistakenly taken to be. Following this, I will critically evaluate these principles from the perspective of ideal theory before examining the case for regarding animal welfare as an appropriate nonideal theory.

What Is Animal Welfare?

In seeking to define what I mean by an animal welfare ethic, it is useful to discuss it in the context of what it is not. First and foremost, it is not equivalent to an indirect duty view. As we saw in chapter 2, contractarian theorists, such as Rawls and Barry, exclude animals from their theories of justice, but this does not mean that they are arguing that we have no direct moral duties to them. Such duties, for Rawls and Barry, are part of a broader moral landscape, although neither sought to explore it in any detail. An animal welfare ethic might be regarded as part of that broader moral landscape in which we have direct moral duties to animals. Alternatively, we might reject contractarian theories of justice and regard animal welfare itself as a theory of justice, in the sense that what animal welfare prescribes is what animals are due as a matter of justice.

This latter position is taken by Galston (1980: 125–6). He argues that:

> If we grant that animals have interests the moral weight of which is considerably greater than zero, then they must for some purposes be included within the sphere of justice when distributional problems arise.

For example, Galston asks us to imagine a situation in which a dog is deprived of sustenance when there is enough food to go around. Such a situation, he argues, is "unjust" since the "dog is *entitled* to sustenance, not on the grounds of generosity or sympathy, but for the same reasons as humans." However, humans have some interests that animals lack and "these distinctively human interests impart a greater weight to human existence, but not an infinitely greater weight."

I argued in chapter 3 that animals stand to gain a great deal by being regarded as recipients of justice. Whether or not we regard animal welfare in such a light, what is clear is that it is an ethic that does recognize that we have direct moral duties to animals. That is, they have moral standing. It is not the case, therefore, that an animal welfare ethic suggests that animals can only be protected when it is in our interests to do so. Nor is it the case that it is equivalent to showing them charity. Rather, we humans owe them something and they have an entitlement to expect us to fulfill our obligations.

Nor, finally, is animal welfare equivalent to being kind to animals or not being cruel. As Regan (1984: 198–9) points out, kindness may be a positive virtue but "the good that kindness is must be kept distinct from judging a kind act right." Likewise, cruelty, defined in terms of an individual gaining pleasure out of harming animals[1], can, similarly, be separated from the rightness or the wrongness of the act. That is, animal welfare is distinct from the motives behind an act. The infliction of unnecessary suffering is wrong irrespective of the character traits of those inflicting the suffering. Imagine, for instance, that a scientist conducts a painful experiment on an animal despite the fact that, unbeknown to the scientist, there is an equally effective alternative that does not involve the infliction of harm. The fact that the scientist is of good character and believes, erroneously as it turns out, that she need not have conducted the experiment is of little relevance from the perspective of the animal welfare ethic. The experiment was morally wrong whatever the mental state of the scientist.

From an animal welfare perspective, what we humans owe animals however, is very different from what we owe them if they possessed rights. The according of rights to individuals assumes a degree of moral equality that does not figure in animal welfare. Rather, an animal welfare ethic accepts that humans are morally superior to animals, but that because the latter are sentient and conscious beings, they have some moral worth, albeit less than humans.[2] A useful way of understanding this is to distinguish between moral standing and moral status or significance. Following Goodpaster (1978), the former I take to mean the existence of *any* degree of direct moral considerability, the latter I take to mean the *degree* of moral worth, so that, as Attfield (2003: 43) clarifies, "moral standing... is compatible with different degrees of moral significance."[3]

Despite having moral standing, then, the animal welfare ethic accords greater moral status to humans. Traditionally, this has been taken to mean that killing animals, providing it is done painlessly, is not an ethical issue (on the grounds that it does not harm animals).[4] In addition, we can inflict suffering on animals, but only when that suffering is necessary. To put it another way, we owe it to animals that they be spared suffering that is unnecessary. Robert Nozick's comment that animal welfare amounts to "utilitarianism for animals and Kantianism for humans" has yet to be bettered as a concise description of the animal welfare ethic (Nozick, 1974: 35–42). We are therefore entitled to sacrifice the fundamental interests of animals if by so doing benefits to humans, and perhaps other animals, accrue. Humans, as possessors of inviolable rights, on the other hand, cannot be treated in the same way.

This emphasis on sentience and utilitarianism gives a clue to the origins of the animal welfare ethic. Some, for example Haynes (2008: chapter 2), regard animal welfare as a twentieth-century phenomena. In reality, however, it is an ethic whose conceptual roots (if not the label) date back to the nineteenth century. It is true that early statutes, which had the effect of protecting animals, were designed, partly at least, not to directly protect animals but to improve humans (Ritvo, 1987). However, as Tannenbaum (1995: 568) correctly points out about animal welfare statutes in general, "if one were to ask legislators, prosecutors, judges, and employees of humane societies... they would say, virtually *universally*, that the primary purpose of these laws is to protect animals." Moreover, the dominant justification for this sentiment is a recognition that animals are sentient.

Particularly important in transforming the moral climate was the influence of utilitarianism and its privileging of sentience as the benchmark of morality. Bentham's famous statement that the moral status of animals derives not from their ability to reason or talk but from their capacity to suffer (Bentham, 1948: 311) was therefore important for the development of animal welfare as an ethic. As we will see in chapter 7, the logical conclusion of utilitarianism is to provide for animals a higher moral status than animal welfare allows for. However, Bentham, aware, no doubt, of the conventions of his own society, did not draw this conclusion, opting instead for a version of animal welfare. Crucially, though, his philosophy established that animals were worth at least something morally, independently of their instrumental value to humans.

Animal welfare dictates, then, that we ask if any particular use of animals is necessary. This is not an easy task, not least because what is deemed to be necessary is likely to vary geographically and historically (see below). Applying the principle to animal experimentation, in particular, is problematic. It is possible to say convincingly that testing another brand of a cosmetic on animals is less necessary than developing and toxicity-testing a drug that will have a significant positive impact on human (and animal) health. The problem here, though, as McCloskey (1987: 660) points out, is that "In advance of the experiment, it is impossible to know which experiments will provide useful knowledge and useful outcomes," and, likewise, it is often difficult to know in advance what level of suffering will result from a particular experiment. What we can ask, though, is whether we already have the knowledge sought, whether the experiment is set up in a way that is likely to produce good results, whether the hoped for benefit is worthwhile, whether the experiment has been done before, and whether it can be achieved in a way that does not involve the use of animals.

Three Observations about Animal Welfare

Three initial observations about the animal welfare ethic, as outlined, are worth making at this point. In the first place, the inclusion of animals in a utilitarian cost-benefit calculus raises question marks, despite what Galston argues, against regarding animal welfare as a theory of *justice* for animals. At one level, animal welfare is appropriate as a theory of justice for animals if we define justice as giving an individual what they are due. In this sense, each individual animal is due whatever is consistent with complying with the unnecessary suffering principle. However, if we take a fundamental feature of justice to be treating like cases alike, then animal welfare clearly does not satisfy as a theory of *justice* for animals.

From an animal welfare perspective, what is deemed to be the morally correct way to treat an animal in any particular circumstance depends not upon any particular characteristic of the animal but upon the purpose for which the animal is being used. This leads to the odd situation, which many have commented upon, that an animal of the same species, with the same characteristics, can be treated in very different ways, and the law, based upon the animal welfare ethic, explicitly allows this. So, for example, whilst keeping a rabbit as a companion animal, it is an offense to inflict suffering on that rabbit, but if the same rabbit were in a laboratory, then a license may well be given to researchers to do exactly that. It is this emphasis on *purpose* in the animal welfare ethic that, I think, explains some of the apparently schizophrenic attitudes to animals that occur in Britain and elsewhere. That is, we dote on our companion animals whilst happily tucking into our meat dinners and, at the same time, endorse the use of animals in painful experiments in order to cure the health problems that arise largely because we eat too much meat!

The second initial observation I would make about animal welfare as an ethic is the extent to which it differs from animal welfare as a science. The claim by Mench (1998: 91) that "ethical and scientific questions about animal welfare have become hopelessly entangled," is apposite, and one of the major aims of this chapter is to untangle the knots of uncertainty. As a matter of historical chronology, the former predates the latter (Haynes, 2008: chapter 2). The study of animal welfare in a scientific context dates back to the 1960s and is now a recognized and respected part of veterinary science (Phillips, 2009: 137–45). This discipline studies what is necessary for the physical and psychological well-being of animals. It is, in general, true that the development of animal welfare science was largely a product of ethical concerns about the well-being of domesticated animals (Fraser and Weary, 2004: 40). Likewise, a scientific evaluation of an animal's welfare is a crucial component in assessing the ethical validity of a particular practice. The fact, for instance, that animal welfare scientists tell us that a certain husbandry system causes animals to suffer is clearly morally significant. Such an empirical observation, however, does not, by itself, determine whether or not this husbandry system is permissible from an ethical perspective since it does not tell us whether or not it is deemed to be necessary.

There is some evidence of confusion in the public mind between animal welfare as a science, on the one hand, and as an ethic and a guide to public policy involving animals, on the other. As I will suggest in chapter 8, this has implications for the validity of a version of animal rights as a nonideal theory of justice for animals. Haynes (2008) recognizes the distinction between animal welfare as a scientific evaluation of an animal's well-being, on the one hand, and as an ethical principle, on the other. He suggests that animal welfare scientists have "illegitimately appropriated the concept of animal welfare" from those who seek the complete liberation of animals from human use. Whether or not this is true, what can be said is that animal welfare as a science is ethically neutral and can be made compatible with an animal liberation position. That is, taking animal welfare in its scientific guise, it would be possible to argue that no uses of animals are justified ethically, on the grounds that they all compromise the welfare of animals.

The third observation about animal welfare is to notice how vague the concept of *unnecessary* suffering is. This, as I will show below, has its political advantages. From an ethical point of view, however, it is less than ideal. A number of scholars have sought to fill in the gaps here by offering more rigorous accounts of what exactly this means for animals, in terms of how far their interests are discounted. A typical analysis is the one offered by Rachels (1990: 182), who distinguishes between a "radical speciesism" and a "mild speciesism."[5] The former is where "the relatively trivial interests of humans take priority over the vital interests of non-humans." The latter is where "we may choose for the non-human" when "the choice is between a relatively trivial human interest and a more substantial interest of a non-human." Becker's category of "absolute speciesism' goes further than Rachels's radical speciesism" by refusing "to rank any animal interest (no matter how serious) above any human interest (no matter how trivial)" (Becker, 1983: 235–6). Such a position, though, comes close to denying any moral concern for animals and therefore might be regarded as inconsistent with an animal welfare ethic. To complicate the matter further, Van De Veer's definition of what he calls "radical speciesism" is equivalent to Becker's absolute speciesism whilst his "interest sensitive speciesism" (where "one may not subordinate a *basic* interest of an animal for the sake of promoting a *peripheral* human interest") is close to Rachels's mild speciesism (Van De Veer, 1979b: 59–61).

Rachels's two categories are best seen as representing both extremes of the animal welfare ethical continuum, a position he describes as "qualified speciesism" (Rachels, 1990: 184). Which point on the continuum is chosen in practice, and enshrined in law, will depend upon geographical and historical factors. Brody (2001), probably correctly, suggests that the US operates a regime for animal experimentation that is closer to radical speciesism, as Rachels defines it, whilst the European approach is closer to a mild speciesism position.

A Normative Critique of the Animal Welfare Ethic

Can the animal welfare ethic be defended in ideal-theoretical terms? The key task is to find a valid reason or reasons for the claim that humans are morally superior to animals. A number of familiar defenses have been suggested over the centuries. Descartes, for instance, based a great deal of his case on the claim that humans, unlike animals, have immortal souls. Such a justification for differential treatment in our more secular age can be given short shrift. Obviously, such an assertion cannot be proven and, in any case, it is not clear why it might be morally significant. If anything, it would seem to lead us to the opposite conclusion—that we are obliged to treat animals well since they, unlike humans, do not have the prospect of an afterlife.

Another obvious defense, of course, is to adopt a position that regards species membership alone as sufficient to justify differential treatment. A speciesist version of this position holds that the interests of human beings are to take precedence simply by virtue of the fact that *they are* human beings, irrespective of the characteristics individual humans possess. Cohen (Cohen and Regan, 2001: 37) adopts this position when he writes that, "Rights are not doled out to this individual person or that one by somehow establishing the presence in them of some special capacity...On the contrary, rights are *universally* human, arise in the human realm, and apply to humans generally."

This type of argument, as we shall see in chapter 9, is used as a device to challenge the so-called "argument from marginal cases." For now, we should note that it is a position that has, as many critics have pointed out, counterintuitive implications. It would mean, for instance, that if we persist with the argument that species membership has moral significance, then should the Earth be invaded by super-intelligent aliens they would automatically have a moral status inferior to that of humans (DeGrazia, 2002: 24–5; Rowlands, 2002: 39–40). Yet, discounting their interests in such a way would seem arbitrary and unjust. In addition, the same kind of justification being used to privilege human moral status could be used to grant a privileged moral status to, say, a particular gender or race (DeGrazia, 1996: 60).

If the speciesist argument fails, then defenders of the animal welfare ethic are dependent upon being able to show convincingly that humans are morally superior to nonhuman animals because they have morally significant characteristics not possessed by nonhuman animals. In reality, this is the defense most often mounted. Even Cohen, whilst claiming, as we saw above, that it is species membership alone that is the key, does go on to suggest (Cohen and Regan, 2001: 38) that it is the inability of animals to be moral agents that is a crucial determinant of their inferior moral status. Steinbock (1978: 247), too, states that, "We do not subject animals to different moral treatment simply because they have fur and feathers, but because they are in fact different from human beings in ways that could be morally relevant." In this version of the defense of human moral superiority—and therefore of the animal welfare ethic—speciesism is not to be compared with racism and sexism because, unlike these illegitimate positions, *there are* morally relevant differences between humans and animals. Indeed, as Cushing (2003) points out, those who hold this position seek to label the moral preference for humans as "humanism" rather than speciesism because of the latter's negative connotations.

Humans, it is typically said, are rational, self-conscious, autonomous persons, able to communicate in a sophisticated way and to act as moral agents. This is often converted into a shorthand claim that humans are persons whilst animals are not.[6] From this empirical evidence, it is argued, can be derived a moral justification for regarding humans as morally superior to nonhumans. Note that, typically, no consideration, in these defenses of the moral orthodoxy, is given to delineating the circumstances in which human interests should prevail. For example, is it when human lives are at stake? Or is it when we are comparing the capacity of animals and humans to suffer? Rather, it is simply stated that in all cases, human interests ought to be given priority over those of nonhumans. As Steinbock (1978: 253–4) argues, "if we can free human beings from crippling diseases, pain and death through experimentation which involves making animals suffer, and if this is the only way to achieve such results," then it is justifiable.

These morally significant differences between humans and nonhuman animals do not necessarily mean that animals have no moral standing whatsoever, although, in the hands of philosophers such as Kant, as we saw in chapter 4, it does. Rather, the orthodox view now, enshrined in the animal welfare position, is, as we have seen, that it is wrong to inflict *unnecessary* suffering on animals but whenever human benefits are at stake, or at least nontrivial human benefits, then any suffering inflicted becomes necessary. In practice, too, the animal welfare ethic has been taken to mean that the lives of animals are of no importance morally and that, provided that animals die without suffering, then killing them is not morally problematic, *even if* they are killed unnecessarily. Clearly, as we will have cause to reiterate in chapter 8, there is a considerable difference between the claim that animal lives are of no importance morally, and the argument that their lives are worth less than human lives. Those philosophers who seek to defend the moral inferiority of animals tend toward the latter position.

Challenging the Animal Welfare Ethic

One dominant response to the moral orthodoxy is to either deny the differences between humans and animals, or to deny that they are morally significant. One version of the former category points to the cognitive capacity of "higher" nonhuman animals, such as the great apes, which, it is argued, ought to put them on a par morally with normal humans (Cavalieri and Singer, 1993). It is clear that some species of nonhuman animals—the great apes and cetaceans in particular—have at least some of the characteristics of personhood. It makes sense, therefore, to give these species the benefit of the doubt and treat them as if they have the same interests as most humans. However, important though it is to acknowledge that more needs to be done to protect the interests of the higher nonhuman animals, all this recognition does is to create a new moral boundary. Above this new moral boundary are most humans and those nonhuman species who possess at least some of the characteristics of personhood. Below this new boundary line are the vast majority of other nonhuman animals. It does not, in other words, provide a justification for the kind of broad application of rights to animals that is usually regarded as the aim of animal rights advocacy.

There is a second, seemingly more promising, version of the denial that there are differences between humans and animals. This is the account offered by Tom Regan (1984). For him, at least some animals (to be precise, mammals one year of age and over) are, along with humans, what he calls "subjects of a life," characterized by beliefs and desires and capable of acting intentionally to satisfy their preferences. All subjects-of-a-life have inherent value. Inherent value does not come in degrees. One either has it or one does not. This equal inherent value translates into strong moral rights. In particular, subjects-of-a-life with inherent value must be treated with respect as ends and not as means to an end.

Although Regan is right to draw attention to the fact that at least some animals have various psychological characteristics and are not merely sentient, it is still, as I will show in chapter 8, difficult to establish that these characteristics are anything remotely approaching those possessed by most humans. Regan's primary aim, it should be said, is to find a level of mental complexity that will allow him to incorporate both some animals (mammals one year and over) and marginal humans. The validity of his theory will, to a large degree therefore, depend upon the success of the argument from marginal cases, consideration of which will be left until chapter 9.

The argument that the differences between humans and animals are not morally significant is the early position of Tom Regan (1975, 1979, 1980) and the one currently stated by Gary Francione (2008) and Gary Steiner (2008). Regan invokes the argument from marginal cases to enable according to animals a similar set of rights to humans (see chapter 9). Francione (2008: xiii), on the other hand, explicitly rejects the "notion that humanlike cognitive characteristics are required for full membership in the moral community." Rather, the fact that animals are sentient is "sufficient to be self-aware and to have an interest in continued existence" (11).

One of the problems with Francione's analysis is that he appears to conflate *full* membership of the moral community with *any* membership of the moral community. Thus, he points out (2008: 141) that cognitive differences between humans and animals "cannot serve to justify our treatment of non-humans as things." This suggests that if we do not grant animals equal moral status to humans, then the only alternative is to regard them as mere things, with no moral standing whatsoever. Now, it may be the case that the granting of some moral status to animals (as suggested by the animal welfare ethic) has, in practice, not amounted to very much because animals remain the property of humans who insist upon doing what they want with them. This, indeed, is Francione's position (1995). But this is to confuse an empirical assertion with a moral one. From the latter perspective, the awarding of some moral status is different from the denial of moral standing, so that if we grant to animals an inferior moral status then this does not amount to saying that we are entitled to treat them as things.

Equally, though, the regarding of animals as morally considerable does not, at least without additional convincing arguments, equate with a moral status on a par with humans. Indeed, the problem with Francione's denial of the importance of differential psychological characteristics is that, as we shall suggest in chapter 8 (as with the critique of Regan's mature theory above), it is difficult to argue against the claim that the differences between "normal" adult humans and adult animals *are* substantial and *are* morally significant.

A more fundamental argument in favor of rejecting the mental complexity model of moral significance (and in support of Francione and the early Regan) is to deny the validity of the model itself. One strand in this argument would be to point to its counterintuitive implications (Aaltola, 2005). For, isn't it the case that some humans have greater psychological capacities than others, and doesn't this mean that, according to the mental complexity model, there is a hierarchy of moral worthy *within* the human species as well as between humans and animals? Doesn't this mean, then, that it is morally permissible to sacrifice the interests of the less-mentally endowed humans in order to further the interests of those who are endowed with greater psychological capacities? (Steiner, 2008: 91, 111). Intuitively, for most of us this would amount to "sanctioning intraspecific injustices" (Van De Veer, 1979b: 74).

As we shall see in chapter 9, there *is* a strong case for saying that the moral worth of so-called marginal humans—infants and those who are severely mentally disabled—*is* lower than that of "normal" adult humans, and this, of course, does raise some important ethical questions. The objection to the mental complexity model being made here, though, is slightly different. Here, it is being claimed that it allows us, erroneously, to differentiate morally between those who can be classified as "normal" adult humans. What is envisaged, then, is a sliding scale, with the most endowed having considerable moral status and the least well-endowed having the least moral status, with gradations of moral status in between.

A possible answer to this objection is to identify a threshold position, above which includes all of those with the equal moral status of personhood (McMahan, 2002 249; Van De Veer, 1979b: 74–5). It is justifiable, it seems to me, to say that those above this threshold position, exhibiting the characteristics of personhood, have a similar interest in life, liberty, and the avoidance of suffering, even though there may be variations in the psychological capacity of individuals above this threshold. McMahan (2002: 161) makes a similar suggestion, identifying the existence of two ranking comparison classes, one consisting of marginal humans, the other consisting of "normal" humans. The idea here is that there is a point at which differences in psychological characteristics do not significantly impact upon individuals' moral worth, and, more specifically, all of those above that point, even though they exhibit a range of psychological characteristics, share equal moral worth.

Of course, there may still be an objection to the threshold argument, along the lines that if we take a comparative view—whereby moral worth is related to psychological capacities—then consistency demands that the interests of some humans must count for more than those of others. I would make two points in response to this. In the first place, the identification of a threshold does not mean that we are not still entitled to make some choices based on the degree of mental ability of the group above the threshold. It would be regarded intuitively as unjust, for instance, not to award places to university courses on the basis of intelligence but on the basis, say, of some irrelevant characteristic such as height or weight! However, when it comes to more fundamental issues relating, in particular, to life and death, then the threshold ought to be applied. Secondly, the notion that it is equally wrong to kill any person is a powerful moral intuition. I therefore concur with McMahan (2002: 251) in suggesting that such a widely accepted intuition should not be dispensed with lightly.

One additional response to those who seek to justify the animal welfare ethic does invoke the argument from marginal cases. It is argued here that since not all humans are rational and autonomous, or able to communicate in a sophisticated way, then we are not justified in regarding all humans as morally superior to all animals. In order, then, to remain morally consistent, it is argued that if we insist upon treating animals as morally inferior to humans and are basing moral value upon the characteristics that individuals possess rather than species membership alone, we ought to treat marginal humans as if they are on a moral par with animals. There is such a considerable reliance on the argument from marginal cases in much of the animal rights literature that I will consider its role and importance in chapter 9.

Leaving all references to marginal cases aside, for now, there is another response to the moral defense of the animal welfare ethic that, in this author's view at least, is much more convincing. There is one overwhelming problem with the argument that we are entitled morally to sacrifice the interests of animals whenever a significant human benefit is likely to accrue by so doing. This is that it is assumed the identification of one characteristic that humans possess and animals do not—in this case rationality, autonomy, language, and so forth—is sufficient for the claim that *all* human interests are morally superior to *all* animal interests.

McCloskey (1987: 80), Warren (1986), and Van De Veer (1979b) provide representative examples of this position. For McCloskey, "the rights to health, to bodily integrity, to self development of persons…outweigh the rights of mammals such as dogs to life, and freedom from suffering." Warren, similarly, defends what she calls a "weak animal rights" position since, although arguing that animals have rights, she also contends that the rights of most animals may be overridden to serve human benefits on the grounds that the rights of animals are weaker. Finally, Van De Veer (1979b: 64) advocates what he calls "two-factor egalitarianism" in which when there is a conflict of interests between an animal and a human being, it is morally permissible "if B lacks significant psychological capacities of A, to sacrifice the like interest of B." These authors are right to contend that the greater psychological capacities of humans are morally significant. Warren, for instance, is correct, as we shall see in chapter 8, to reject the "strong" animal rights position (what I describe as species egalitarianism) associated with Regan and Francione, and therefore is right to deny that animals and humans are

morally equal in all respects. She is right, in other words, that the characteristics of personhood have moral relevance.

It does not follow, however, that we are therefore entitled to override *any*
interests animals have in order to defend *any* of the interests humans have,
at least without an additional argument explaining why we are entitled to
do this.[7] In particular, if humans and animals are capable of suffering in an
equivalent manner, then why is this capacity of animals downgraded on the
grounds that humans also possess the characteristics of personhood? In other
words, what has personhood got to do with suffering? James Rachels (1990:
186) sets out the illogicality of this argument nicely. He asks us to consider
the case of cosmetics testing on animals—say, for example, putting chemicals
in rabbits' eyes to test the safety of a new shampoo. He writes, "To say that
rabbits may be treated in this way, but humans may not, because humans are
rational agents, is comparable to saying that one law school applicant may be
accepted, and another rejected because one has a broken arm while the other
has an infection."

What I am arguing here, then, is that the fact that humans are persons
and animals are not cannot justify the whole range of differences between
our treatment of humans and animals in the way that the animal welfare ethic
wants it to. To put it simply, torturing an animal is wrong because it hurts.
Here, the fact that the animal does not have the characteristics of personhood would seem to be irrelevant. As Rachels (2004: 167) points out then:
"Autonomy and self-consciousness are not ethical superqualities that entitle
the bearer to every possible kind of favourable treatment."

Animal Welfare as Nonideal Theory

However ethically flawed the animal welfare ethic might be, it could still
provide the basis for a viable nonideal theory of justice for animals. Indeed,
it has been so regarded in the animal ethics literature and by many animal
rights advocates. The label "New Welfarist" has been applied, usually by its
critics, to those who are philosophically critical of animal welfare, but who
regard it as a necessary stepping stone to the achievement of animal rights
goals (Francione, 1996; Francione and Garner, 2010).

In the past, I have defended animal welfare as strategically important for the
animal protection movement, despite its obvious normative flaws (Francione
and Garner, 2010). For good reason, too. For one thing, animal welfare has
the advantage of strong name recognition. It is difficult to find anyone now
who does not accept the goal of animal welfare. Indeed, the concept of animal

welfare has dominated discussion of the treatment of animals and has been the main rationale behind the improvements to the treatment of animals that have occurred in recent decades. Indeed, legislation governing the treatment of animals is based almost universally on the unnecessary suffering principle (Garner, 1998).

Moreover, what is characterized as unnecessary is not static. Over the past few decades what is regarded as unnecessary suffering has expanded. Some practices—such as the wearing of fur, the testing of cosmetics on animals, and the worst excesses of factory farming—were regarded as morally acceptable thirty or so years ago but for many they are now examples of the infliction of unnecessary suffering. This has, in turn, impacted upon public policy. In Britain, for example, fur farming has been prohibited and no licenses are now given for cosmetic testing on animals. Likewise, many aspects of factory farming—such as the debeaking of poultry, the use of veal crates, pig stalls, and tethers, and the battery cage—are now being seriously challenged throughout Europe. It is now thought by many that it is unnecessary to keep hens confined in battery cages or broiler chickens cooped up in windowless sheds.

Such is the flexibility of the animal welfare ethic that it can justify the cessation of all animal exploitation. Francione (2000), for instance—although in reality a committed advocate of the species-egalitarian strand of animal rights—adopts this approach in his book-length text on animal rights. We can all accept, he suggests, what he calls the "humane treatment principle," which prohibits the infliction of unnecessary suffering on animals. But, he continues, we do not practice what we preach because "the overwhelming portion of our animal use can be justified *only* by habit, convention, amusement, convenience or pleasure." As a result, "most of the suffering that we impose on animals is completely unnecessary *however* we interpret that notion" (Francione, 2000: xxiii–xxiv).

Animal welfare has also been the focus of virtually all mainstream groups within the animal protection movement. That is, they have been primarily concerned to show not that the use of animals is morally wrong irrespective of the benefits to humans, but rather that most, if not all, of the ways in which animals are currently treated are unnecessary in the sense that they do not produce human benefits or that such benefits can be achieved in other ways. The classic example here is the tendency of animal rights groups to adopt a "practical anti-vivisection" strategy—animal experimentation does not work or is unnecessary because it is trivial or the results can be found through using alternatives to animals—rather than an "ethical anti-vivisection" strategy—animal experimentation is morally wrong whatever the benefits it produces.

However, as a nonideal theory, animal welfare does possess severe limitations. Francione has provided a critique of "New Welfarism" that, if correct, would mean that the animal welfare ethic does not meet Rawls's criteria for a valid nonideal theory (Francione and Garner, 2010). In particular, Francione has argued not only that the property status of animal obstructs effective animal welfare measures, but also that insofar as the welfare of animals improves—or is perceived to improve—through animal welfare measures, then this hinders the achievement of the animal rights end point by making the treatment of animals more acceptable. If true, the pursuit of animal welfare as a nonideal theory falls foul of Rawls's effectiveness criterion whereby the validity of a particular nonideal theory can be judged by the degree to which it moves society toward the ideal position.

I do not intend to replicate in detail here the debate Gary Francione and I have had about the alleged counterproductive nature of animal welfare (the debate can be found in Francione and Garner, 2010). In brief, my challenge to Francione's argument is based partly on the fact that I offer an alternative ideal theory, one that is not based on abolitionism. As a result, improvements to the welfare of animals short of the abolition of particular uses of animals are, I believe, worth having for their own sake irrespective of whether they do hinder an abolitionist end-point (see chapter 8). In addition, I deny that animal welfare reforms are in any way counterproductive, as Francione suggests. The notion that improvements to the way animals are treated makes it much harder to achieve the eventual abolition of animal exploitation is flawed partly because it is based on an unprovable counterfactual and partly because it flies in the face of the evidence that, despite widespread publicity of the iniquities of factory farming, there has not been a major increase in the number of vegetarians and vegans. Thus, the argument, or, in reality, the implication, that people will only desist from consuming animal products if their welfare is shown to be inadequate, does not fit the facts.

Despite my rejection of Francione's counterproductive argument, however, I do share some reservations about the use of animal welfare as a nonideal theory. This contention stems partly from the objection that the animal welfare ethic is so clearly normatively flawed. A viable nonideal theory, it seems to me, should try, as Sher (1997: ch. 11) has argued, at achieving a reasonable balance. That is, it should try to combine the rigor and imagination of ideal theory with the realism of nonideal theory. In the context of the animals debate, it should not only be a position that the public and decision makers can be persuaded to accept. Rather, it should also be one that is a reasonable compromise between the objectives of elements of the animal protection movement.

I would suggest that animal welfare is not such a reasonable balance. Because it allows for no side-constraints limiting the use of animals for human benefit, it permits fundamental animal interests to be sacrificed for human benefit, and because of the way it is usually interpreted, leads to too much animal suffering. Part of the problem has been that animal welfare has been co-opted by those with an interest in the continued exploitation of animals, to serve their ends. As a result, despite the improvements to animal welfare that have undoubtedly occurred, they remain relatively minor in scope and animals still pay a heavy price as a result of the application of the animal welfare ethic. Satz (2009: 6) is right here to argue that in practice a great deal of what she refers to as "legal gerrymandering for human interests" goes on when "the natural baseline for the legal protection of animals—premised on their inherent capacities—is redrawn to facilitate human use of animals." This is precisely why, according to the animal welfare ethic, whether or not it is justifiable ethically to inflict suffering on an animal depends first and foremost, as we saw above, on the purpose for which the animal is being used.

According to the animal welfare ethic, however, there is no inconsistency here. That is, as I pointed out earlier, the reason why we dote on our companion animals, and the law will take action against us if we do not, is because no purpose is served by inflicting suffering on them. Indeed, the purpose of keeping companion animals is precisely not to inflict suffering on them. Rather, the purpose is to provide us with company that aids our psychological and physical well-being. This discrepancy can only be alleviated if we dispense with animal welfare as the dominant ethical discourse.

As a result, although animal welfare is not counterproductive and is therefore effective (or at least not ineffective)—in the Rawlsian sense of the term—it is not morally permissible in the sense that it does not remove the most grievous, or most urgent injustice, the one that departs the most from the ideal theory. This is because it fails to prevent extreme levels of suffering being imposed on animals if there is a chance that humans will benefit as a result. In contrast to a theory based on rights, the animal welfare ethic contains no trumps or automatic constraints that can prevent the exploitation of animals irrespective of the greater good that might result.

There will be those, of course, who will, and do, say that animal welfare is the best that animal advocates are going to get at the moment, and therefore, they have little option but to accept it, even if their ultimate goal is the achievement of an animal rights agenda. It is certainly the case that the abolitionist, or species-egalitarian, version of animal rights is an unrealistic objective. However, as chapter 8 will attempt to show, this is not the only strand of animal rights available, and there are alternative versions that can, arguably, serve us better at the ideal and nonideal levels. Before I engage with that task, I will, in the next chapter, identify the constituent elements of an alternative animal rights position.

6

Animal Rights and Justice

IN THIS CHAPTER, I outline the constituent parts of my preferred theory of justice for animals. Put simply, it is a rights-based theory, an interest-based theory, and a capacity-oriented theory. One criticism of rights theory we encountered earlier pointed to the "mysterious" way in which rights, for humans and for animals, are often justified. It is true that, shorn of their religious origins, the moorings of rights have often been somewhat slippery. As this chapter will show, however, this need not be the case. Indeed, a rights-based approach built upon the principles of the equal consideration of interests and moral individualism, suggested by a number of animal ethicists, offers a very precise and intuitively beguiling ethic. Moreover, an ethic built upon rights, focusing on the equal consideration of the interests of individuals, not only has a good fit with the concept of justice, but also allows for the inclusion of animals in a convincing manner.

Rights and Justice

The adoption of a rights-based approach would seem to be particularly appropriate for a theory of *justice* for animals. As we saw in chapter 3, justice represents a special kind of morality, in that claims based on justice ought to be urgently addressed and enforced. To say that an individual has a right to something does seem to offer this kind of urgency in that rights are usually associated with entitlements that confer correlative duties. As Nussbaum (2006: 377) points out in the context of animals: "When I say that the mistreatment of animals is unjust, I mean to say not only that it is wrong *of us* to treat them in that way, but also that they have a right, a moral entitlement, not to be treated in that way. It is unfair *to them*." McCloskey (1987: 79), in even stronger terms, writes, about rights in general, that:

> To violate a person's right is not simply to fail to carry out a duty
> to another person comparable with failing to carry out a duty of

benevolence to a needy friend who has no moral claim on us. It is to wrong the possessor of the right and to engage in a morally much more reprehensible act than that of simply failing in our duties towards him. When a person demands respect for his moral rights, he is asking for no favours or privileges. He is demanding what is his, what is owed to him.

The link between rights and justice is heightened by the fact that a rights-based approach focuses on the individual. We do not, intuitively, think it is just to sacrifice the interests of an individual even if by so doing a gain in aggregative social welfare is made. The employment of rights, unlike a utilitarian approach, specifically rules out such an outcome (see chapter 7). Indeed, the growing importance of rights discourse was at least partly a product of "a deep moral unease" about the way in which utilitarianism resolved conflicts (Waldron, 1989: 507). Whatever else rights are, exponents agree that their effect is to build protective fences around individuals, defending them "from becoming mere instruments for the attainment of the common good" (Cavalieri, 2001: 91). As Dworkin (1977: 199) insists, "the institution of rights rests on the conviction that the invasion of a relatively important right…is a grave injustice."

Seen in a negative sense, rights are what Nozick (1974) calls "side constraints," limiting the extent to which individuals are entitled to interfere in a person's activities. They therefore act as "trumps," in that protecting individual rights takes priority over the promotion of the common good when our interests are in danger of being traded off (Dworkin,1977: xi, 90–4, 364–8). Even though few would want to claim they are absolute, not least since rights can conflict, we must think long and hard before infringing a right. The notion that even though gains might be made by sacrificing the interests of individuals, these gains are illegitimate because they are ill-gotten, is very powerful. To label such sacrifices as *unjust* would seem to be entirely appropriate.

Rights and Interests

The second component of my preferred theory of justice for animals centers on the notion of interests. Conceptually, the key debate in the rights literature has been between exponents of a will or choice theory of rights, on the one hand, and exponents of an interest theory of rights, on the other. The former, Kantian, approach holds that the function of rights is to establish arenas within which individuals can exercise choices (Hart, 1967; Steiner, 1998). By contrast, the interest theory of rights maintains that the function of rights is to uphold individual well-being (Raz, 1986; Kramer, 1998). The possession of an interest therefore leads to a duty on others to ensure that this right—following directly from the possession of an interest —is upheld. As in Raz's famous formulation, "an aspect of X's well being (his interest) is a sufficient reason for holding some other person(s) to be under a duty" (Raz, 1986: 165).

This conceptual debate within political and moral philosophy has direct relevance to the debate about animal rights, since exponents of the will theory hold that only those who are able to claim and waive their rights can be rights holders. This has the effect of excluding animals, as well as marginal humans (infants, and the seriously mentally deficient). The purpose of adopting this position is to emphasize and promote individual self-determination as a morally important characteristic. Thus, only those who are able to claim and act upon a domain "within which the choices made by designated individuals…must not be subjected to interference" (Steiner, 1998: 238) can be possessors of rights.

The will theory has been explicitly, and approvingly, used by some philosophers as part of their case against according rights to animals. For example, McCloskey, although in an earlier work claiming that having interests is all that is necessary for an individual to be capable of being a bearer of rights, later rejects this view as "mistaken, misconceived and misdirected" (McCloskey, 1979: 36). Instead, animals are excluded as possessors of rights because "the exercise of moral rights involves the capacity for moral judgments, namely, moral awareness of the extent of the liberty the right confers" (McCloskey, 1987: 79. See also Cohen and Regan, 2001: 55 and Hills, 2005: 123–6).

Echoing the discussion in chapter 3 of this book, both Steiner (1998: 259) and Hart (1967: 58), although rejecting the case for according rights to animals, recognize that we may still have moral duties to them. However, in the same way that excluding animals from a theory of justice is problematic because of the high status accorded to justice, the exclusion of animals as rights holders is likely to diminish the importance attached to these moral duties precisely because of the high status accorded to rights in modern society (Campbell, 2006: 49). Since it is largely accepted that animals, and marginal humans, can have interests—on the grounds that their sentience means they can be valued for their own sake and not for the benefits it gives to others—it is obvious that a theory of animal rights would be wise to adopt the interest, rather than the will, version (Feinberg, 1980; Cochrane, 2012).

Critics of the will theory of rights usually focus on the fact that it also excludes some humans: those—such as infants and the severely mentally disabled—not capable of exercising choice. This has been regarded by many philosophers as a weakness because it is not in accord with our commonsense understanding of rights (Wenar, 2005: 240). By contrast, the interest theory, concerned with promoting the well-being of the rights holder, is applicable to any individual who has interests, including marginal humans.[1] More substantively, it is not clear why it is necessary for the rights holders themselves to be able to claim and waive their rights, as opposed to someone else doing it on their behalf (Feinberg, 1980: 163–4). After all, this is the way the interests of children and the mentally deficient are expressed and protected. To insist that rights only exist when they can be waived or claimed, then, seems overly dogmatic (Campbell, 2006: 45).

However, although defining rights in terms of interests does enable us to incorporate animals, which is the purpose of this chapter, there would appear to be some problems with associating rights with interests. Thus, McCloskey (1979: 36) rejects the interest theory on the grounds that rights and interests are "completely distinct things." Moreover, even if we accept that animals have interests, it may be that they do not translate into rights because, for instance, humans have interests with a higher priority. Indeed, a major part of chapter 8 in this volume is concerned with attempting to elucidate which animal interests can be translated into rights. There is an assumption here, of course, that rights are more important morally than interests, that the former can trump the latter (Cohen and Regan, 2001: 18).

It is also argued that an interest-based theory of rights fails to account for cases where the rights holder is not the beneficiary (Wenar, 2005: 240). For example, certain occupational roles contain rights—such as the right of a judge to pass sentence, or the right of a traffic warden to hand out parking tickets—the exercise of which do not benefit the rights holder. Similarly, in cases where third parties are beneficiaries, it is not the rights holders whose interests are being served. Thus, if I promise X to benefit Y in some way, it is X who has a right to insist that I fulfill the promise and not Y, despite the fact that Y is the beneficiary.

We can respond in a number of ways to these objections. In the first place, advocates of an interest-based theory of rights are not suggesting that all interests can be translated into rights, only that rights derive from interests. It may be that we decide that some, relatively trivial, interests are not strong enough to be translated into rights whereas others clearly are, or that some interests ought not to be promoted because they harm others (Cochrane, 2012: 42–3). In response to the argument that an interest-based theory is unable to account for those cases where the rights holder is not the beneficiary, we can argue that the kind of rights that do not benefit the right holder are not actually rights at all; adopt the will theory, which does allow us to include them (but at the expense of excluding animals); or adopt an alternative version that encompasses rights based on both choice and discretion *and* benefits (a position endorsed by Wenar, 2005, and Campbell, 2006: 46). The key point for the purposes of this chapter, though, is that it is not fatal for a theory of animal rights if we adopt this more inclusive principle because it does not exclude rights grounded in interests that allow for the inclusion of animals.

The case for adopting this more inclusive theory is amplified when it is recognized that neither theory of rights is based on purely abstract principles but is inextricably linked with the values that each theory is designed to promote (Campbell, 2006: 46). Thus, advocates of the will theory are concerned with highlighting the importance of autonomy as a normative goal, whereas advocates of the interest theory are concerned with promoting a broader range of goals. In a sense, then, it is difficult to divorce the question of what rights are from the question of who should have them. In the context of the subject matter of this book, therefore, we are justified in adopting an interest theory of rights precisely because of our preexisting belief in the moral importance of animals.

Animals and the Interest-Based Theory of Rights

Applying the notion of interests in the case of animals has been a common, albeit submerged, undertaking. The use of interests to ground a theory of rights has often been implicit. Singer (1990), the first to popularize the equal consideration of interests principle, is, of course, a utilitarian. Neither Rachels (1990) nor DeGrazia (1996), two other key exponents, are primarily concerned with advocating a rights-based ethic.[2] It was Joel Feinberg (1980) who first suggested applying a combination of an interest-based ethic and a rights position to nonhuman animals, and his work has been built upon by Alasdair Cochrane (2012), who is the first to put forward a comprehensive interest-based theory of animal rights.[3]

The use of arguments centering around interests in the animal ethics literature have tended to be submerged by the dominance of the species-egalitarian abolitionism associated, above all, with Regan. Utilizing an interest-based theory, however, enabled, as we saw in chapter 5, an effective critique of the animal welfare ethic and, on the same grounds, enables us to challenge the normative validity of the abolitionist, species-egalitarian, version of animal rights, too (see chapter 7). Central to this critique of both the animal welfare ethic and the species-egalitarian version of animal rights is the principle of the equal consideration of interests, an idea initially developed by Peter Singer (1990, 1993) and utilized by other animal ethicists such as James Rachels (1990) and David DeGrazia (1996).

DeGrazia (2002: 19) sums up the equal consideration of interests principle when he writes that "whenever a human and an animal have a comparable interest, we should regard the animal's interest and the human's interest as equally morally important." The key feature of the principle is to emphasize the importance of individual interests independently of species. In other words, it is not the species one is a member of that is morally important but the interests we have as individuals. As Singer (1980: 329) points out, "no being should have its interests disregarded or discounted merely because it is not human." Equal consideration, of course, is not synonymous with moral equality and equal treatment. It commits us to treating like interests in a comparable fashion, a key principle of justice, but it does not tell us what interests particular individuals have. To determine that is where the hard work for moral philosophers starts.

Rachels's version of the equal consideration principle is a position he describes as "moral individualism." For him, how "an individual should be treated depends on his or her own particular characteristics, rather than on whether he or she is a member of some preferred group" (Rachels, 1990: 5). Once attention is directed away from species membership and toward particular characteristics of individuals, the door is left open to emphasize those characteristics possessed by nonhuman animals, which are shared with humans, in addition to an awareness that not all humans have the same characteristics. In this way, the prevailing doctrine of "human specialness," derived initially from religious teachings, can be challenged.

The key point here is that, as Rachels (1990: 186) argues, "the observation that humans are rational autonomous agents cannot justify the whole range of differences between our treatment of humans and our treatment of nonhumans. It can justify some differences in treatment, but not others." That is, an approach that insists upon finding a single characteristic that justifies the possession of rights in general is flawed, and ought to be replaced with one that seeks to identify characteristics relevant to the possession of a particular right. Rachels (1990: 179) asks us to contemplate the considerations involved in assessing the characteristics relevant morally in denying a university education, on the one hand, and torture, on the other. Clearly, in the case of the former, it would be ridiculous to regard it as morally wrong to deny a university education to an individual lacking the capacity to read and write. In the case of the latter, however, the relevant characteristic would not be the level of cognitive capacity, but the capacity to suffer.

As we saw in chapter 5, this approach—identifying characteristics that might be relevant in any particular case—avoids the blanket inegalitarianism contained in the animal welfare ethic. In addition, as we will see in chapter 7, it enables us to avoid the blanket egalitarianism that is a central feature of the species-egalitarian strand of animal rights. Both these approaches, by contrast, are concerned with identifying a single characteristic (personhood in the case of the former and inherent value in the case of Regan's version of the latter) that can explain the denial of rights possession in the former, and the possession of rights in the latter. In addition, one of the key consequences of seeking to decouple moral worth from species membership, of course, is to raise question marks about human moral equality. Singer's willingness, in particular, to consider whether human life should always be regarded as sacrosanct has, indeed, provoked more controversy than his views on animals.

The full implications of adopting an interest-based theory of animal rights is drawn out by Cochrane (2007; 2009; 2012). He argues that animals do not possess an intrinsic interest in liberty, because, unlike humans, they are not autonomous agents "possessing the ability to frame, revise and pursue their own conceptions of the good" (Cochrane, 2009: 661). As a result, the adoption of animal rights does not mean that the use of animals by humans is necessarily prohibited morally since, because they do not possess an *intrinsic* interest in liberty, they do not have an automatic right to liberty. As the title of his book indicates, the effect of this analysis is to "decouple animal rights from animal liberation" (Cochrane, 2012). This is not to say that, for Cochrane, all uses of animals are thereby deemed morally acceptable. Animals, for him, do have an interest in avoiding suffering (and therefore a right not to have suffering inflicted on them) and so in cases where the use of animals does infringe this right, it ought to be prohibited.

Cochrane (2012: 68–71) also suggests that, although animals may not possess as great an interest in continued life as humans, the fact that we regard marginal humans as if they have the same interest in life as nonmarginal humans (even when they clearly do not) signifies we should regard animals in the same light. The granting of a right to life to animals means that Cochrane's practical program is, to all intents and purposes, not that different from the species-egalitarian version of animal rights that regards all uses of animals as morally unacceptable. This end result, however, comes about not so much because of his adoption of an interest-based theory of animal rights, but because of Cochrane's acceptance of the argument from marginal cases. This, by itself, is not a criticism—unless one rejects the argument from marginal cases. However, Cochrane's analysis may be open to the charge of inconsistency. For, if the argument from marginal cases is applied in the same way to the issue of liberty as it is for life, might it not be argued that animals ought to be also granted a right to liberty? Cochrane avoids this conclusion by claiming that marginal humans are, to some extent at least, also denied a right to liberty. This issue is revisited in chapter 9.

Capacities, not Relations

The third major component of my preferred theory of justice for animals is the adoption of what Palmer (2010: 5) has described as a "capacity-oriented" ethic. According to the capacity-oriented approach, moral status or worth is granted on the basis of the possession of some ability or other, whether it be mere sentience or greater cognitive capacities. It is therefore based on the view that, "How a being ought to be treated depends, to some significant extent, on its intrinsic properties—in particular its psychological properties and capacities" (McMahan, 1996: 31). A major alternative approach is the adoption of a relational ethic, whereby, in its pure sense at least, the moral status of an individual is based not upon her capacities or interests but upon the relationship she has with others.[4]

A relational ethic can be used to justify the importance of species. One account of this is that our closest relationships tend to be with other humans—a position most associated with Midgley (1983). Equally, though, one can point to relationships that humans have with animals, too. Indeed, this would seem to account for the different ways humans regard companion animals, on the one hand, and those animals that live wildly, on the other. Thus, utilizing a relational ethic can justify leaving wild animals alone, and therefore avoid the need to get embroiled in debates about whether we ought to intervene to prevent the suffering of wild animals, not least when this suffering is caused by other animals, as in predation. By contrast, domesticated animals, because of the relationship we have with them, can expect us to intervene in a positive fashion to prevent and alleviate suffering, at least when it is not against our interests to do so.

However, an ethic that suggests that all of our moral obligations, or a large part of them, derive from our relationships, and not the capacities of individuals, is seriously flawed. In particular, it would have the implication that we owe no obligations—positive or negative—to those with whom we do not have a relationship. Such a position—to regard those humans with whom we do not have a relationship as being owed nothing morally—is intuitively problematic. As DeGrazia (1999: 126) remarks, "giving extensive weight to social bonds might destabilize the moral status of many humans; unloved loners, people from very different cultures or highly isolated countries." To put it bluntly, we do not think that prohibitions on killing apply only to our friends.

It is equally the case that utilizing the relational ethic as the main ingredient of an animal ethic results in morally counterintuitive conclusions. For it follows that if moral status is accorded merely on the basis of relational factors, then those animals with whom we do not have a cooperative relationship have no moral worth at all. This provides some odd outcomes. It would mean that we would be morally obliged to treat animals with the same cognitive capacities very differently according to whether or not we do have a cooperative relationship with them. The contrast between domesticated and wild-living animals is the obvious example here.

It is also questionable whether moral worth deriving from our relationships can be divorced entirely from moral worth based on capacities. It is plausible to argue that the moral importance of the relationships we are said to have with those with whom we have relationships (such as friends, family members, and companion animals) stems from a recognition of moral worth deriving from their capacities (Scanlon, 1998: 166). Thus, we do not regard our houseplants as having moral worth whereas we do recognize the moral worth of our companion animals, precisely because the latter have the capacity of sentience whereas the former do not. Therefore, the question of whether we should grant moral preference to our houseplants rather than, say, our neighbor's houseplants or the plants on the local park, does not arise.

It is not being claimed here that a relational ethic has no importance in moral theory in general, and in animal ethics in particular. Clearly, the perception that our moral obligations to those to whom we are close have a special resonance is intuitively appealing. What *is* being claimed here, however, is that moral preferences based on special relations can only be seen as supplementing the moral worth of entities determined by their capacities. To illustrate this point it is worthwhile examining the position taken by, perhaps, the two best known relational accounts in animal ethics.

In the first of these, Donaldson and Kymlicka (2011: 6) take the animal rights tradition to task for not paying sufficient attention to the moral importance that ought to be attached to the "geographically and historically specific relationships that have been developed between particular groups of humans and particular groups of animals." This enables us, they argue, to transcend the traditional focus in animal rights discourse on negative rights. In an innovative analysis, applying Kymlicka's long-held advocacy of group-differentiated rights, they argue that it is useful to map our obligations to animals through the utilization of citizenship theory (Kymlicka, 1995). In other words, the moral worth of animals is cashed out, at least in part, through their membership of political communities.

Donaldson and Kymlicka envisage three categories of animals, informed by a relational ethic based on citizenship theory. Domesticated animals, those who are part of our societies, are equivalent to co-citizens, and have certain particular rights because of their relational status with humans (chapter 5). Those animals who live amongst us but are not domesticated, so-called liminal animals, are equivalent to co-residents who do not have the rights of full citizenship but to whom we must have moral guidelines given their close proximity to us (chapter 7). Finally, genuinely wild animals are equivalent to separate sovereign communities that ought to be regulated by norms of international justice (chapter 6).

There is no doubt that Donaldson and Kymlicka's relational approach provides a rich analysis of human-animal relations. However, the relational approach plays a rather small role in their analysis, and, as a result, the case for regarding their approach as genuinely different and innovative can be challenged. This is because their starting point is the acceptance, as a baseline, of a traditional species-egalitarian abolitionist animal rights agenda based on a capacity-oriented ethic (Donaldson and Kymlicka, 2011: chapter 2). That is, they accept that animals have a right to life and liberty that "prohibits harming them, killing them, confining them, owing them, and enslaving them" (40). This has the effect of ruling out of account the domestication of animals for exploitative human purposes. Animal agriculture and animal experimentation are therefore morally illegitimate on the grounds that to use animals in such a way is to infringe their rights. When Donaldson and Kymlicka talk about those animals who should be regarded as citizens, then, they are only referring to companion animals.

Now, as we saw in chapter 2, it is difficult, albeit not impossible, to show that the domesticating of animals for, say, agricultural purposes represents a genuine cooperative relationship, as opposed to one based on exploitation. In other words, extrapolating a relational ethic beyond companion animals is contentious. Donaldson and Kymlicka, though, do not have to get involved in this debate because they adopt an animal rights ethic that rules out the use of animals for food and for experimental purposes. It is a capacity-oriented ethic, then, that is doing most of the work here. Indeed, because their point of departure is the species-egalitarian version of animal rights, a great deal of the book is concerned with refuting the position that all domestication of animals is morally wrong because it makes animals dependent on humans, or because it is still using animals for human ends (Donaldson and Kymlicka, 2011: 62–84).

There is some doubt, too, whether animals can be regarded as citizens in any meaningful sense. More to the point of this chapter, however, is that in order to show that companion animals can be equated as citizens, even in a weaker sense, Donaldson and Kymlicka, it seems to me, are somewhat dependent upon a capacity-oriented approach. Clearly, as they recognize (55), animals do not qualify if a traditional definition of citizenship (a member of a political community who is endowed with a set of rights and a set of obligations or responsibilities) is invoked. Animals cannot engage in democratic political agency, at least in the traditional sense of the notion. They can have rights, but cannot exercise responsibilities.

Donaldson and Kymlicka's case for applying citizenship to animals is based, at least partly, on the fact that the traditional notion of active citizenship does not apply to many so-called marginal humans either, a fact that has been well-documented by disability campaigners and advocates of disability theories of citizenship (Donaldson and Kymlicka, 2011: 105–8). The weaker form of citizenship envisaged, however, is more about animals expressing their needs, to which we are obliged to respond, than about the exercise of responsibilities (108–22). Even a weaker form of citizenship, however, depends upon certain capacities, as Donaldson and Kymlicka (2011: 108) recognize, namely, to "have and communicate a subjective good", to "comply with schemes of social cooperation" and to "participate as agents in social life." Their relations of citizenship, therefore, are mediated through a capacity-oriented approach, thereby confirming its central place in animal ethics.

The second well-known relational account in animal ethics is provided by Clare Palmer (2010). This work focuses on the ethics of assisting animals, and argues that traditional approaches in animal ethics find it difficult to account for the "laissez faire" intuition whereby it is permissible morally to leave wild animals to their fate whilst it is unacceptable to neglect domesticated animals in the same way. That is, a capacity-oriented ethic would not be able to account for the widely held intuition that we should treat animals with the same or similar cognitive capacities in very different ways.

The problem for a capacity-oriented ethic, then—according to Palmer, at least—is that it cannot justify the conferring of differential rights (positive rights for domesticated animals and negative rights for wild animals) on the grounds of psychological capacities alone. Donalsdon and Kymlicka (2011) share this position, too, of course. Only those domesticated animals who are citizens have certain particular positive rights because of their relational status with humans. By contrast, genuinely wild animals are equivalent to separate sovereign communities and the assumption here is that they should be left alone by other, human, communities.[5] Only the adoption of a relational ethic allows us to make this distinction, since only a relational ethic enables us to differentiate between wild animals (where positive duties of assistance are thought not to be required) and domesticated animals (where they are thought to be required).

What should we make of this defense of a relational ethic as far as animals are concerned? Three specific responses can be made. We could argue, firstly, that the intuition that we should not intervene in the wild is mistaken. We might not want to go as far as engaging in the kind of human engineering of the wild that Nussbaum seems to think is necessary when she makes the claim that the natural world must be replaced by the just world (see chapter 7). Such a scenario does look decidedly odd. But, as Cochrane (forthcoming) points out, we do already recognize a right to protection from predation in the case of some wild animals. For instance, human predation is sometimes severely curtailed, as in the case of the ban on whaling. We do not think it odd, either, to protect, what Donaldson and Kymlicka would describe as, liminal animals from domesticated animals. Preventing cats from killing birds, for example, is a common practice, and not regarded as counterintuitive in the slightest. In other cases, as Cochrane (forthcoming) rightly argues, we take the view that intervening to protect prey animals is not a reasonable option given the costs involved, the likelihood that it will not be effective, or the impact it would have on predator animals. The key point, though, is that we have not just assumed in these cases that wild animals should be left to their own devices. Rather, we have concluded after much deliberation that it is the right course of action.

The second response to the argument that a relational ethic ought to be a valuable part of the animal ethicist's armory is to repeat a general point I made earlier. It is one thing to compliment a capacity-oriented ethic with a relational ethic, but quite another to replace the former with the latter. Palmer, at least in her earlier work (2003), seems to veer toward the latter option. Donaldson and Kymlicka (2011), as we have seen, adopt the former approach, although the capacities approach does more work in their account than is, perhaps, appreciated.

Finally, it can be argued utilitarianism and the capabilities approach (which we will consider in more detail in chapter 7) find it more difficult, than a rights-based ethic, to account for the intuitively plausible claim that we ought not to accord assistance rights to wild animals. Since the origin, and the perpetrator, of animal suffering is unimportant for utilitarians, it is an ethic that requires humans to intervene in the wild if by so doing it results in a surplus of pain over pleasure, or it maximizes preferences (Palmer, 2010: 28–9). Palmer (2010: 29) recognizes that utilitarians such as Singer would respond by arguing that we do not know enough about the ecosystem to determine what the consequences of our actions will be. She is not convinced, however, by this retort, and for good reason, too. It might be argued, for instance, that the more we intervene in the ecosystem, the greater our knowledge would become. The fact remains that *were we* to have the full facts of the impact of our intervention to hand, then the case for intervening in the wild would be unanswerable.

A rights-based capacity-oriented ethic, on the other hand, it might be thought, would be able to deal with the assistance problem that Palmer identifies. Regan, for instance, seeks to defend negative rights. He does advocate a duty to assist animals, but only when they are being harmed by moral agents (Regan, 1984: 285). This avoids a rights-position from committing itself to intervening in predation, to stop the prey animals from being harmed. As a result, his mantra about wild animals is that we should leave them alone. However, such a position fails to account for the positive assistance rights that the laissez faire intuition suggests ought to be accorded to domesticated animals. "There are no rights-generated duties" in Regan's thought, Palmer (2010: 38) argues, "to assist any subjects-of-a-life, in cases where a threat or some past harm is not from a moral agent."

In the case of rights theory, therefore, negative rights based on capacities can be supplemented with assistance rights derived from the moral duties that derive from relationships. At the same time, we are not committed to protecting wild animals against threats from other animals or from the impact of nature as a whole. Utilitarianism and the capabilities approach, on the other hand, seem committed to assisting wild animals in ways that are intuitively problematic, and cannot therefore be complimented by a relational ethic in a helpful way.

Conclusion

This chapter has been concerned with outlining the constituent elements of my preferred ideal and nonideal theory of justice for animals. It is a rights-based theory, since there seems to be a close fit between the according of rights to individuals and behaving justly to them. It is, secondly, an interest-based theory of rights. Animals are entitled to rights, and are therefore entitled to be recipients of justice, because they have interests. Finally, it is also, despite the claims of a relational approach, predominantly a capacity-oriented theory. The next step is to analyze what rights animals are due as a matter of justice. That is, what interests do animals possess that can be translated into rights? Before that, though, chapter 7 seeks to utilize the theory sketched out in this chapter to examine, and ultimately reject, three separate positions in the animal ethics debate.

7

Three Positions Rejected

THE STRENGTH OF the rights-based approach outlined in the previous chapter can be illustrated if it is compared and contrasted with three of its chief rivals in the animal ethics literature. This chapter, then, examines two non-rights-based positions in the animal ethics debate—based, respectively, on utilitarianism, and capabilities—and one rights-based approach to animal ethics. It is argued that, taking into account the constituent elements of my preferred theory of justice for animals, all are deficient as ideal and nonideal theories of justice for animals.

Utilitarianism, Rights, and Justice

Utilitarianism, as advocated most notably by Singer (1990; 1993) and largely supported by Dale Jamieson (1990; 1999), represents an important approach within animal ethics.[1] There are some grounds, too, for regarding utilitarianism as an appropriate theory of justice for animals. In the first place, as we saw in the context of the animal welfare ethic, by focusing on sentience as the benchmark of moral standing, utilitarianism draws attention to what links humans and animals (Nussbaum, 2006: 339). Moreover, central to utilitarianism is the equality principle. Individuals are to count equally. This equal consideration, or equality, principle appears consistent with a formal theory of justice. Therefore, in Regan's words (1984: 212), utilitarianism has a "predistributive requirement of just treatment" in the form of the equality principle, which, as Singer states, requires that "the interests of every being affected by an action are to be taken into account and given the same weight as the like interests of any other" (Singer, 1989: 77).

Another issue is that some argue that Singer's utilitarianism is equivalent to an animal welfare position, with the normative flaws we encountered in chapter 5 (Anderson, 2004: 227; Francione and Garner, 2010: 6–13). This is partly because Singer emphasizes the moral importance of sentience and partly because he does not base his theory on the according of rights to animals. In this sense, he *is* a welfarist in that he is a consequentialist, concerned to maximize welfare, as opposed to an advocate of a deontological position that argues that individuals should be protected even if by so doing welfare is not maximized (Donaldson and Kymlicka, 2011: 260). However, if we combine the moral importance of sentience with the equality principle, then it can be seen that Singer's position is very different from an animal welfare ethic. That is, Singer is committed to treating like interests alike, in accordance with the equal consideration of interests principle. As a result, although human personhood may count for something morally, it is illegitimate to regard human interests in avoiding suffering as more important morally than animal interests in not suffering. Indeed, in this respect, Singer's argument here deals with the key weakness of the animal welfare position as enunciated in chapter 5.

There is a widely held perception that Singer maintains there is nothing wrong morally with killing animals, provided that replacements are forthcoming to maintain the same amount of pleasure in the world, and that what is morally wrong about our treatment of animals is the infliction of suffering on them. Hare (1999: 238) adopts this interpretation when he writes that, "For utilitarians like Singer and myself, doing wrong to animals must involve harming them. If there is no harm there is no wrong." As a result, killing them is not a moral problem. All that matters is that those animals that are killed are replaced by others who live equally pleasant lives.

However, this is not entirely Singer's position. It is true that he accepts that in the case of animals who are not self-conscious, and therefore have no sense of themselves existing over time, it is permissible morally to kill them providing that they are replaced by beings who live equally pleasant lives. In this sense, eating animals who have had pleasant lives and who are killed painlessly presents no moral problem (Singer, 1999: 326). However, Singer also argues, although not in the first edition of *Animal Liberation*, that for animals that are self-conscious, there *is* a direct loss to them caused by death (in the form of the denying of the preference that such individuals have for continued life) and therefore these preferences should be taken into account (Singer, 1993: 27). In other words, the individual lives of self-conscious individuals do count morally. Additionally, Singer would seem to be giving too much away here anyway in the sense that the value of individual lives would not seem to be dependent on self-consciousness. That is, the knowledge and fear of death—available only to the self-conscious—is not the only harm that can be caused by it. Rather, there are also the lost opportunities caused by death, which are independent of entities' awareness that death will remove them (see chapter 8).

Against Singer, and the case for regarding utilitarianism as an ideal theory of justice for animals, however, are the weaknesses inherent in failing to combine the equal consideration of interests principle with a rights-based ethic. Rather, Singer is an act utilitarian. As such, when judging the ethical permissibility of a particular use of animals, he is required to weigh up the total number of preferences, including preferences to go on living, which would be satisfied if that use is prohibited. It is this aggregative character of utilitarianism that creates problems for its claim to be an appropriate theory of justice for animals.

In the first place, if we factor in all of the consequences likely to follow a particular improvement to the way that animals are treated, it may prove not to be justified on utilitarian grounds. Thus, Singer's claim that such a utilitarian calculation does result in farming animals for food or using them as experimental subjects being deemed objectionable morally is dubious, to say the least. Assuming that we can realistically hope to weigh up all of the preferences involved, there would seem to be numerous human preferences that would be served by continuing these practices. In the case of animal agriculture, for instance, it is clearly not the case that all we have to do is simply weigh up the most fundamental interests of animals against the most trivial interests of humans. A surprising number of accounts do make this claim (see Gruzalski,1997; Nobis, 2002: 140–1).[2] Rather, to what might be regarded as a trivial interest—the fact that many humans like the taste of meat—must be added less trivial human interests such as the undoubtedly significant economic costs of the elimination of factory farming or of all forms of animal agriculture (Frey, 1983: 197–203; Regan, 1980b: 310–11; 1984: 221–3).

Indeed, the calculations can get even more complex (and somewhat surreal) if one was to factor in farm animals, and the claim that the pleasures resulting from their existence are maximized *because* we eat them. That is, if vegetarianism became the norm, there would be less utility in the world because fewer animals would be likely to exist (Narveson, 1983: 55). The key point is that, at the very least, "it is not *obviously* true" that the end of animal agriculture would result in a surplus of preferences met (Regan, 1980b: 311). A utilitarian calculation does not even necessarily justify the end of factory farming, although there is clearly a stronger case for this conclusion since animals do not live pleasant lives in factory farms and, as we saw in chapter 4, there are plenty of human-interest grounds for eliminating it. One would have thought, too, that a utilitarian case for ending all animal experimentation would, if anything, be even harder to sustain given the claim that the use of animals can have very beneficial health consequences for both humans and animals in addition to the economic costs of abolishing it.[3]

Of course, as Singer (1980: 326–7) rightly remarks, Regan and others have not succeeded in criticizing utilitarianism as a moral theory, only that, they argue, it cannot justify vegetarianism or an end to animal experimentation. This criticism of utilitarianism is still valid, though, if one is intent upon finding a theory that is most appropriate for the protection of animals if that goal matches one's moral convictions. However, there is a more fundamental criticism of utilitarianism that Singer has to contend with. This is that there is also a strong case for saying that the aggregative approach adopted by utilitarianism is at odds with a theory of justice because, for utilitarians, justice is a secondary concern—subordinate to the primary concern of maximizing utility. As Vincent (2004: 123) correctly observes, "utility trumps all comers." Singer would be justified in claiming that the equality principle—treat like cases alike—offers a predistributive requirement that is consistent with a formal principle of justice. However, as many commentators have remarked, the aggregation of interests inherent in utilitarianism is inconsistent with the separateness of persons that most take to be a central feature of justice.[4]

That is, utilitarianism neglects the individual. Its aggregative character results in allowing "some people to be treated as less than equals, as a means to other people's ends" (Rowlands, 2009: 42). In other words, the way that humans and animals are treated in utilitarianism is not a product of the characteristics they possess as individuals, "but of the effects of their treatment on others" (56). This would still be the case *even if* there is a valid claim for saying that this or that way animals are treated is, in fact, illegitimate morally on utilitarian grounds. In short, utilitarianism does not give people what they are due. Indeed, it distorts "the concept of equal consideration beyond recognition" (Regan, 1984: 213). A classic example of this is that unrefined act utilitarianism would justify the punishment of the innocent if by so doing utility is maximized.

The Capabilities Approach

A new approach to animal ethics has emerged in recent years with the aim of challenging well-established contractarian, utilitarian, and rights-based accounts. This is the capabilities approach associated with Martha Nussbaum. The emphasis on capabilities originates from the work of Amartya Sen, who developed the idea as an alternative to the dominant model of resource distribution (Sen, 1993). That is, rather than focusing on, say, the distribution of income and wealth, the state should instead ascertain the degree to which a particular resource distribution allows individuals to flourish. This, in turn, necessitates the identification of basic capabilities that are required for individuals to lead a dignified life.

Nussbaum has developed and popularized Sen's approach, identifying a list of capabilities initially to be applied to humans only, but then extended to encompass animals, too (2001, 2004, 2006), on the grounds that the treatment of animals is "one of the most urgent moral issues of our time" (Nussbaum, 2001: 1549). These capabilities are required in order to enable humans, and animals, to flourish, and ought to be upheld at least to a threshold level. For Nussbaum (2006: 75), "a society that does not guarantee these to all its citizens, at some appropriate threshold level, falls short of being a fully just society." Nussbaum adopts the same capabilities for animals as she does for humans, although she recognizes that not all of the capabilities will apply to all nonhuman sentient species. These capabilities are (Nussbaum, 2004: 315–17): (1) life, (2) bodily health, (3) bodily integrity, (4) senses, imagination, and thought, (5) emotions, (6) practical reason, (7) affiliation with others, (8) a meaningful relationship with other species and with nature, (9) play, and (10) control over one's environment.

Strengths of the Capabilities Approach

The question we need to ask here is, does the capabilities approach add anything to our understanding of animal ethics, and in particular does it, as Nussbaum claims, offer a viable, and indeed preferable, alternative theory of justice to the existing accounts available, and particularly to the rights-based approach I outlined in chapter 6? The portents look promising. In the first place, the fact that Nussbaum argues the case for regarding animals as recipients of justice is also consistent with the approach taken in this book and, for the reasons I have explored, is therefore preferable to contractarian and utilitarian accounts.

In addition, although generally sympathetic to Rawls's contractarian account, Nussbaum recognizes that it has difficulty in including those entities—the serious mentally impaired and animals—who are not moral agents, and because of this the theory is deficient, and needs complementing with the capabilities approach (2006: chapter 1). Nussbaum (2004: 300–1) argues that, just as we intuitively think it is wrong to exclude marginal humans as recipients of a theory of justice, so it is for animals. The mistake contractarian theories make, Nussbaum argues, in line with the discussion in chapter 2 of this book, is to conflate two distinct questions: "By whom are society's basic principles designed?" and "For whom are society's basic principles designed?" (Nussbaum, 2006: 16).

So far, so good. It is also the case that by focusing on the capabilities and flourishing of individuals, Nussbaum moves beyond species as a benchmark of moral importance. Echoing Rachels, it is the characteristics of individuals, whether human or nonhuman, that are morally significant (2004: 309). Moreover, the identification of animal capabilities and the conditions of animal flourishing is a very useful benchmark against which public policy involving animals can be judged, in the same vein as the "five freedoms" have for the welfare of farmed animals (see chapter 8) (Ilea, 2008: 559). As Nussbaum (2006: 70) herself writes, capabilities are the "source of political principles for a liberal pluralistic society." What is more, they allow for the possibility that animals may pursue goods (such as freedom of movement) the absence of which does not cause pain and suffering (Nussbaum, 2006: 345).

In Search of a Theory

Of course, for Nussbaum, there is a normative purpose in identifying capabilities. It is not just that these are the characteristics that will enable animals to flourish, but rather, and in addition, that these are the capabilities that must be protected, at least to a threshold level, if justice is to be served. Thus, she writes (2004: 306) that "it is wrong when the flourishing of a creature is blocked by the harmful agency of another." But this normative intent presents a problem for Nussbaum. Given the list of capabilities identified, this approach ostensibly represents a radical position to take. For, to choose the obvious example, if animals require life in order to flourish, as Nussbaum confirms they do, it follows that this capability must be protected. Thus, for Nussbaum (2004: 314), "all animals are entitled to continue their lives, whether or not they have such a conscious interest."

The implications are obvious. It would seem to suggest that animals should not be used by humans in ways that will result in their lives being taken. Clearly, without any additional argument, this means that animals cannot be eaten for food or used in scientific experiments in which they are killed. We have here, then, exactly the same prohibition on killing animals as insisted upon by the species-egalitarian, or abolitionist, strand of animal rights. Moreover, Nussbaum's position would also seem to rule out the exploitation of animals in general, whether or not they are killed, since such uses are likely to conflict with other capabilities such as bodily integrity.

Nussbaum's position also leads to a radical conclusion about the treatment of wild animals (2006: 366–79). Under the guise of fulfilling the eighth capability, involving the creation of a meaningful relationship between species, Nussbaum (2004: 316–17) "calls for the gradual formation of an interdependent world in which all species will enjoy cooperative and mutually supportive relationships with one another." She recognizes, however, that: "Nature is not that way and never has been." As a result, she continues, the capabilities approach "calls, in a very general way, for the gradual supplanting of the natural by the just."

I will leave aside the position Nussbaum arrives at in connection with wild animals, which is regarded by some as absurdly utopian (Schinkel, 2008: 49; Wissenberg, 2011; Cripps, 2010). I want to focus, instead, on her position as concerns domesticated animals. As critics have not been slow in pointing out, Nussbaum does not arrive at the radical conclusions her theory would seem to presage (Schinkel, 2008). She does, consistently, recommend the ending of those practices—such as the worst vestiges of factory farming—that inhibit the functioning of bodily integrity and health. However, Nussbaum does not, when it comes to it, regard the eating of animals as morally unacceptable, nor does she think that all animal experimentation ought to be prohibited (2004: 317–18). As Schinkel (2008: 60) comments: "A society that regards animals in the way required by Nussbaum's approach, undermines its own willingness to use them for food or in research."

A sympathetic reading of this apparent inconsistency would hold that Nussbaum is trying to distinguish between what is ethically desirable from what is politically acceptable. If so, particularly given the central theme of this book, this approach should be regarded as laudable. There is some evidence for this interpretation (Nussbaum, 2006: 388–90). She argues (2006: 393) in one place, for instance, that "it seems wise to focus initially on banning all forms of cruelty to living animals and then moving gradually towards a consensus against killing at least the more complexly sentient animals for food." And again (2006: 394), she recognizes that the capabilities approach does not have to get involved in a utilitarian cost-benefit calculation concerning, for instance, the economic costs of abolishing meat eating. In terms of animal experimentation, likewise, Nussbaum (2006: 403) argues that research that inflicts pain and suffering on animals is "morally bad" as "a matter of ideal entitlement theory," irrespective of what is politically possible.

This sympathetic reading of Nussbaum, however, does not suffice. For there is evidence, too, that the normative framework she adopts is, at best, unclear, certainly derivative, and yet inconsistent with the rights-based (linked with capabilities) approach she seems to endorse (2001: 1512; 1527).[5] These characteristics are evident in the way that Nussbaum conceptualizes both the eating of, and experimentation on, animals as tragic conflict situations, in which all of the possible courses of action lead to severe harm. That is, eating animals for food and experimenting on them involve the sacrifice of fundamental capabilities (in the case of the former this is always the life of an animal, as is usually the case with the latter). Therefore, if we take on board Nussbaum's commitment to the need to protect equivalent human and animal capabilities, a genuine tragic conflict situation would be where a prohibition on the eating of animals for food or using them for experimental purposes would result in similar restrictions on human capabilities (2006: 401–5).

Take the killing of animals for food first. Nussbaum (2004: 315) regards this as a "difficult" case to which she does not have a clear answer. This is partly, it seems, because she doubts whether animals do, in fact, have a right to life or, in terms of her discourse, whether continued life is a capability necessary for animals to flourish. As she writes in an earlier work (2001: 1542), "I share Singer's doubts about whether a painless death is really a deprivation." This interpretation of Nussbaum would hold her as adopting a classic animal welfare position, which, whilst seeking to avoid unnecessary suffering being inflicted on animals, is prepared to accept animal exploitation (and the sacrifice of animal capabilities) if significant human interests are at stake. According to this scenario, animals could be eaten even where a tragic conflict does not exist.

If this *is* Nussbaum's position, then it is not difficult to justify exploiting animals. But, it is not clear if this is indeed her stance. That is because the question of meat eating is also "difficult" for Nussbaum (2004: 318), because she is not sure what the consequences will be for humans, particularly children in developing countries, living on a vegetarian diet. In other words, she is also saying that meat eating is morally acceptable because to prohibit it might lead to equivalent damage to human flourishing that is caused by slaughtering animals for food. In other words, the decision whether or not to morally prohibit killing animals for food is difficult because it represents a tragic conflict situation.

In response to Nussbaum here, however, it is possible to argue that the question of whether or not eating animals ought to be morally prohibited is not an example of a tragic conflict. This is because the universal conversion to a vegetarian diet will not have detrimental consequences for most humans. That is, humans, as we saw in chapter 4, can still flourish, and indeed may be better off—in health and environmental terms—by adopting vegetarianism (Schinkel, 2008: 55). Of course, this is an empirical question, but the empirical evidence would not appear to be on Nussbaum's side here.

Animal experimentation, in certain circumstances, is certainly closer to being a tragic conflict situation, or at least it is if one accepts that using animals produces therapeutic benefits that contribute to the saving of human lives. In such a so-called lifeboat case a choice has to be made to sacrifice someone if the others are to survive. This is because in a genuine lifeboat scenario, all will lose unless some are sacrificed. In such a scenario, therefore, the circumstances of justice do not apply. The outcome becomes a tragic necessity rather than a matter of justice. However, for some thinkers, such as Franklin (2005), Pluhar (1995: 297), and Schinkel (2008: 56), scientific experimentation on animals is not a lifeboat scenario and therefore not a tragic conflict situation. This is because animals are not in the lifeboat in the first place. Therefore, they stand to lose nothing, and gain an awful lot, if animal experimentation is prohibited. In other words, animals are only in the lifeboat because humans choose to put them there by making human suffering the concern of animals.

Whether or not we regard animal experimentation as, strictly speaking, a lifeboat case, it is clearly the case that situations where whatever we do results in serious harms to either humans or animals are examples of conflicts that are difficult to resolve. This applies as long as we are weighting the moral status of animals and humans as equivalent, which Nussbaum appears to do when she makes the claim that the same capabilities for humans and animals must be protected (2001: 1542). Both eating and experimenting on animals can, in theory, be examples of such cases, although the degree to which they are is dependent on empirical analysis.

Two further points need to be made here about Nussbaum's characterization of animal experimentation as a tragic conflict situation. The first is to say that one option for a rights-based ethic in such a situation is to say that rights are sufficiently inviolable that, even if the consequences of not using animals in scientific experiments will result in humans not being able to avoid serious harm, the rights of animals should not be sacrificed (Jamieson, 1990: 362). Secondly, and relatedly, what is interesting is Nussbaum's unwillingness to consider the case of sacrificing the flourishing of some humans to benefit other humans, and maybe animals, too. There is certainly a strong empirical case for saying, for instance, that experimenting on humans, say, to find a cure for a fatal human disease, stands far more likelihood of success than using animals. This is never entertained, in terms of moral theory at least (see chapter 9), because it is argued that humans have rights that prohibit them being used in this way. But, then, Nussbaum appears to be committed to the position that similar capabilities should be protected irrespective of whether the holders are humans or animals. Her failure to entertain the idea that humans might lose out in tragic conflict situations suggests that she does not, in fact, weight human and animal capabilities in the same way, and that animals are regarded as morally inferior to humans.

Nussbaum's capabilities approach, then, is not as distinctive as it perhaps presents itself. Despite the fact that she regards her approach as a subset of rights, it is clear that she is unwilling to follow the logic conclusion of a right to life approach, sometimes reverting to a conventional animal welfare position in the process. One option is to retain an emphasis on the capabilities of animals but make clear that they, or at least some, are not to be regarded as morally significant as the capabilities of humans. This is the approach I take (see chapter 8). To make such an argument, however, requires the adoption of a prior normative moral theory, whether it be based on rights, welfare, contractarianism, utilitarianism, or any other alternative. In my view, the absence of such a distinctive normative ethic within Nussbaum's thinking about animals disqualifies it as a substantive alternative theory within animal ethics.

The Species-Egalitarian Version of Animal Rights

The third approach in animal ethics that is challenged in this chapter is a version of animal rights. The dominant version of animal rights has been of the species-egalitarian variety.[6] The egalitarianism I am referring to here is about equal rights based on equal moral value. This can be distinguished from an egalitarianism that claims that those things that are valuable, or the means to get them, should be distributed equally. Egalitarianism in this second sense can conflict with egalitarianism in the sense that it is being used in this chapter. For example, rights theorists would oppose reaching a more egalitarian situation by violating someone's rights, something that egalitarians, in the second sense above, may be willing to do. The species-egalitarian version of animal rights differs, too, from the equal consideration of interests principle. The latter, as we saw in chapter 6, only argues that we should *consider* all interests equally, but it does not tell us that these interests should be regarded as of equal moral weight. Indeed, as Singer, most notably, has argued, the value of human lives are, all things being equal, greater than those of nonhuman animals. By contrast, the species-egalitarian version of animal rights does want to suggest that the interests that human and animals have in life and liberty are to be regarded as equally valuable morally.

The species-egalitarian version has been the dominant strand of animal rights, both for those working within animal rights discourse and for the philosophical opponents of animal rights (for an example of the latter see Cohen's contribution in Cohen and Regan, 2001, particularly 6–7). This perception reflects the dominance of its chief advocate, Tom Regan. As we saw in chapter 5, Regan argues that at least some animals (to be precise, mammals one year of age and over) are what he calls "subjects of a life," and all, human and nonhuman, subjects-of-a-life have inherent value. This equal inherent value translates into strong moral rights. In particular, subjects-of-a-life with inherent value must be treated with respect as ends and not as means to an end. Regan, therefore, posits only one fundamental right, the right to respectful treatment, which derives from the inherent value of both humans and nonhuman animals.

The implication of this is that to use animals, irrespective of what is done to them whilst they are being used, is illegitimate. As Bryant (2007: 209) concurs, "The animal rights perspective calls for freedom from any and all exploitation by humans." Thus, just as slavery is unjust for humans because it infringes their right to liberty, the confinement of animals, whether or not such confinement causes them suffering, is unjust because it fails to treat animals with the respect they deserve. It is for this reason that animal rights advocates often draw a "dreaded comparison" between human slavery and the use of animals (Spiegel, 1988). It goes without saying, too, that, according to the species-egalitarian version of animal rights, to kill animals for human purposes also infringes their right to respectful treatment.

A prohibition on the confinement and killing of animals would, of course, rule out most of the ways in which animals are currently used by humans, as sources of food and as subjects of animal experimentation in particular. For Regan, animal experimentation is not wrong because it causes animals to suffer or because it is unnecessary. Rather, it is wrong because "animals used in research are routinely, systematically treated as if their value is reducible to their usefulness to others, they are routinely, systematically treated with a lack of respect" (Cohen and Regan, 2001: 212). Similarly, the "fundamental wrong" with raising and killing animals for food is not that this causes them suffering or that humans do not really need to eat meat, but that they are "viewed and treated merely as means to human ends, as resources for us" (Cohen and Regan, 2001: 213). As Francione, a key exponent of the species-egalitarian version of animal rights, points out (2008: 2), then, this strand of animal rights thinking "maintains that our use of animals cannot be justified" and "seeks to *abolish* all animal use." As a result, I have elsewhere (Garner, 2011) described this strand of animal rights as the use position, because it is associated with the belief that all *uses* of animals are morally impermissible.[7]

A Critique of Species Egalitarianism

We saw in chapter 5 that the animal welfare ethic is flawed morally because it does not take into account the fact that, like humans, animals have important interests—such as avoiding suffering—that are not dependent upon possessing the characteristics—rationality, autonomy, language, and so forth—of personhood. Likewise, the species-egalitarian version of animal rights is similarly guilty, but rather than failing to take into account the importance of nonpersonhood interests, it fails to take into account the moral significance of those interests associated with persons. In other words, the species-egalitarian strand of animal rights is flawed because it is difficult to argue against the claim that the differences between "normal" adult humans and adult animals *are* substantial and *are* morally significant. In short, the level of complexity of an individual affects what can be a harm for it.[8]

In particular, the fact that most animals lack the characteristics of personhood challenges the claim that they have equivalent levels of interest in life and liberty to "normal" humans. In other words, it is not possible to justify moral egalitarianism between humans and animals because it is not the case that humans and animals have equally important interests in life and liberty. I argue in chapter 8 that it is extremely likely that at least some species of nonhuman animals have an interest in being protected from the infliction of suffering. Equally, though, it is extremely unlikely that most nonhuman animals have an interest in, or an interest equivalent to humans in, life or liberty.

It is my contention, then, that *both* the conventional defense of the animal welfare ethic, *and* the typical species-egalitarian response to it, are flawed. And they are flawed because they fail to draw the correct moral conclusions from the differential characteristics possessed by different species. By contrast, an alternative strand of animal rights thinking *has* recognized the moral importance of these differential characteristics. As Cochrane (2012: 2–7) has astutely observed, what I have described as the species-egalitarian version of animal rights is only one strand of animal rights philosophy, albeit perhaps the dominant strand given the high profile Regan has within the discipline. Another, partly submerged, strand offers a more convincing account of animal rights.

This alternative account of animal rights, to reiterate the analysis provided in chapter 6, is based on invoking the principles of the equal consideration of interests, and the version of it—moral individualism—developed by Rachels (1990). Applying the equal consideration of interests principle enables us to differentiate between the interests of humans and nonhuman animals in a way that the species-egalitarian strand of animal rights is unable to do. As a result, just as my preferred approach denies the blanket inegalitarianism adopted by exponents of the animal welfare ethic, it also rejects the blanket egalitarianism of the abolitionist use position adopted by most exponents of animal rights. Thus, adopting an animal rights position, or at least a particular version of an animal rights position, does not equate necessarily with moral equality between humans and animals. Instead, the like interests of humans and animals are to be treated equally, and their unlike interests are to be treated unequally. This, it should be noted, is an essential principle of justice. Differentiating morally between the interests of humans and animals allows us, then, to paint a much more complex, and realistic, picture of our moral obligations to animals than both the animal welfare ethic and the species egalitarianism of the dominant strand of animal rights thinking.

There is another ground on which the species-egalitarian version of animal rights ought to be rejected as an ideal theory of justice for animals. Not only is the theory normatively flawed, but it can also be suggested that it does not constitute what Rawls refers to as a "realistic utopia." That is, even if the ethical principles are sound, in the sense that they prescribe accurately what morality demands of it, we should still reject abolitionism because it demands too much of human beings. As Nagel (1989: 904) notes: "An ideal, however attractive it may be to contemplate, is utopian if real individuals cannot be motivated to live by it."

Abolitionism is confronted by some hard facts about the world. No country in the world has prohibited the use of animals as sources of food or as experimental subjects on the grounds that it is unacceptable morally to do so. Countries differ significantly over the degree to which the use of animals is regulated, but nowhere have these fundamental uses of animals been abolished or challenged to any great extent.[9] Moreover, there is not the slightest chance that these practices will be abolished in the foreseeable future. As Donaldson and Kymlicka (2011: 2) point out, "animal exploitation underpins the way we feed and clothe ourselves, our forms of entertainment and leisure, and our structure of industrial production and scientific research." The species-egalitarian version of animal rights challenges "our cultural heritage"

(Donaldson and Kymlicka, 2011: 4). It is, then, utopian to believe that an end to animal use will occur.

There will be those, of course, who argue that the charge of utopianism has been leveled against all radical social movements; that in the past, for instance, the same charge was made against the antislavery movement and the women's movement. To some extent, we have to rely, as Rawls suggests, "on conjecture and speculation" in determining whether a particular set of principles represents a realistic utopia (Rawls, 1999: 12). There are some reasons for thinking, however, that the species-egalitarian strand of animal rights is qualitatively different from other social movement causes now and in the past. This is because it represents a paradigmatic leap in the way that, for example, the ending of slavery and the gradual assimilation of women into social and political life did not. This leap is, of course, over the species divide.

As I have pointed out in the past, the abolitionist objectives of the animal rights movement are exceptionally altruistic, asking us to give up significant advantages (potentially our health, a major source of food, clothing, entertainment) in order to protect members of different species (Garner, 1998). In this sense, the abolitionist animal rights position "functions as a mythical *Paradise Island*." As Ingrid Robeyns (2008: 344–5) points out:

> We have heard wonderful stories about Paradise Island, but no one has ever visited it, and some doubt that it truly exists. We have a few maps that tell us, roughly, where it should be situated, but since it is in the middle of the ocean, far away from all known societies, no one knows *precisely* where it is situated.[10]

As a result, it is difficult to foresee a time when the human species will be prepared to accept the implications of the moral egalitarianism postulated in the abolitionist position, to contemplate putting another species on a moral par with our own.

The species-egalitarian strand of animal rights might also be regarded as counterintuitive because it eschews the idea of beneficial relationships between humans and animals. That is, there is a tendency within animal rights abolitionism to regard animals and humans as operating in different realms so that it is our moral obligation to leave them alone. This leads to the expectation that once the exploitation of domesticated animals is abolished, the very notion of domesticating animals for any purpose— however benign—ends, too. So, for Francione, "we ought not to bring any more domesticated nonhumans into existence," including animals we intend to have as our companions (quoted in Donaldson and Kymlicka, 2011: 7). For Dunayer (2004: 117), likewise, "Animal rights advocates want laws that will prohibit humans from exploiting and otherwise harming nonhumans. They don't seek to protect nonhumans within human society. They seek to protect nonhumans *from* human society."

Thus, human/animal relationships are regarded as inherently exploitative, and all uses of animals are therefore deemed unacceptable morally. Instead, animals ought to be freed from domestication and human control so that they can live separate lives. As Donaldson and Kymlicka (2011: 7) argue convincingly, however, this is to deny the beneficial relationships between humans and animals that do exist, and from which a viable nonideal theory of justice for animals can be built. The animal rights movement therefore needs to bring on board those who already have relationships with animals but who cannot be described as animal rights advocates (257). The failure to recognize the practical importance of these relationships is regarded by Donaldson and Kymlicka (2011: 79) as a "strategic disaster" for the animal rights movement.

This latter critique of animal rights theory and the animal rights movement is only partly correct. It is certainly the case that the species-egalitarian version of animal rights does lend itself to the criticism that it sees domestication as the problem, as opposed to what is done to animals through domestication. Some animal rights advocates, as a consequence, do have an ambiguous attitude toward the keeping of animals as pets. The fact that the phrase "companion" animal is widely used as an alternative is symbolic of this ambiguity. It would be wrong, however, to regard animal rights advocates as somehow indifferent to animals in practice as this critique suggests, and I do not think there is a widespread public perception that the animal rights movement can be characterized in such a way. Indeed, if anything, the public "problem" with the animal rights movement is that it is too much on the side of animals, thereby subordinating human interests in the process.

Conclusion

In this chapter we have rejected three possible candidates for an ideal and nonideal theory of justice for animals. The utilitarian approach fails to qualify as a theory of *justice* because it does not appreciate sufficiently the separateness of persons—which must be a central feature of any valid theory of justice. Both Nussbaum's capabilities approach and the approach deriving from Regan's species egalitarianism are rights-based. However, the former is somewhat confused and adds little to a rights-based discourse. Most importantly of all, the latter is flawed as an ideal theory, both because it fails to account for the moral importance of the significant differences between most humans and animals, and because it does not qualify as a realistic utopia. In the next chapter, the constituent elements of a rights-based animal ethic will be utilized to identify my preferred ideal and nonideal theories of justice for animals.

8

Animal Rights as Ideal and Nonideal Theory

I ARGUED IN the previous chapter that the species-egalitarian version of animal rights—at least when shorn of the implications deriving from the argument from marginal cases—does not sufficiently take into account the morally important differences between animals and most humans. This does not mean, however, that we have to dispense with a rights-based theory of justice for animals. Rather, applying moral individualism and the equal consideration of interests, outlined in chapter 6, enables us to provide a much more nuanced animal rights position. Two versions of animal rights are modeled in this chapter, what I label, for want of a better phrase, the "sentience position" and the "enhanced sentience position."[1] Both avoid the pitfalls of the species-egalitarian version of animal rights whilst neutralizing the conventional critique of animal rights. It is further argued that whilst the latter, enhanced sentience, position is more adequate from an ethical perspective, the former, whilst fulfilling a large part of the animal rights agenda, is also likely to be more acceptable socially and politically, therefore offering a more appropriate nonideal theory of justice for animals.

The Sentience Position

Utilizing the interest strand of animal rights thinking, I suggest that it is possible to model at least two approaches to animal rights, both of which are preferable to the species-egalitarian version. The first might be described as the sentience position. As its name suggests, it is based on the assumption that at least some nonhuman animals have an interest in not suffering. As a result, they have a prima facie interest in avoiding suffering that might be inflicted on them by humans. If we are prepared to say that humans have a right not to suffer at the hands of others, then, given that animals have a similar, although by no means identical, capacity to suffer, consistency demands that we also accord a right not to suffer to animals. If this is granted, and we do not try to identify additional interests animals possess to which we might attach a right, then this is a position claiming that what is wrong with our treatment of animals is not their use per se but is a product of what we do to them whilst they are being used.

Clearly, we need to clarify what is meant by sentience and suffering. Sentience, defined as the capacity to experience pleasure and pain, is narrower than suffering if the latter is defined to include a variety of negative states including pain, anxiety, boredom, frustration, and so on. DeGrazia (1996: 262), for instance, describes suffering as "a highly unpleasant emotional state associated with more-than-minimal pain or distress." One can therefore experience pain—in the sense of momentary pain for my own good—without suffering, and one can suffer without experiencing pain. It is credible to claim that all mammals are capable of suffering as so defined (see the evidence in Palmer, 2010: 15–18). For instance, although some common factory farming practices may not cause physical pain, they undoubtedly cause suffering. Having said this, some forms of suffering—such as disgust, embarrassment, grief, and shame—can only be experienced by self-conscious beings that probably exclude most animals.

Clearly, not all the things that make us suffer, when we also consider the positive effects that may derive from it, are detrimental to the interests of humans or nonhuman animals. Fleeting pain may serve as a warning that is to the benefit of the sufferer. Likewise, the infliction of suffering may—as in treatment for a disease or injury—produce, or be designed to produce, a beneficial result for an individual. In practice, adopting the sentience position prohibits morally those activities that inflict more than trivial suffering on animals that is not in their interests.[2] What is to count as an acceptable level of suffering is inevitably imprecise, but, given that we are conferring to animals a *right* not to have suffering inflicted on them by humans, all but insubstantial cases would be prohibited. It is important to understand the difference between this position and the animal welfare ethic we encountered in chapter 5. According to the animal welfare ethic, it is permissible morally to inflict suffering on an animal provided that the benefits to be gained from so doing are perceived to be sufficiently large. The sentience position, on the other hand, rules out such a cost-benefit approach. *Whatever* the benefit that might accrue to humans, or other animals for that matter, practices that inflict suffering on animals are prohibited.[3]

An Objection to the Sentience Position

A major objection to the sentience position can be advanced at this point. This is the claim that suffering is a greater harm for humans than it is for animals. If this is established, then, applying the equal consideration of interests principle, we should attach less than equal moral weight to their comparable interests in not suffering since humans have a greater interest in avoiding suffering. Two slightly different versions of this objection can be made. In the first place, it might be argued that those who possess the characteristics of personhood *do* in fact suffer more. Therefore, in the event of a conflict, human suffering ought to be relieved. This would lead, for example, to a moral justification for inflicting suffering on an animal in a laboratory procedure the aim of which is to reduce human suffering.

It is the case that, as Singer (1990: 10) points out, "Normal adult human beings have mental capacities that will, in certain circumstances, lead them to suffer more than animals would in the same circumstances," and our moral judgments should reflect this fact. For example, humans are likely to suffer from their greater capacity to anticipate pain and suffering and there may be greater long-term psychological damage endured by humans that would not apply to the same degree to animals (Rachels, 1990: 193). A number of responses are possible to this argument, however. In the first place, it may well be the case that animals can suffer some psychological damage following the infliction of pain. Anyone who has seen the dysfunctional behavior of dogs that have been poorly treated would attest to this. Of course, too, we can imagine situations where the experiences of persons have been factored out. In cases where there is no time to anticipate the pain and where death follows soon after we would be committed to concluding that animals and human persons suffer equally (Holland, 2003: 33–4).

In some circumstances, finally, it is possible to imagine situations where an animal's suffering might actually be greater than a human's in a similar situation (Singer, 1990: 16). Rowlands (2002: 14–15) provides an example to illustrate this point. Imagine, he asks, that

> you and your dog are taken into a room where you are both given a very painful injection. However, the situation is explained to you (the injection is necessary to save your life, the pain will be relatively short lived, there will be no complications, and then you will be allowed to go)... Your dog, however, knows none of these things, and so in

addition to the pain of the injection, it has the anxiety associated with unfamiliar surroundings, strange people restraining it, and so on. In this case, your dog seems to suffer more than you do.

The impact of pain for someone not possessing the characteristics of personhood may, then, make things worse. The sentience position models animals as living totally in the present. As a result, they cannot remember what not being in pain is like or imagine it disappearing in the future. For such an individual to be in pain, "their whole universe is pain. There is no horizon; they are their pain." (Rollin, 2011: 157). That outcome is grim indeed.

All of the above suggests that we should apply the principle, whereby moral judgments derive from differentiated interests, in each case. The general rule is that animals can suffer in a variety of ways and sometimes this suffering will be greater than that experienced by humans in similar circumstances, sometimes it will be equal, and sometimes it will be less. The bottom line here, though, is that we have no reason to believe that the pain suffered by an animal is any less than a pain suffered by a human in similar circumstances, and morally we should not act as though it is. As Feinberg (1980a: 194) writes: "An intense toothache is an evil in a young person or an old person, a man or a woman, a Caucasian or a Negro, a human being or a lion."

A slightly different variant of the objection against the sentience position is the claim that human suffering is worse because it precludes the living of a *life* that is more valuable than that of an animal (Steinbock, 1978: 254). What is being claimed in this critique of the sentience position is not that humans suffer more than animals but that their suffering precludes the enjoyment that derives from the possession of the characteristics of personhood. It follows, of course, that if we grant animals a right not to suffer, then humans, too, have such a right. By itself, though, this does not justify infringing an animal's right to suffer in order to prevent a human from suffering, any more than it would justify sacrificing a human's interest in not suffering for another human's. To answer to the contrary would require us to show that the suffering of humans is greater, which, as I argued above, I do not accept. It is true, as I will contend below, however, that there is a strong case for saying that the life of a normal human *is* more valuable than that of an animal. Does this mean, then, that we are morally obliged to inflict suffering on an animal if by so doing we can relieve the suffering of a human, thereby allowing for his or her life to flourish? If so, there is not much left of the claim that animals have a right not to suffer.

There is no doubt that the infliction of pain can hinder seriously the living of an autonomous life, so, on instrumental grounds, the infliction of pain on a human would seem to cause greater harm than the infliction of equivalent amounts of pain on an animal. Following Rachels (2004: 169) and DeGrazia (1996: 272), however, I am inclined to think that this amounts to an additional reason why inflicting pain is wrong, but that it does not undermine the claim that the infliction of pain is wrong because it hurts, and, in intrinsic terms, is therefore similarly evil for both humans and animals in equal measure, irrespective of the greater instrumental effect it has on the former. As Campbell (2006: 57) points out: "Whilst it is true that torturing usually.... undermines their (autonomous being's) capacity for rational decision-making, this is hardly the core reason why we disapprove of it" (my addition in parentheses).

Of course, one way of completely avoiding this objection to the sentience position is to invoke the argument from marginal cases. That is, we could say that the suffering of marginal humans, like animals, causes less instrumental harm than the equivalent suffering of nonmarginal humans. As a result we have two options. We could treat marginal humans in the same way as animals, and regard their suffering as less important than that endured by nonmarginal humans. Or, alternatively, we could argue that if we are prepared to treat marginal humans as if their suffering is as significant as nonmarginal humans, then consistency demands that we do the same for animals. Since the former option is not at all palatable for most people, we should adopt the latter. By so doing, the objection to the sentience position disappears.

A key response to the latter version of the argument from marginal cases, as we shall see in chapter 9, is that family ties exist for marginal humans and this explains why harming them is a greater wrong than harming animals. As DeGrazia (1996: 272) points out, however, it may be that there would be less concern from relatives about the infliction of suffering on marginal humans as opposed to the loss of their lives. This, however, is surely a subjective matter that may vary. One can conceive of relatives being deeply disturbed at the infliction of suffering on their mentally disabled loved ones, however temporary and whatever the benefits that might accrue from so doing, and the effects may even be worse than the loss caused by their deaths.

Questions of Life and Death

From the other end of the moral spectrum, many animal rights philosophers and advocates would argue that the sentience position does not go far enough. That is, it is incorrect ethically to limit rights to animals in this way, and that granting to animals only a right not to suffer is insufficient in meeting the

conventional goals of the animal rights movement. These goals are abolitionist, so that they require us to adopt a position that prescribes the *use* of animals, and not just the infliction of suffering on them, as illegitimate.

Animal rights critics might argue, then, that ethically, at least some animals possess much more extensive capacities than allowed for by the sentience
position, so that they have interests in not just avoiding suffering but also, for
instance, in avoiding death and confinement. As a result, it is claimed, it is
wrong to use animals as sources of food or as experimental subjects because
to do so is to infringe these interests, irrespective of whether or not suffering
is inflicted.

Such critics of the sentience position would be right to claim that many
species of animals have more extensive psychological capacities than mere
sentience. The possession of sentience suggests a being that lives entirely in
the present without psychological connections with the past and the future
(McMahan, 2002: 75-6). It would therefore be wrong to claim that all of the
characteristics of personhood are possessed completely by normal humans,
and not at all by animals. The extent to which members of different species
possess them is a matter of degree, a point established by Darwin (Rachels,
1990). However, to claim that many species of animals are more than merely
sentient is one thing. To claim that animals possess psychological characteristics giving rise to interests that are equivalent in strength to those held by
humans is quite another. Such a position is very difficult to sustain.

A critique of Regan's philosophy of animal rights is instructive here. It
will be remembered that Regan argues that at least some animals are subjects-
of-a-life because they have the capacities that should deem us to treat them
with respect. Regan is not claiming, however, that to be a subject-of-a-life
is equivalent to personhood (Cohen and Regan, 2001: 209). Indeed, as we
shall see in chapter 9, the particular value of the subject-of-a-life criterion for
Regan is precisely that it enables the inclusion of some animals as well as marginal humans amongst those beings who are autonomous. However, this still
leaves open the possibility that those humans who *are* persons have differing
morally significant characteristics that we ought to take into account.

The distinction we are grappling with here is well drawn out by Frey (1987).
Frey distinguishes between control and preference autonomy. Autonomy
matters, he argues, because of what it enables us to make of our lives. Normal
humans can exercise the control version of the concept, which is equivalent to
a Kantian notion of autonomy. This involves individuals themselves choosing
what they want to achieve and organizing their lives in pursuit of this goal. We
will not be autonomous to the extent that we allow ourselves to be coerced by

others and to the extent that we allow our life plan to become subservient to our "first-order" desires—eating, drinking, drugs, and so on.

Animals, Frey continues, can only exercise what he and Regan call preference autonomy, which requires merely that beings be able to have desires, or preferences, and have the ability to initiate actions with a view to satisfying them. Gone from this notion of autonomy are the key features of his "control" sense of the term. The latter involves a much higher quality of life concerning a rational assessment of desires and a willingness to shed or moderate some, particularly first-order, desires if they are not consistent with an individual's conception of the good life. At most, then, animals are only capable of dealing with a very basic set of first-order desires, which denies them "means to that rich full life of self-fulfilment and achievement" and which is "quite apart from any satisfaction and fulfilment that comes through the satisfaction of our appetites."

This distinction is of crucial importance when we come to the issue of the respective interest humans and animals have in life itself. Philosophers have written endlessly on this question. It is tempting to agree with DeGrazia (1996: 249) that this "whole area is quite baffling," impossible of resolution and therefore ought to be avoided at all costs. At the risk of not heeding my own advice, though, it is worthwhile exploring, relatively briefly, the respective interests that humans and animals have in continued life.

Here it is clear that many, if not most, animal ethicists who agree that animals ought to be granted a higher moral status than the moral orthodoxy allows, do accept that, although at least some animals have an interest in continued life, those normal adult humans who possess the characteristics of personhood—rationality, autonomy, a sophisticated communication system, moral agency, and so on—have a greater interest in continued life. The argument that the duty not to kill animals is as strong as the duty not to kill humans is, in DeGrazia's words (1996: 233), "very hard to believe." Likewise, for McMahan (2002: 190) it is "uncontroversial" to regard the killing of an animal as less seriously wrong than the killing of a human.

This becomes clear if we consider the harms caused by death.[4] There are two distinct ways in which harm might be caused by death. The first, what DeGrazia (2002: 59–61) calls the "desire-based account," postulates that death causes harm because it denies a desire to stay alive. It is probably right to assert here that it is extremely doubtful if any animals, except perhaps the higher mammals, even understand the concept of staying alive, let alone the desire to do so. To desire to go on living requires a being to be self-conscious, aware of itself as a distinct entity with a past, present, and future. As a result, if we assert that most species of animals lack self-consciousness to the requisite degree, then death is not a harm for most animals according to this account of the harm caused by death. Normal adult humans, on the other hand, clearly do possess the concept of death, because they are self-conscious, and therefore have a desire to stay alive. "To take the lives" of such self-conscious beings, as Singer (1993: 90) points out, "is to thwart their desires for the future. Killing a snail or a day-old infant does not thwart any desires of this kind, because snails and newborn infants are incapable of having such desires."

The thwarting of a desire to continue living, however, is not the only harm that death can cause. The obvious reason why death might be a harm is if we are made worse off by it. This is what DeGrazia (2002: 61) calls an "opportunities-based" account of the harm caused by death. Unlike the desire-based account, this view does not depend upon an individual's awareness of the opportunities lost by death, but they may exist nonetheless. These are, then, harms of deprivation. Thus, "the degree to which death is bad is a *function* of the value of" the particular life under scrutiny (McMahan, 2002: 98). That is, harms of deprivation refer to things that might have happened but now will not because of death.

If we adopt a quantitative measure, there would not seem to be any great case for saying that humans have greater opportunities than animals, not least because they are difficult to tabulate. Clearly, animals will lose some opportunities by death that humans will not, and vice versa (DeGrazia: 1996: 238). Having said that, on a purely quantitative measure, humans in general live longer lives than nonhumans so that there are more opportunities to lose for the former (McMahan, 2002: 196) A qualitative account of the opportunities lost by death is more likely to reveal that humans have more to lose. It is not, then, that humans lose more opportunities by death, but that the opportunities they do lose are richer, as suggested by Frey's distinction, described above, between preference and control autonomy. This reminds one of Mill's (2002) famous, and ultimately flawed, attempt to justify a preference for what he regarded as the "higher" pleasures over the "lower" ones. "It is better to be a human being dissatisfied than a pig satisfied, better to be Socrates dissatisfied than a fool satisfied," Mill wrote, arguing in support of the statement that those who had experience of both forms of pleasure would always prefer the higher ones.

Thus, for beings that are merely sentient, death causes harm because it prevents the future possibility of pleasurable experiences. Therefore, whilst even nonhuman animals that lack self-consciousness do lose something by death, the greater the psychological capacities, the greater the qualitative loss will be.

For more complex beings, greater opportunities are lost by death, including "a constellation of experiences, beliefs, desires, goals, projects, activities, and various other things" (Rowlands, 2002: 76). McMahan (2002: 195) concurs: "Because of their limited cognitive and emotional capacities, most animals lack the capacity for many of the forms of experience and action that give the lives of persons their special richness and meaning." Most animals, for instance, are incapable of deep personal relationships, have little imagination and no aesthetic awareness, and no sense of achieving long-term goals and ambitions. The lives of persons contain plans to bring to fruition, and mistakes to remedy or apologies to be made, all of which might be thwarted by death (McMahan, 2002: 196–8).

Of course, not all animal species have the same degree of cognitive complexity and therefore, on the opportunities account of the wrongness of killing, the death of a member of one nonhuman animal species may be a greater wrong than the death of a member of another species. Indeed, Regan, if not others such as Francione, is, as we saw, prepared to admit this, and only grants subject-of-a-life status to mammals one year of age and over. We would, then, be much less concerned morally about the death of a reptile than a mammal, and much less concerned morally about the death of some species of mammals, such as rodents, than about the death of others such as dogs or cats. The general point, though, is that, with the possible exception of the higher mammals—such as the great apes and cetaceans—the opportunities account of the wrongness of killing suggests that humans have more to lose by death. As a result, it would be justified morally to choose the life of a human over an animal on the grounds that this would cause less harm.

It should be noted that this conclusion has been disputed. In the first place, it is argued, particularly by Sapontzis (1987), that it underestimates the capabilities of animals. However, it is difficult, as we have seen, to deny major differences in the intellectual capacities of humans and animals. It has been further claimed that even if we accept that animal experiences are less sophisticated than those of humans, animals have experiences humans do not and these may be extremely enriching and satisfying. As Sapontzis (1987: 219) remarks, "we cannot enjoy the life of a dog, a bird, a bat, or a dolphin. Consequently, we cannot appreciate the subtleties of smell, sight, sound, and touch that these animals can apparently appreciate." Comparing average human lives with the unalloyed joy apparent in the lives of well-cared for dogs, for instance, McMahan (2002: 195) comments that: "There are, I confess, moments when one doubts the superiority of the goods of human life." But then, a person's life, as a whole, contains the same fleeting moments of joy as experienced by a dog and, as we have seen, much more besides. Against this, it is true that beings with more sophisticated psychological characteristics may be capable of greater suffering, too, in the form, say, of greater mental anguish caused perhaps if their lives do not go as well for them as they had anticipated. At the very least, therefore, we should exercise caution before claiming that the subjective experiences of animals are somehow inferior to human experiences.

Nevertheless, despite these apparent difficulties, there is, as DeGrazia (1996: 248) remarks, a "stubborn conviction" among many philosophers "that the lives of normal humans *must* be of greater value than the lives of many, if not all, nonhuman animals." Likewise, we tend to regard, intuitively, some human lives as less valuable than others, a viewpoint reflected in much of the literature on abortion, euthanasia, and so on (Rachels, 1990: 209). Whether this "stubborn conviction" is correct will have to persist, to some degree, as an open question for now. At the very least, it remains extremely contentious to continue to insist, as advocates of the species-egalitarian strand of animal rights do, that the value of animal lives is as great as the value of human lives.

The characteristics of personhood can also be utilized to show that adult humans have a greater interest in liberty than animals. As I noted in chapter 6, Cochrane (2012) argues that because animals lack autonomy, and therefore do not have the ability to "frame, revise and pursue their own conceptions of the good" they, unlike humans, do not have an intrinsic interest in liberty. Curtailment of freedom can harm animals but only in an instrumental sense, as a cause of suffering. For humans, on the other hand, to be constrained from pursuing their life plans causes harm, irrespective of whether it produces suffering. Slavery, for a human, is therefore harmful even if whilst enslaved she is treated well. For animals, on the other hand, lacking the interest in being autonomous, confinement does not cause harm unless it is accompanied by pain and suffering. Cochrane utilizes this insight to show that the use of animals is not, per se, illegitimate morally, and therefore challenges the species-egalitarian position that holds that any such use of animals is an infringement of their rights.

Even if we challenge Cochrane's nuanced argument that humans have an *intrinsic* interest in liberty—and merely state that, because of their greater psychological characteristics, humans have a greater interest in liberty—then the argument about human moral superiority still holds. As DeGrazia (1996: 234) points out, "If the goods that my freedom permit are, on the whole, more prudentially valuable than what a bird's freedom permits, then equal consideration does not confer equal moral weight on my freedom and the bird's."

The Enhanced Sentience Position

Given the greater strength of the interests possessed by normal adult humans, then, the species-egalitarian position would seem to be mistaken. Such humans have a greater interest in liberty and in continued life. As a result, from the perspective of a rights-based discourse, it seems plausible to say that such humans ought to have a stronger claim on a right to life and a right to liberty than do animals. The only means of challenging this conclusion, as we shall see in chapter 9, is to invoke the argument from marginal cases.

Nevertheless, it is also true that, since at least some animals have some interest in continued life and also perhaps in liberty, too—even though the strength of these interests is less than it is for most adult humans—it ought to be taken into account morally, although not, perhaps, in the form of the according of a right because it can be overridden for the benefit of those with a stronger interest in life and liberty. This amounts to what I would describe as the *enhanced sentience position*. Here, the greater interest of humans in continued life ought to take precedence in the event of a conflict. Since at least some animals have an, albeit lesser, interest in continued life, however, we ought to take it seriously and, when possible, protect this interest.

The enhanced sentience position places much greater limits on what it is morally permissible to do to animals than does the sentience position. According to the latter, the lives of animals are of no moral concern. Provided that suffering is, at the very least, minimized, we are morally permitted to use animals in whatever way we see fit. In the case of the former, on the other hand, the lives of animals can only be sacrificed if very significant human benefits accrue. Clearly, if we had to make a choice between saving the life of an animal and saving the life of a human, all things being equal, we would be morally obliged to choose the latter. When the human costs of saving an animal's life are less than this, the morally correct outcome to choose is less obvious.

Guidance here is provided by Hon-Lam Li (2002, 2007). He points out that there are two sets of variables to consider in resolving such conflicts; the level of moral status of the competing parties and the relative moral weight of the claim being made. Where either of the two variables are the same, a moral judgment can be made. Thus, in the event of a situation where the moral status is the same, the most weighty claim ought to be chosen. Where, for instance, we regard the moral status of humans and at least some animals as the same (as in the species-egalitarian version of animal rights), then in the event of a choice between saving the life of a human and inflicting nonfatal suffering on an animal (or another human), we ought to choose the former. Likewise, where the claim being made is constant (say, saving the life of a human or an animal), then a resolution to a moral conflict will depend upon differences in the moral status of the entities under consideration. In other words, we should save the life of an entity that has higher moral status. Problems occur, for Hon-Lam Li, where the moral status and the claim both differ or are both the same.

In the case of the enhanced sentience position, the moral status of animals is less than that of normal humans, and indeed, the moral status of some nonhuman animals may, of course, be greater than others. Where the claim being made is the same (for example, one life or another), the moral conflict can be resolved in favor of the being with higher moral status. Problems occur when the claims being made differ, such as where, for example, the choice is between killing an animal and reducing the suffering of a human, or merely depriving her of the satisfaction of a good meal. What, in other words, does the higher moral status of humans permit us to do in such situations?[5] Hon-Lam Li (2002: 598–99) provides a solution here in terms of the rule of approximation. In terms of the enhanced sentience position, this would mean that the closer the claims approximate to each other, the more difficult will be the moral evaluation. If the choice, for instance, is between a trivial human interest and a highly significant animal interest, then the decision to be made is obvious. If, however, the choice is between, say, the death of an animal and severe, and prolonged, pain for a human, then the two claims approximate to such a degree that a choice is more difficult.

The application of the enhanced sentience position, then, would rule out meat eating, even from animals raised in free-range conditions and slaughtered humanely, except where consuming meat is necessary for human health and survival. It is clearly the case that a meat-free diet is not necessarily damaging to human health, certainly in the developed world, and indeed, as I noted in chapter 4, meat eating may have detrimental effects on human health (Pluhar, 1992). The use of animals in scientific research is more problematic since it is claimed that some such research does have very substantial benefits to humans. Only when it is shown to do so, however, is animal experimentation justified, and even then, this would have to be research that does not inflict suffering on animals, since humans and animals, all things being equal, have an equivalent interest in avoiding suffering.

The Sentience Position as Nonideal Theory

The claim being made here so far, then, is that, from the perspective of normative ethics, the enhanced sentience position would seem to represent an ideal theory of justice for animals. That is, it describes accurately what animals are due as a matter of justice. Readers will also be aware that the enhanced sentience position is very demanding in terms of what it requires of human beings in their dealings with animals. Indeed, it is not that far away, in terms of its practical implications, from the species-egalitarian version of animal rights. As a result, the conclusion of this book is that the sentience position ought to be regarded as the nonideal route by which the enhanced sentience position is achieved.

At this point, there will be objections from those who think that the sentience position does not go far enough *and* from those who think that it is politically unrealistic. In order to demonstrate that both of these objections are misplaced, I will consider the sentience position in the context of the Rawlsian characteristics of nonideal theory identified in the introduction to this book. In terms of moral permissibility, there is a strong claim that the sentience position seeks to remove the most grievous, or most urgent, injustice inflicted on animals. The ideal theory developed in this chapter accepts that most humans have a greater interest in continued life and liberty than most animals. However, it is argued that animals and humans have an equal interest in avoiding suffering. It follows that the most urgent injustice to eradicate is the practice of inflicting suffering on animals for any, nontrivial, human purpose. This is precisely what the sentience position advocates.

The sentience position is also effective in the sense that it does not hinder progress toward the ideal theory. In particular, it does not, unlike the animal welfare and the utilitarian ethic, involve the trading off of animals' interest in not suffering. The sentience position insists that animals have an inviolable right not to have suffering inflicted upon them, irrespective of the benefits that might be forthcoming from so doing. It is true that the sentience position does permit the sacrificing of animals' interest in continued life but this is only permitted when animals do not suffer in the process. It is a relatively small step from this to the acceptance of the additional principle that animals do have an interest in life and liberty, albeit not to the same extent as most humans, and that this interest ought to be taken into account in our moral deliberations.

In actual fact, upholding animals' right not to suffer can, in practice, take us a long way toward the achievement of abolitionist animal rights goals. Take, firstly, the use of animals as experimental subjects. A situation where animals do not suffer in the laboratory environment can, for sure, be envisaged. Imagine that environmental enrichment was such that animals did not suffer from boredom or stress, and that procedures were carried out under anesthetic, with the animal killed before it regained consciousness. The problem with this scenario is that it is very far from the reality of most animal experimentation where, for many procedures, suffering is inflicted and the animal must remain conscious, sometimes even without any pain relief. A "no pain and suffering" principle, then, would have the effect of ending many, if not most, procedures on laboratory animals.

It is feasible, too, to imagine a form of farm animal husbandry that reduced significantly the suffering of animals. It has been well documented that so-called "factory" farming causes enormous suffering in terms of pain as well as boredom, stress, anxiety, and so on (see DeGrazia, 1996: 281–4; Mason and Singer, 1990). Genuine "free-range" husbandry systems are the obvious alternative option here, although, looking into the future, at least two additional options might be feasible. The first is the production of in vitro, or laboratory-cultured, meat. Animals would still be required as cell donors but, provided they are treated well, this should not raise any ethical problems.[6] The real problem is the likely limitation on the type of meat that could be produced and the current cost, which at present does not make it a viable option (Pluhar, 2010: 463–4).

The second option is a "technological solution to the problem of animal suffering" in which factory-farmed livestock can be genetically engineered so as not to suffer pain or to have that capacity reduced significantly (Shriver, 2009). If possible, and there are considerable doubts as to whether it *is* possible, this would make even factory farming more acceptable from the perspective of the sentience position. In addition, it would be a move consistent with a nonideal theory given that, as Shriver (2009: 120) points out, people would be more likely to eat genetically modified meat than give up meat all together. Producing so-called "knockout livestock," however, is not entirely compatible with the sentience position. This is because, as was pointed out earlier, suffering involves more than mere pain, so ending or vastly reducing the amount of pain suffered by animals in factory farms would not reduce suffering entirely or even substantially.

Genuine free-ranging husbandry systems do reduce much of the suffering evident in factory farming. However, even assuming that genuine free-range enterprises are able to satisfy animals' interest in not suffering—and it should be noted that *all* husbandry and slaughtering systems must involve the infliction of at least some suffering[7]—they are currently few and far between (Pluhar, 2010: 461–3). There is a good reason for this. Factory farming was created in the first place in order to mass produce animal products at the lowest price possible. It is clear that alternative free-range systems could not produce animal products for consumption in anything like the amount required or the price desired. To insist they become the norm would, then, have radical implications involving the dismantling of the present dominant structure of factory farming, and the consequent reduction in supply, and increased price, of meat and associated animal products. At present, such an eventuality would be given a positive welcome by most animal rights activists.

Of course, this will lead to a further objection, that the sentience position is just too far-reaching and therefore does not meet Rawls's criterion that a nonideal theory should be politically possible. I would make a number of points in response to this objection. In the first place, there is a great deal of utility for a social movement in presenting its case in terms of rights, precisely because, as with the concept of justice, rights have such a high status in political discourse. As Campbell (2006: 3) remarks: "There is little chance that any cause will be taken seriously in the contemporary world that cannot be expressed as a demand for the recognition or enforcement of rights of one sort of another." Of course, Campbell adopts an anthropocentric perspective and, it might be argued, his claim has greater credibility when it is applied to humans rather than animals. The demand that animals' interests in not suffering should not be traded off in the search for human benefits still, it might be argued, looks unrealistic in the light of current practices.

One response to this charge is to make the point that utilizing the sentience position still allows for animals to be used. As we saw above, for instance, farming animals for food and using them for scientific purposes are not ruled out. What is ruled out is the infliction of suffering. In particular, much important scientific research can still go ahead. For example, much contemporary animal research (about 15 percent in terms of the procedures undertaken in Britain) uses rodents that are reared solely to generate tissues for experiments (Spedding, 2000: 150). That is, the animals are killed for their tissues and not actually experimented on. The sentience position would see no ethical problem with this provided that the animals receive adequate space and nutrition. Moreover, it is worth speculating that the prohibition on suffering in the laboratory would encourage the development of alternatives to the use of animals. Presently, very few resources are put into this area precisely because animals are available to be used with relatively few constraints.

Another response to the charge of a lack of political realism is to make the point that, even if there is a substantial gap between the current moral orthodoxy and the sentience position, it can still be claimed that the latter does represent a reasonable balance between competing perspectives, a position advanced by Sher (1997). The sentience position, it might be argued, is a valid attempt to reconcile those animal rights advocates who want the complete abolition of the use of animals, on the one hand, with those decision makers and most of the public who would appear to be only willing, at present, to embrace a moderate welfarism. Seen in this way, the sentience position is sufficiently aspirational and cannot be accused of being too conservative.

There is a case for saying, in addition, that the focus on suffering in the sentience position does strike a chord with public opinion in the way that the fundamental objection to the use of animals in the species-egalitarian version of animal rights does not. The sentience position does not have anything negatively to say about uses of animals that do not involve suffering. It does not, therefore, have to get involved in debates about whether an animal rights ethic precludes owing animals as pets or companion animals. Providing that suffering is not involved in the provision or keeping of companion animals, then it is morally legitimate. Of course, there are practices—such as puppy farms—where suffering is involved and these become illegitimate according to the sentience position. Nevertheless, the sentience position, unlike the species-egalitarian version of animal rights, is not at odds with the fact that many humans do have relationships with animals that enrich the lives of both the human and the animal involved.

Moreover, the sentience position, unlike other versions of animal rights, involves no contentious speculations about the respective value of human and animal life. All it requires is the acceptance that animals, like humans, can experience pain and suffering and that pain and suffering is experienced by humans and animals in similar ways. As a result, it avoids the "clash of entrenched views and theories" associated with the question of the value of life. By contrast, an emphasis on pain and suffering "almost certainly has a better chance of gaining acceptance ... than does some case resting upon a sus-pect account of the morality of killing" (Frey, 1983: 101).

An additional point to make here is that we should not assume that the moral position enshrined in animal welfare statutes and administrative arrangements reflects public opinion accurately. It is important to distinguish between the values and interests of those centrally involved in the exploita-tion of animals and the wider public. It may be, then, that an animal rights stance based on suffering, if properly explained, is likely to be much more amenable to the public than it will be to an elite that includes those who ben-efit directly from exploiting animals. Indeed, the way in which public policy in Britain and elsewhere is made may well disguise the level of support for more far-reaching reforms to the way animals are treated.

Support for this can be found in political science research, which shows that animal welfare public policy tends to be made in insulated so-called policy communities that are isolated from public opinion. These policy communities tend to be dominated by those—such as research scientists, representatives from pharmaceutical companies, agribusiness interests, and so forth—who stand to gain from the continuation of animal exploitation (Lyons, forthcoming). The logic of this argument is that if policy making becomes more open and transparent, then animals will fare better, since the power of vested interests will be reduced. To this end, campaigns by British anti-vivisection groups to challenge the secrecy central to animal experimentation law is potentially a very profitable move.

It is being suggested, then, that whilst it may be unrealistic to expect research scientists to accept the sentience position, it may not be unrealistic to get a majority of the public to accept it. Two examples from the practice of animal protection politics can be used to suggest that the sentience position might be closer to the public's position than the skeptics might think. The first relates to the so-called "five freedoms," consisting of: freedom from hunger, thirst and malnutrition; freedom from fear and distress; freedom from physical and thermal discomfort; freedom from pain, injury, and disease; and freedom to express normal patterns of behavior.[8] These were identified in the 1960s by the Brambell Committee—a committee set up by the British Government to investigate the welfare implications of modern animal agriculture—as the major characteristics of good animal welfare (Brambell Report, 1965).[9] Since then, in Britain and elsewhere, they have become, however symbolically, the goal of a variety of public bodies.

It is important to notice that the five freedoms are not equivalent to animal welfare in an ethical and public policy sense. Rather, what it represents is an aspirational list of what good animal welfare would look like from an empirical perspective, from the perspective of the animal welfare scientist. From an ethical and public policy perspective, on the other hand, the five freedoms might not be what animal welfare mandates. This will largely depend upon whether the infringement of any of these five freedoms in any particular case is regarded as necessary.

Animal welfare, in an empirical scientific sense, therefore, may well, and is often, not met by animal welfare in an ethical and public policy sense. But an interesting thought follows from this. If it is the case that what most people understand by animal welfare is the empirical and scientific version, then it may well be that they would reject the ethical and public policy version of animal welfare as not far reaching enough. In other words, they would advocate the sentience position, since only a rights-based ethic can ensure that the five freedoms are maintained because only then can they avoid being sacrificed if some human interest or other demands it. At the very least, this is an empirical proposition worthy of further study.

The second example of the political saliency of the sentience position is the emphasis on suffering in antivivisection campaigns. Because some procedures undertaken in the laboratory do involve cutting (that is, vivisection proper), it is easy for antivivisection campaigns to utilize the gruesome pictures that sometimes come their way. What is interesting is that antivivisection campaigns rarely say whether or not in the case of a particular image the animal was conscious. I am not saying here that the absence of this information is deliberate but it can surely not hinder a campaign for the public to think that the animal was suffering.

There is, in fact, some polling evidence that suggests it is the suffering of animals in scientific procedures that really exercises the public mind, as opposed to the benefits such research produces. One survey, for instance, asked whether "scientists should be allowed to do research that causes pain and injury to animals like dogs and chimpanzees if it produces new information about human health problems" (Pifer and Shimizu, 1994). The intensity of the opposition to such scientific procedures varied but in many countries (such as Japan and the United States) it was approaching half and in France and West Germany a sizeable majority opposed the proposal. Now, not a great deal should be made of these findings. The species focused on may well have tilted the findings (different results would probably have been produced had the dogs and chimpanzee been replaced by rodents) and the question emphasized the suffering rather more than the possible benefits. Nevertheless, at the very least, it is illustrative that the infliction of pain and suffering on animals is a cause of concern for the public. Further empirical research, well beyond the scope of this study, is clearly necessary here.

Conclusion

In this chapter, I have outlined my preferred ideal and nonideal theory of justice for animals. Both are built upon the characteristics identified in chapter 6. That is, they are both rights-based theories justified by reference to the interests humans and animals have, which, in turn, are based upon the differential capacities possessed by animals and humans. Whilst the enhanced sentience position is a more valid ideal theory—because it takes into account the interest that animals have in continued life—it was argued that the sentience position is an appropriate nonideal route, meeting the terms of the characteristics identified by Rawls.

It may be thought that there is little more to be said now in this book and we can come to a speedy conclusion. This is not quite the case because the species-egalitarian version of animal rights has one more arrow in its bow. This weapon is the so-called argument from marginal cases and, because of its importance, the last chapter is devoted to a critical analysis of it.

9

The Argument from Marginal Cases Revisited

IN AN INTRODUCTORY account of the political philosophy of Hegel, Peter Singer confesses, at the halfway point of the book, that he has been cheating. He admits that, to aid understanding, he has not been telling the full story about Hegel's philosophy (Singer, 1983: 45). Somewhat further into this book, I confess, we have reached a similar point. I have not been telling the whole story about animal ethics, or at least I have only hinted at the full story. It has been argued so far that humans and animals have different cognitive capacities and that these differences are morally significant. This assertion, however, is vulnerable to the so-called argument from marginal cases (hereinafter amc), a discussion of which constitutes the content of this last chapter. This chapter examines the use of the amc within the animal ethics literature before going on to consider how valid it is as an ethical principle, particularly in light of the animal rights positions identified in this book. Following this, it is argued that the amc can probably be discarded as a central piece of the animal rights armoury since it is counterintuitive, unnecessary, and probably underestimates the degree to which marginal humans are in any case in practice regarded as having an inferior moral status to other humans.

The amc is ubiquitous in the animal ethics literature. This is not surprising given the important role it can, and has, played in the accounts of those who seek to argue for an enhanced moral status for animals. Anderson (2004: 279) goes as far as to claim, inaccurately as I will explain below, that the amc represents "the central argument behind the claim that nonhuman animals have rights." There are, in fact, two versions of the amc, both of which are concerned with maintaining consistency in moral thinking.

In what Pluhar (1995) describes as the "bioconditional" version, it is argued that *if* "marginal" humans—infants, anencephalic babies (a condition where a baby's brain is seriously underdeveloped), the permanently comatose, the severely retarded, those who have suffered severe mental impairment through strokes, those with advanced dementia, and so on—are regarded as if they have the same moral status as other—nonmarginal—humans, then consistency demands that animals of similar cognitive ability ought to be accorded the same moral worth.[1] The second version of the amc, what Pluhar (1995) calls the "categorical" version, holds that *because* marginal humans (or human nonpersons) are deemed to have maximum moral significance, then consistency demands that animals with an equivalent cognitive capacity are accorded the same moral status. The difference between the two versions is that the former, bioconditional, version could be used to justify excluding *both* animals and marginal humans from maximum moral significance.

The Argument from Marginal Cases in Action

The amc is central to debates within the discipline of animal ethics in that most defenders of an enhanced moral status for animals use it and virtually all defenders of human moral superiority respond to it (see Dombrowski, 1997). It is particularly central to the abolitionist species-egalitarian version of animal rights we encountered in chapter 7. The case against this position—that animals do not have a right to life or liberty because their interests in life and liberty are less than those of humans—can be countered by the argument that marginal humans do not have the same level of interest, either. Therefore, if we persist in claiming that marginal humans have an interest in life and liberty that is as great as nonmarginal humans, then consistency demands that we accord the same moral status to those animals that have similar psychological capacities to marginal humans.

As Singer (1993: 132) remarks, whilst animals do not have the same level of self-consciousness as the average human, the case against killing them "is as strong as the case against killing permanently intellectually disabled human beings at a similar mental level." In other words, the success of the abolitionist animal rights project—to make the death of animals as morally important as the death of humans—depends upon the success of the argument from marginal cases. If we do not accept it, then, as we suggested in chapter 8, the case for regarding human lives as more morally important than animal lives would seem to be strong.

Virtually all animal ethicists make some use of the amc, although not always in the same way. Particularly illustrative is Regan's argument. We saw in chapter 8 that Regan rejects the ethical significance of the Kantian notion of personhood, and seeks to replace it with a weaker preference autonomy, enshrined in the concept of a subject-of-a-life. This move is justified by reference to the argument from marginal cases. That is, Regan recognizes that marginal humans would not be accorded rights under the Kantian notion of personhood. In order to avoid this counterintuitive conclusion, he adopts a weaker sense of autonomy to enable the inclusion of marginal humans, which, for consistency's sake, demands the inclusion of at least some species of animals, too (Cohen and Regan, 2001: 209). Thus, as he writes (Cohen and Regan, 2001: 271), "because these (marginal) humans are subjects-of-a-life, such (direct) duties are owed, and correlative rights possessed. And because other animals are like these humans in the relevant respects, the same is true in their case" (see also Rollin, 2009: 497–8).

Singer also makes use of the amc, but adopts a position that is less reliant on it. As Dombrowski (1997: 9–11) explains, because Singer does not adopt a rights position, and does not hold that human life should be preserved at all costs, he does not need to accept the categorical version of the amc. That is, he does not need to accept the position that, because marginal humans are treated as if they have a right to life, then so should animals with similar psychological capacities. Rather, he is prepared to accept that sometimes, the life of, say, a severely mentally disabled adult is not worth living. Singer does not, therefore, accept that human lives are of equal value, and likewise, as we saw in chapter 7, he does not accept that human and animal lives are necessarily of equal value, either. However, he falls short of saying, unlike another philosopher, R. G. Frey (see below), that we are therefore entitled to sacrifice the lives of such humans if by so doing a greater social benefit would be the consequence.

To give one more example, Cochrane's conclusion, in a more recent work (2012)—that the vast majority of animals do not have an interest in liberty, and therefore a right to liberty, because they are not autonomous—is reached by adopting the bioconditional version of the amc. That is, he argues that, in practice, marginal humans are treated as if they do not have the same interest in liberty as nonmarginal humans. The adoption of this version of the amc commits Cochrane to the position that it is justified to deprive marginal humans of their liberty not only when it is in their interest to do so but also when it is not. Thus, he writes that "humans such as babies and the severely mentally disabled have no interest in not being used in experimentation that is painless and which does not result in death" (Cochrane, 2007: 316). This latter claim is, of course, controversial and does not meet with accepted practice. In his defense, Cochrane (2007: 316–17) then suggests that the use of marginal humans in experiments is rarely morally permissible, either because it causes suffering or because such a move will be unacceptable to caregivers or parents (see below).

By contrast, Cochrane employs the categorical version of the amc in the case of issues surrounding the value of life. Thus, he argues, consistency demands that we grant to animals the same interest in continued life as we grant to humans on the grounds that we would not wish to deny such an interest to marginal humans. Such a use of the categorical version of the amc in the case of continued life is, of course, dependent on the truth of the assertion that the value of marginal human life is regarded, in practice, as the value of nonmarginal human life. This is an issue that we will come back to later in this chapter.

Defending Differential Moral Worth

Given the importance of the amc in the animal ethicist's canon, and its apparent impeccable logic, the key question to ask is whether there are any justifications for regarding marginal humans as more morally considerable than animals? The first, and most common, justification for so doing is the "appeal to thwarted potential" (Pluhar, 1988: 60). Here, it is argued that it is justifiable morally to treat those with the potential to become persons as if they were persons, since to fail to do so is to thwart this potential personhood. This obviously applies to infants. The death of an infant may represent a loss in terms of the goods that will be forfeited, and since these will be, for the most part, the goods that derive from the psychological characteristics of personhood, they are likely to be considerable (see chapter 8).

There is, however, a question mark against the moral importance of potential. One implication of taking potential into account is that it makes abortion, and even the use of contraception, a serious wrong (McMahan, 2002: 192). To abort a fetus, or to prevent one from developing, clearly has the effect of thwarting potential.[2] One way of countering this, should we decide it is necessary, is to factor in the "extent to which it matters, for his sake now or from his present point of view" that the fetus or the potential fetus should continue to live (McMahan, 2002: 105). The consequence of doing this is, of course, to reduce the moral force of potentiality. As we argued in chapter 8, just as the desire to continue living (which is a reflection of a being's recognition of what will be lost by death) of animals is low, or nonexistent, it can be argued that it will be lower for infants than for nonmarginal adults and nonexistent for fetuses. This reflects the idea that "we do not generally accept that

individuals who have the potential to obtain a particular status already have
the rights that go with that status" (Palmer, 2010: 22).

Whatever the merits of the thwarted potential argument, it only applies,
in any case, to those marginal humans who *have* potential. It therefore
excludes those who acquired a diminution of cognitive capacities, and those
whose cognitive impairments are congenital. Another argument that seeks
to defend the moral superiority of marginal humans over animals, and that
covers all marginal humans and not just infants, focuses on the claim that
marginal humans are the same "kind" as "normal" humans and are therefore different from animals. Cohen provides a representative example of this
position. He recognizes that marginal humans do not have the same characteristics as "normal" humans, but still argues that the former have rights
whereas animals do not, on the grounds that the latter "are not beings of
a kind capable of exercising or responding to moral claims" (Cohen, 1986:
866; see also Machan, 2007: 53–54).

As has been regularly remarked (Nobis, 2004; Palmer, 2010: 22; Rachels,
1990; Cohen and Regan, 2001: 278–79), it is not clear why the normal characteristics of a species are morally more important than those of particular
individuals within that species. It is difficult to see, in other words, how a
biological criterion such as species can have any moral significance. To do so
involves according the same moral status to individuals within a species who
have certain characteristics to those members of the same species who do
not. To pursue this, clearly speciesist, line of reasoning results in some odd,
and surely incorrect, consequences. For example, it means, fallaciously, to
imply that because an anencephalic infant is a human being (and therefore
has the same moral value as other human beings), she has the same capacities
as nonmarginal human beings (Cohen and Regan, 2001: 278). Imagine, to
put it another way, that you were a member of a class where all of the stu-
dents but you had the property of being able to do well in exams. Whereas
the other members of your class passed, you failed. The "kind" argument, in
this context, would allow you to say, implausibly, that because you are in a
class of people who can pass exams, you, too, have the capacity to pass exams
(Nobis, 2004: 53).

Other philosophers have sought to justify the "kind" argument in different ways. Levy (2004) seeks to defend Cohen's focus on species membership, as opposed to individual characteristics, by arguing, firstly, that "our
moral intuitions seem to track species membership quite closely" (216), so
that it is morally counterintuitive, for example, to imagine using marginal
humans in scientific experiments. Secondly, he appeals to the origin and

function of morality, which, he suggests, has evolved with only humans in mind so that, whilst not equating morality entirely with species selfishness, "the rootedness of morality in our evolutionary history might give us reason to extend the highest form of moral considerability to members of our own species, whatever their non-relational properties." It is true that species solidarity can be enormously powerful, particularly when a species is faced with a common external threat. As I pointed out in chapter 7, human species solidarity is a key reason why the species-egalitarian strand of animal rights might lack the characteristics of what Rawls describes as a realistic utopia. Nevertheless, in answer to this justification of Cohen's position, it should be noted that the *fact* that morality may have evolved to serve the interests of humans is not a comprehensive argument in defense of why it *ought* to continue to do so.

Another dimension to the kind argument is to point to one difference between marginal humans and animals: that the former have a damaged or unfortunate life, in the sense that they lack the characteristics common to their species, whilst animals do not. (Feder Kittay, 2005: 110–12). This distinction is important, it is argued, because it would seem intuitively wrong to be prepared to morally subordinate someone who is already regarded as unfortunate. It is difficult to see, however, how this distinction is morally relevant. This argument would seem to be speciesist in the sense that a being's moral status is determined by their species (to be precise, what is normal for their species) and not by the characteristics of individuals. To illustrate what would seem to be intuitively wrong with this notion, McMahan (1996: 13–15) asks us to imagine a chimp that is given human cognitive characteristics, which are then eliminated through brain damage. To claim, as the species norm argument does, that the chimp is not unfortunate would seem to be intuitively problematic, and that therefore falling below the level normal for your species is not necessary in order for suffering or loss to occur. As Pluhar (1988: 65) points out, then, a nonperson's moral status "cannot depend on the purely contingent question of what *most* members of his or her species are like."

Another defense of regarding marginal humans as morally superior to animals is the so-called "difference in kind" argument. This differs from the "kind" argument discussed above in that the latter is a mere appeal to group membership whereas the former argues that there is a genuine difference between marginal humans and animals. Thus, Cohen (1986: 15) argues that "what humans retain when disabled, animals never had." Likewise, Feder Kittay (2005: 126) argues that we should not underestimate the cognitive capacities of even severely mentally retarded humans. Most can speak at least a few words, and can be involved in activities and relationships so that they are far from being unresponsive to their environment.

This objection to the amc depends, of course, on an empirical examination of the respective psychological characteristics of marginal humans and animals. Much will therefore depend on the level of cognitive impairment encountered by the "marginal" human, and the species of animal it is being compared with. It is certainly true that those, such as Singer, who make much use of the amc, do not generally distinguish between the cognitive capacities of those classified as marginal humans, and yet it is a large category covering humans with widely different capacities.

Even though it is difficult to compare accurately the psychological capacities of marginal humans and animals in all cases, it is undoubtedly true that in some cases the psychological capacities of some animals compares favorably with those of some marginal humans. Anencephalic infants, for example, are born without the capacity for consciousness. Those with advanced Alzheimer's disease have little capacity for thought and perception to the point that they have ceased to exist as a person. (McMahan, 2002: 44). In addition, those with severe pathological states, who live their lives entirely in the present, with no memories or future plans (McMahan, 2002: 76), are equivalent to the psychological state of animals modeled in the sentience position. As was argued in chapter 8, this position seriously underestimates the capabilities of many species of animals.

A subsidiary part of the difference in kind argument is to accept that in some cases—such as the ones described above—the psychological capacities of some humans may be equal to, or inferior than, many species of animals, but to deny its salience. This is based on the position that such humans are extremely rare and that, in any case, these humans *are* regarded as having an inferior moral status to other humans, even from some who might also be classified as marginal (Benson, 1978; VanDeVeer, 1979b; Williams, 1980: 160).

We will deal with the second clause of this claim later in the chapter. The first clause, the argument based on rarity, is, of course, dependent upon an empirical examination. It is notoriously difficult to get accurate figures on the percentage of the population that can be classified as "marginal" and then interpret what this means in terms of their capabilities. To give some guidance, it was estimated in the 1970s that 2.3 percent of the population in the United States could be described as retarded (defined in terms of level of IQ), amounting to some six million people. However, the category of severely and profoundly retarded constituted only about 5 percent of this total, amounting to 0.15 percent of the population (Rose-Ackerman, 1982: 83). It is claimed that only this latter category can really be classified as lacking personhood in the sense that they would not pass a minimal autonomy or rationality test (Rose-Ackerman, 1982: 85). Of course, these figures exclude infants. They might be deemed to be covered by the thwarted potential argument discussed above. It has also been claimed that even infants under two years of age possess some characteristics not possessed by most animals (Pickering-Francis and Norman, 1978: 509).

As a result, there would seem to be some merit in the claim that those whose psychological characteristics are equivalent, or on a par with, many species of animals constitute a very small minority of the human population. A relevant aside here is that it is only relatively recently that life expectancies for the severely cognitively impaired have improved. Prior to the middle of the last century, the proportion of the profoundly retarded who survived was small (Becker, 2005: 9–10). Of course, the argument from marginal cases is not entirely dependent on maximizing the number of those humans who might be genuinely described as "marginal." Nevertheless, it might reduce the force of the claims made. More importantly, if it can be shown that this small group of genuinely marginal humans is, in fact, regarded as morally less considerable than other humans—including those who are moderately or mildly retarded—and therefore treated very differently in practice from other humans as a consequence, then the validity of the argument from marginal cases would be seriously diminished. We examine this question further below.

Yet another argument for maintaining an ethical distinction between animals and marginal humans focuses on a slippery slope justification (Carruthers, 1992: 114–17; Devine, 1978: 495–502). The argument here is that if we treat marginal humans as inferior morally to rational and autonomous persons, then, given that there are no sharp boundaries between humans who have the characteristics of personhood and those who do not, this is the first step toward treating some persons, or near persons, in an inferior way to other persons. It therefore creates "too large a risk of error, and too much cost in anxiety among the mildly retarded and their relatives" (Devine, 1978: 497), as well as other picked-on groups of humans. This, of course, is an empirical claim that would have to be shown to be true in any particular case (Cavalieri, 2001: 82). Certainly, the slippery slope argument is not supported by the evidence that has been derived from those societies in which marginal humans have been regarded as morally inferior (Dombrowski, 1997: 128).

The "kind" argument discussed above is distinctive because it does not seek to try to identify morally relevant differences between animals and marginal humans that are based on psychological capacities. A more promising version of this approach is the adoption of a relational argument, of the kind we discussed in chapter 6. That is, the relevant difference between animals and marginal humans relates to extrinsic relational factors and not to intrinsic psychological characteristics. A general account of the moral importance of these relational factors is provided by Midgley (1983: 125). Human beings, for Midgley, bond with other humans on the basis of their species membership, just as parents have particular bonds with their children. Humans also, she argues, create "mixed communities" that also contain animals, some of with whom we can develop strong bonds. This is why animals matter to us, hence the title of her best-known book on animal ethics (Midgley, 1983). The assumption here from those who wish to invoke a relational argument to challenge the amc is that relations between humans are deeper and more significant than those between humans and animals.

A critique of this relational approach is that without an additional argument, it is difficult to see how the *fact* of our bonds with other humans and certain animals, such as those we keep as our companions, can generate an obligation to regard them as *morally* more important. One possible additional argument is proffered by McMahan. It can be argued, he suggests, that it is the special relations we have with marginal humans—primarily as relatives— from which we can derive moral reasons to treat them more favorably than animals with similar psychological characteristics (McMahan, 2002: 217–20; see also Pickering-Francis and Norman, 1978). This turns out to be a version of an indirect duty view in that the benefit of showing greater compassion to marginal humans than to animals is not owed to marginal humans themselves but to those close to them who will suffer if they are not regarded as morally considerable.

One implication of such an approach is that, because the moral worth of an individual is linked not to her own psychological characteristics but to the benefits likely to accrue to those with an interest in upholding her moral worth, it opens up the possibility of a nonanthropocentric application. That is, it is possible to claim that an individual's closeness to a particular animal justifies greater respect for that animal. Others should therefore respect my special relation with, for example, my companion animal. As Horta (2010: 262) points out, bonds of sympathy are not restricted to human relationships with other humans, nor are they always present in human relations. However, this may not be fatal for the relational justification for a differential moral status for animals and marginal humans. It can be argued that such an argument *is* used to justify the preferential treatment given to some animals, such as those kept as companions. And in any case, the bonds of blood are likely, empirically, to mean that there will be a greater desire to protect marginal humans than animals. The fact that we are members of the same species may give us a reason to care for marginal humans that we do not have in the case of animals.

Where the relational view comes up short is its implications for intra-human interactions. In the first place, it would seem to justify additional moral worth being attached to those with whom we are close. Imagine, then, that we feel closest to those of the same race or gender, as well as those marginal humans to whom we are attached. Would this result in members of our own race or gender having additional moral worth, so that in a situation where we are forced to choose between, say, helping a black or white person, we should choose the latter if we are white and feel ourselves closer to those with the same skin color? (Cavalieri, 2001: 80). This is a position that most would find intuitively problematic.

Applied to marginal humans, the situation is even more problematic. In the case of race, we are referring to moral worth above and beyond that which is granted to autonomous and rational human beings. Ordinarily then, skin color or gender is irrelevant to our granting to humans a high moral status. That is, if a white man has a right to life, so does a black man, and so on. In the case of marginal humans, on the other hand, they are dependent for the existence of the full panoply of rights on relations they have with other, non-marginal, humans. In other words, those marginal humans—such as orphans or those with callous and unfeeling caregivers—who do not have such relationships do not, according to the relational position, possess the same moral status as nonmarginal humans. In these cases, the challenge to the amc has not worked. Again, most of us would find the cause of such differential moral status as problematic (Gunnarsson, 2008: 309).

Should We Discard the Argument from Marginal Cases?

The debate about the argument from marginal cases has, as we have seen, continued to rage in the pages of philosophy journals with little sign of resolution either way. Given this lack of consensus, it ought to be asked if there is a case for discarding it. There are two main grounds for doing so. In the first place, we might discard it on the grounds that it is intuitively unacceptable to equate marginal humans with animals. In this context, there is some disquiet from advocates of animal rights, whom I have regularly heard complain that to compare animals with "damaged" human beings is disrespectful to both. More importantly, whatever its merits from the perspective of analytical moral philosophy, it still remains counterintuitive to equate marginal humans with animals.

Even though the amc might be correct in theory, then, its lack of support in society means that it does not pass the ought implies can test, a vital ingredient, as we saw, of any viable nonideal theory of justice. That is, humans will simply not allow the marginal members of their species to be regarded as morally inferior to other humans such that they are treated in the same way that animals are currently treated. As Sztybel (2000: 340) points out, "it is a fact of our contemporary, human nature that normal humans *cannot* pan-fry, say, mentally challenged humans." So, "if we *cannot* treat marginal humans on a par with nonhumans, let it not be said that we *ought* to do so." Of course, it might be argued in reply that it is precisely this response that the categorical version of the amc relies upon. That is, we would not treat marginal humans in the way that we currently treat animals, and therefore we should not treat animals with similar psychological characteristics in the same way. This is, however, to miss the point being made here, which is not a technical philosophical one but an empirical one to the effect that humans do not, by and large, regard animals as on a par morally with marginal humans.

It might also be argued, secondly, that the amc is unnecessary. It is usually employed to challenge the animal welfare ethic (outlined in chapter 5) and to justify the abolitionist, species-egalitarian, version of animal rights (discussed in chapter 7). Its usefulness here is obvious. The animal welfare ethic argues that *all* animal interests can be sacrificed if it results in a significant benefit for humans. The purpose of the amc is to undermine this animal welfare ethic, however, by challenging its central principle that all humans have interests that carry greater moral weight than animals. The effect of the amc here is to eliminate the force of this view by pointing out that, even if we accept that nonmarginal humans have greater moral worth than animals, the same does not apply to marginal humans. Therefore, if we are prepared to sacrifice the interests of fundamental animal interests, we should also be prepared to sacrifice the similar interests of those marginal humans who have equivalent psychological characteristics. This is a very useful argument for exponents of the abolitionist animal rights position since it follows that if we are to say that marginal humans have a right to life and an intrinsic interest in liberty, then consistency demands that those animals who have similar psychological characteristics do, too.

The amc is not as necessary, however, in the case of the sentience position, outlined in chapter 8. Exponents of the sentience position can readily admit that humans, or at least those humans who are not classified as marginal, have a higher moral status than animals—possessing, for instance, a greater interest in life—without having to give up the nontradeable interest that animals have in not suffering. In other words, the sentience position challenges the animal welfare ethic's insistence that all fundamental interests of animals can be sacrificed to promote a significant human interest.

Of course, provided that we accept the force of the amc, it still has consequences for the sentience position. The sentience position does not accord to animals the full range of moral entitlements possessed by nonmarginal humans, and is not therefore consistent with the moral egalitarianism that follows from adopting the categorical version of the amc. Moreover, since consistency demands that we treat marginal humans in the same way as those animals with similar psychological capacities, applying the bioconditional version of the amc to the sentience position demands that marginal humans possess a right not to suffer at the hands of humans, but no moral importance ought to be attached to their lives. Clearly, many would still maintain that it is counterintuitive to suggest that the lives of marginal humans, even of those most severely damaged, are of no moral import.

There are two responses we can make here. One is that, as we saw in chapter 8, there is a strong case for saying that at least some, perhaps most, of the goals of the abolitionist animal rights movement can be achieved by recognizing the moral obligations that derive from accepting merely that animals are sentient. If this is the case, there is no need to invoke the amc in order to justify a higher moral status for animals. Secondly, it might be argued that the lives of the very seriously cognitively damaged humans (anencephalic infants, say, and those in the final stages of dementia) *are* of much less importance morally. There would clearly be less concern about using such humans as means to an end (in, for example, nonpainful scientific experiments) than using nonmarginal humans. As we will discuss below, there is some evidence that the lives of marginal humans *are* regarded as of less importance morally, and that this is becoming much more socially acceptable. Echoing a debate described above, a great deal here depends, of course, upon who we include in the marginal human category and whether we ought to differentiate morally within this category.

One final point to make here is that accepting that animals are probably due even greater moral status, as the enhanced sentience position does, challenges the necessity of the amc even further. Applying the bioconditional version of the amc to this position would mean that the lives of marginal humans would be regarded as of less moral importance than those of nonmarginal humans, but that, since they have some interest in continued life, we would not be permitted to sacrifice these interests unless it was to promote a very significant human interest, such as the preservation of human life. It should be noted that in the case of the most severely cognitively damaged humans, it may be going too far to grant them *any* interest in continued life, so in that sense the enhanced sentience position probably awards too high a moral status to such individuals.

Differential Moral Status in Practice?

As I indicated above, another justification for rejecting the amc—or, to be more precise, the categorical version of it—might be that it underestimates the degree to which marginal humans *are* regarded as morally inferior to "normal" humans, thereby reducing or eliminating the inconsistency claim of the amc. The bioconditional version of the amc, as we saw, does allow for this by raising the prospect of regarding marginal humans as morally on a par with animals. Cochrane (2012), as I indicated above, adopts this approach in the case of liberty by suggesting that, in practice, marginal humans are not treated as if they have an interest in liberty. This section is predicated on the assumption that animal rights advocates of the amc usually fail to engage in a discussion of how marginal humans are regarded morally, and therefore treated, in practice. That is, it is merely assumed that the sanctity of *all* human life and liberty is a principle that is observed in practice.

There is, of course, a difference between the argument that we ought to regard morally marginal humans as we do animals, and the argument that, in practice, the difference between the way marginal humans and animals are regarded morally can be exaggerated. This section focuses on the latter point. The best known exponent of the former argument is R. G. Frey. He suggests that the force of the amc means that consistency demands that we either reject animal experimentation, or "condone experiments on humans whose quality of life is exceeded by or equal to that of animals." Since it would be a mistake to forgo the benefits of animal experimentation, we should, according to Frey, choose the latter. This choice is not made "with great glee, and rejoicing, and with great reluctance," but because, "I cannot think of anything at all compelling that cedes all human life of any quality of greater value than animal life of any quality" (Frey, 1983: 115; see also Frey, 2003; 2006).

The main topic of this section is the claim that marginal humans are, in practice, regarded as morally inferior to other humans and, to a certain extent, treated as if they are, although not with the same moral disdain as are animals. The first point to note here is that history is replete with examples of humans being used in experiments as a means to the end of aggregative social benefits. This has included marginal humans, but by no means exclusively so. Indeed, experimentation on humans is still routinely undertaken in the form, for example, of clinical trials. Such use, by itself, is not necessarily morally problematic. Nevertheless, there have been countless "astonishing moral outrages" (Vaughn, 2010: 193) in the history of human experimentation (see McNeill, 1993). The use of humans for various experimental purposes during the Second World War, in Nazi Germany and Japan in particular, represented the nadir here.

The Nazis conducted experiments mainly on Jews but they also used other "inferior" races such as Gypsies, Slavs, and the mentally disabled, many of whom could be classified as marginal. Many experiments—such as testing the limits of human endurance in low-pressure chambers and in iced water—had a military purpose. Others—such as the notorious genetic experiments on twins and sterilization experiments designed to further the Third Reich's "racial hygiene" program—had a wider political and medical purpose (Annas and Grodin, 1992). By the end of the war in 1945, about 85 percent of those disabled German citizens who had been institutionalized before the war had been eliminated (Groce and Marks, 2001: 819).

Experiments on humans in Japan between 1932 and 1945 were, if anything, even more brutal. Conducted largely on Chinese residents for military purposes, these experiments involved such gruesome practices as vivisection without the use of anesthetics, as well as burning, shooting, and the infliction of deliberate infections. Staff referred to the subjects as Maruta, or logs of wood. Somewhat ironically, in the context of this chapter, human and animal experimental subjects were kept together in the same cells (McNeill, 2009: 474).

The discovery of these brutal practices led to the introduction of national and international codes of practice. The Nuremberg Code, drawn up after the trial of Nazi doctors, put forward a set of minimal ethical principles, and these were built upon by the Declaration of Helsinki, a code issued by the World Medical Association in 1964. These included the need for informed voluntary consent, some knowledge of the likely effect of experiments, and a requirement that human subjects should be at liberty to end an experiment at any time (Rollin, 2006: 66–70).

McNeill (2009: 475) claims that these early codes of practice were largely ignored by doctors who regarded the Nazi case as an aberration. It is certainly the case that, since 1945, numerous instances have come to light where the use of humans in experiments has clearly breached what is socially acceptable through a combination of failing to gain consent, the provision of incomplete information, and the withholding of known treatments. There are too many cases to mention here but particularly shocking examples include the Tuskegee syphilis case, conducted between 1932 and 1972 in Tuskegee, Alabama, by the US Public Health Service, which involved studying the natural progression of untreated syphilis in poor, rural black men who thought they were receiving free health care from the US government; the US government's sponsoring of radiation experiments on unsuspecting human subjects between 1944–74; and a study of the natural course of hepatitis in institutionalized children in a New York hospital in 1963 (Vaughn, 2010: 193–94; Rollin, 2006: 72–85).

The response to these revelations was a renewed effort to scrutinize experiments on humans through committee review, and codes of conduct mainly issued by funding bodies at the behest, in the United States, of the federal government. The basic principles behind contemporary codes is a reaffirmation of the central idea that subjects must give their informed, voluntary consent, together with an insistence that risks to subjects must be minimized and must always be offset by the benefits of the research, and that, whatever the expected benefits of an experiment are, experiments involving extreme risk should not be permitted. Interestingly, in the context of this chapter, research on children and the mentally impaired is even more strictly controlled. In the case of the latter, studies are permitted by the National Institutes of Health in the United States provided that consent is secured (either from the individual herself or a proxy), and that the risk is minimal (or if not, that there is a prospect of benefit to the subject herself, or a chance of gaining important knowledge about the subject's own illness) (Vaughn, 2010: 203). Moreover, there is a presumption that nonmarginal adults will be used before children or marginal humans (Rollin, 2006: 93).

In the contemporary world, those uses of humans for experimental purposes that breach the codes of conduct are rare, although even this is disputed by some (Rollin, 2006). Clearly, in the case of marginal humans, there are particular problems with determining consent. Likewise, the treatment of people in the developing world, particularly in AIDS research, is a cause for concern (Vaughn, 2010: 209–10; Luna and Macklin, 2009: 463). More to the point here, though, should coercion or undue influence take place, it would be regarded as morally and legally unacceptable. In other words, there is still a huge gap between what it is socially acceptable to do to marginal humans and what public opinion and government regulation still sanctions in the case of animals. As paragraph 5 of the Declaration of Helsinki states: "In medical research on human subjects, considerations related to the well-being of the human subject should take precedence over the interests of science and society" (World Medical Association, 1964). This clause, of course, represents exactly the opposite position to the one inherent in the moral orthodoxy concerning animals.

We can accept, then, that it is now deemed to be morally and legally unacceptable to use any human in an experiment, without their informed consent, as a means to the end of greater knowledge. This does not mean in general, however, that outside of the sphere of medical research the treatment of marginal and nonmarginal humans is identical, nor that it is widely thought that all of this differential treatment is morally objectionable. In the first place, there is plenty of evidence of the poor care given to the severely retarded, even in an advanced industrial country such as the United States. Institutionalization and a poor level of care, including forced sterilization, were common practice historically and sanctioned by the law (Rose-Ackerman, 1982: 81).

The degree to which marginal humans are still subject to poor treatment (reflecting a perception that they have an inferior moral status), in practice if not by statute, is open to doubt, although only detailed empirical studies can determine the reality. Certainly, the policy of deinstitutionalization and normalization followed by governments in most developed countries (subsequent to the UN "Declaration on the Rights of Mentally Retarded Persons" issued in 1971), has tackled some of the worst examples of poor care and neglect (Anstotz, 1993). However, a high proportion of the most severely retarded do remain institutionalized, and the level of care and compassion shown is variable. Moreover, as Nussbaum (2006: 199–200) points out, children with mental impairments are still often treated as if they have no right of access to public space in addition to being provided with limited educational opportunities.

The poor treatment of the severely retarded described above is universally condemned. In other areas, however, the differential treatment is deemed to be more acceptable, despite the fact that it would seem to reflect a recognition that marginal humans are morally less important. It is not regarded as counterintuitive, for example, to suggest that marginal humans ought to be deprived of an interest in liberty *if* by that is meant greater interference in their lives so that their interest (in not harming themselves) is upheld. It is possible to point to cases where this happens in practice in a noncontroversial way. For example, it was common practice in many parts of the United States for the mildly retarded to be required to seek the guidance of nonmarginal humans before making important decisions such as entering into contracts or getting married (Winkler, 1979: 377).

Similar arguments in support of denying animals and marginal humans an intrinsic interest in liberty can be, and have been, utilized to deny animals and marginal humans an interest in continued life. Letting seriously disabled newborns die does occur on the grounds that their condition is too severe to warrant treatment, and this position is supported by mainstream medical opinion (Kuhse and Singer, 2006: 42, 44–45; Eike-Henner and Kluge, 2009). In this general area of the value of marginal human lives, too, there is some evidence that public opinion, if not legislation, has begun to change. It is much less likely now that a majority of people believe that life is so sacred that it should be preserved even at the cost of a great deal of suffering or lack of quality. For example, public opinion is now much more in favor of assisted suicide than it used to be, and in some cases the law has changed to recognize this. Likewise, although it remains illegal in the United States and elsewhere to kill, or let die, anencephalic infants in order that their organs can be used for transplantation, there has been a public debate about its ethical validity. For example, in 1995 the American Medical Association (AMA) endorsed this course of action, provided that parental approval was forthcoming, only to reverse the policy after public protests (McMahan, 2002: 208).[3] Finally, the issue of whether or not to terminate the life-sustaining treatment of dementia sufferers is likely to become ever more important as the population ages. Here, one sympathizes with Callahan's position that "the expenditure of large amounts of money deliberately to prolong the life of the late-stage demented person would not pass an opportunity cost test or qualify as a high priority matter," and, what is more, overturning the usual bias in favor of treatment is, in the advanced dementia sufferer, a principle already practiced by some (Callahan, 2006: 102).

Of course, there is a huge difference between the argument that we ought to restrict the liberty, or not prolong the lives, of marginal humans in their own interests, and what is done to animals where, with the exception of the euthanasia of animals enduring severe suffering, they suffer and die in order to benefit humans. Thus, the denial of an interest in liberty for animals means that we regard it as legitimate to keep them in captivity, regarding them as our property, and depriving them of self-ownership. Crucially, too, we do this not in their interests but for a variety of human benefits, some more detrimental to the interests of animals than others. Put more starkly, if it is unproblematic morally to regard animals as our property and to treat them as our slaves (on the grounds that they do not possess an intrinsic interest in liberty), then why is it any different for marginal humans?

Similarly, in the case of the lives of marginal humans, we do not think it is intuitively right to kill them, as opposed to letting them die. For many moral philosophers, there is a significant difference ethically between allowing some-one to die and killing them (for a contrary view, see Kushe and Singer, 2006: 44–45). Similarly, the decision not to keep a marginal human alive is based on the consent of the subject or in what is perceived to be her interests. A use-ful contrast, here, is between the modern notion of euthanasia, or "mercy killing," and the version of it practiced by the Third Reich (Macklin, 2006). In the former, the objective is to painlessly terminate the life of an individ-ual who is terminally ill or whose quality of life is below an acceptable level. Consent is to be given by the individual involved or, if not capable of making such a request, by the relatives. In the latter case, the decision to terminate a life was taken by an official body and the criterion was not the welfare of the individual patient but what the value of the individual's life was judged to be, not to the individual herself or her relatives, but to the "community."

In the contemporary world, even in the event of a decision forced by the need to choose between scarce medical resources, a calculation is made based on who can benefit most from treatment and continued life. Doctors may agonize over such quality of life decisions. This is in stark contrast to the treat-ment of animals where animal lives are sacrificed routinely to promote the, sometimes trivial, interests of humans. Having said that, as health care costs rocket as a result of an aging population, life and death decisions concerning marginal humans are increasingly likely to be taken on resource grounds, and may become more routine, and less morally troublesome.

In practice, then, there are differences in the way that marginal and non-marginal humans are treated, *both* in terms of liberty and life, reflecting changing perceptions of their respective moral value. This is a more nuanced position than the one, for instance, adopted by Cochrane (2012), who sug-gests, the reader will remember, that, whilst we treat marginal humans as if they have no right to liberty, we do treat them as if they have a right to life equivalent to that accorded to nonmarginal humans. Of course, a huge gap between what it is deemed acceptable to do to animals and marginal humans remains.

Normative Convergence

Despite the obvious differences in the way that the lives and liberties of mar-ginal humans and animals are regarded, the fact that marginal humans are increasingly being treated differently from nonmarginal humans, and that this reflects a shift in moral attitudes, offers the prospect of some norma-tive convergence between the way we ought to treat marginal humans and animals. There is every possibility, too, that this differential may increase as public morals change further. We may be able to arrive at what McMahan (2002: 206) calls a "convergent assimilation" position, in which "animals and the severely retarded share roughly the same moral status, though the moral status of neither is quite what it has traditionally and popularly been supposed to be" (a view also suggested by Singer, 1980). In other words, perhaps the biggest lesson to be learnt from a consideration of the argument from marginal cases is that "we must accept that animals have a higher moral status than we have previously supposed, while…the moral status of severely retarded human beings is lower than we have assumed" (McMahan, 2002: 228).

The effect of this process of convergent assimilation may provide us with additional support for the enhanced sentience position that was outlined in chapter 8. For example, the fact that inflicting suffering on marginal humans is clearly prohibited morally, whatever the benefits that might accrue to others from so doing, suggests that it is equally wrong to inflict a similar amount of suffering on animals with comparable psychological capacities. Moreover, in the case of the value of lives, "it is doubtful that we can retain our traditional beliefs about the importance of preserving the lives of the severely retarded" (McMahan, 2002: 230). Such a position, of course, undermines the function of the argument from marginal cases for animal rights abolitionists, which is to justify the sanctity of animal life by invoking the sanctity of *all* human life.

McMahan (2002: 230–31), however, steps back from suggesting that the value of a marginal human's life must be identical to that of at least some animals by invoking the relational argument described above. He therefore accepts that it may be justified, only "on occasion," to kill, or let die, a severely retarded human. However, if we reject the relational argument, then consistency demands that the moral worth of animals as described in the enhanced sentience position would also apply to marginal humans. This would mean that whenever human life is at stake, it is morally justified to sacrifice painlessly the life of a marginal human just as it would be justified morally to sacrifice painlessly the life of an animal. Singer (1980: 244), for one, seems to support this view.

Conclusion

If accepted, the amc can justify the abolitionist objectives of the species-egalitarian version of animal rights, although to do so depends upon accepting that all human life is sacred, a position that is being increasingly disputed in practice. There is a case, however, for discarding the amc as a central plank of the animal rights argument, on the grounds that it is intuitively problematic, unnecessary, and probably underestimates the degree to which marginal humans are regarded in practice as having an inferior moral status to other humans. The most robust defense of the differential moral worth of marginal humans and animals is the relational argument. However, because of its counterintuitive implications, it is by no means clear that it ought to be accepted. What a consideration of the amc enables us to do is to consider how much normative convergence in the moral worth of marginal humans and animals is justified. The result, if one dispenses with the relational argument, is a close match between the moral worth of marginal humans and the enhanced sentience model of animal rights sketched in chapter 8.

10

Conclusion

THIS BOOK REPRESENTS an attempt by a political theorist to identify and evaluate a number of positions in the animal ethics debate in the context of the concept of justice and with reference to ideal and nonideal theory. It has been organized around three key questions: can animals be recipients of justice, what do animals gain from being recipients of justice and, finally, what are animals due as a matter of justice? Its conclusions, in brief, are that animals can be recipients of justice, and that the status of justice is such that it should be the preferred discourse of animal advocates. The hard work started with an attempt to answer the third question. I surveyed a number of possible theories of justice for animals and rejected them in favor of an animal rights position. Two variants of this position—the sentience position and the enhanced sentience position—were developed to reflect the need for moral and political philosophers to think in terms of ideal as well as nonideal theory.

The Importance of Justice

One of the distinguishing features of this book is its emphasis on the relationship between justice and the well-being of animals. Most of the animal ethics literature has either ignored the concept of justice or merely assumed that justice and morality are synonymous. It is clear that there is no obstacle to animals being regarded as recipients of justice. A distributive paradigm is consistent with this ambition. Moreover, although contractarian theories have traditionally denied animals this status, theories of justice do not end with contractarian versions, and we are quite entitled to consider alternatives. The fact that, counterintuitively, marginal humans and future generations will also have to be excluded from such theories, adds to the case for this move.

Determining that animals can be recipients of justice does not tell us what they are due as a matter of justice. Nor does it tell us whether, and to what extent, animals can benefit from being regarded as recipients of justice. In other words, why bother to couch the debate about animals in the discourse of justice as opposed to morality or ethics? After all, contractarian thinkers such as Rawls imply that direct duties can be owed to animals independently of justice. However, one of the central claims of this book is that animals benefit enormously from being regarded as the kind of beings that can be recipients of justice, rather than being merely morally considerable.

The benefit for animals of being part of the discourse of justice relates to the status of the concept. The fact that a case of injustice is regarded as something that ought to be remedied urgently means that it is more likely to entail legal compulsion. So, whilst it is possible theoretically to conceive of a moral realm independently of justice, it is doubtful if any direct moral duties to animals, equivalent to or greater in weight than those attached to justice claims, can, in practice, be established. In actuality, in other words, excluding animals from a theory of justice amounts, at best, to the claim that we have very limited direct duties to some animals, and, at worst, that we only have indirect duties to them. Subsuming our obligations to animals in the language of justice avoids this outcome.

Indirect duties to animals come about when it is in the interests of humans to protect them. Such a position, even if it is based on virtue ethics, does not constitute a theory of *justice* for animals because it does not recognize their intrinsic value, that it matters morally what is done to them, irrespective of the consequences for others. Owing direct duties to animals, in turn, is a necessary, but not sufficient, characteristic for including animals within a theory of justice. Whilst there are some benefits in adopting an indirect duty position, not least because it avoids the conflict, endemic in animal ethics, between human and animal interests, it is deeply unsatisfactory.

Not only does an indirect duty position invoke a counterintuitive ethical stance that we owe no direct duties to animals, but it is also often the case that human interests do not coincide with those of animals. Moreover, the attempt to adapt virtue ethics is problematic. It is vulnerable to conflicts between virtues, and depends upon the, dubious, validity of the claim that behaving virtuously toward animals ultimately benefits the virtuous person. At most, then, an indirect duty position can be utilized only as a complement to one deriving from a recognition that we owe direct duties to animals.

Animals and Ideal Theory

Much of the book focuses on what animals are due as a matter of justice. In terms of ideal theory, the animal ethics debate is, more often than not, couched in terms of two extremes. At the one end of the continuum is the animal welfare ethic. At the other end are theories of animal rights. Most animal rights philosophers, and indeed their opponents, too, regard the ideal theory, the goal to which they are aiming, as abolitionist. This is based on a moral egalitarianism that suggests that animals, like humans, have a right to life and liberty. A central concern of this book is to challenge the ideal efficacy of both of those extremes. This is achieved through the adoption of a moral position predicated on a right-based ethic, an interest theory of rights, the application of the equal consideration of interests principle, and a capacity-oriented, rather than a relational, ethic.

The animal welfare ethic is right to draw attention to the fact that humans and animals differ in ways that are morally relevant. I broadly agree with what has become the moral consensus that normal adult humans possess a greater interest in life and liberty than most animals, and that this ought to be reflected in a calculation of the respective moral importance of humans and animals. However, advocates of the animal welfare ethic then take a wrong turn. They conclude from this that *all* human interests are more important morally than *all* animal interests. In other words, they assume that, because most humans have a greater interest in liberty and continued life than most animals, they have a greater interest in other things, too. But this does not follow. Indeed, all things being equal, it is difficult to avoid the conclusion that an animal's interest in avoiding suffering is equivalent to a human's interest in avoiding suffering.

This conclusion—that some animal interests are equivalent in strength to those of humans—is not strong enough to support the species-egalitarian version of animal rights that tends to dominate in the animal rights community and which is also the version challenged by the opponents of animal rights. It is a valid claim that suffering of the same intensity and duration has the same moral weight whether endured by humans or animals. It is also a valid claim that the interest that animals have in not suffering can be translated into a right not to suffer at the hands of humans, so that if humans have such a right, so do animals. However, this does not mean that the moral status of animals is equivalent to humans so that, to all intents and purposes, animals ought to be treated as if they are persons. As a result, the claim that it is our use of animals per se, irrespective of what is done to them whilst they are being used, that is the problem with the current way we regard animals is mistaken.

An attempt to rescue the abolitionist animal rights position can be, and has been, undertaken by invoking the argument from marginal cases (amc). That is, if we persist in treating marginal humans as if they are nonmarginal in moral terms, despite their lack of those cognitive capacities that are deemed to be necessary for personhood, then we should also accord the same moral worth to animals that also lack these capacities. It is not clear, however, that the amc can carry the weight that many exponents of animal rights require of it. There are, as we saw, various reasons for treating marginal humans differently from animals, some of which—the adoption of a relational position in particular—would seem to be credible. In addition, the amc, or at least the bioconditional version of it, which suggests that we should treat marginal humans in a similar fashion to the way animals are currently treated, is counterintuitive.

In addition, the force of the categorical version of the amc is undermined somewhat by the fact that marginal humans are, to some extent, regarded as morally inferior to nonmarginal humans in practice. This offers the prospect of a normative convergence whereby marginal humans and animals ought to be treated differently than they are at present. Such a convergence provides support for my own preferred ideal theory of justice for animals, which, whilst recognizing the morally important differences between nonmarginal humans and animals, does not condemn either animals or marginal humans to suffer at the hands of humans.

I confirm, then, that the species egalitarian version of animal rights fails as an ethical theory. It is not, in other words, what we ought, in the moral sense of ought, to be striving for. What is noticeable, too, is the huge gap between the animal welfare and species-egalitarian positions. Whatever the ethical validity of the latter—and, as we have seen, it has been challenged in this book—I argued, in addition, that it also fails as an ideal theory because it does not pass the Rawlsian realistic utopia test. That is, the species-egalitarian version of animal rights, irrespective of whether it is a valid ethical position, requires too much of human beings, necessitating a transformation of what would seem to be our natural tendency to put our species, at least in some instances, first morally. That is, it fails to take into account the shared heritage of humanity that, from time immemorial, has used animals. In the language of communitarianism, it fails to take into account the history of narrative life stories. As MacIntyre (1981: 204–5) astutely remarks: "I inherit from the past of my family, my city, my tribe, my nation, a variety of debts, inheritances, rightful expectations and obligations. These constitute the given of my life, my moral starting point." Animals have certainly played a part in these narrative life stories, but they have never been the moral equal of humans.[1]

Animals and Nonideal Theory

It should go without saying that an ideal theory of animal rights, whether it be the species-egalitarian version or the enhanced sentience version, is not going to be achieved in practice in the short or medium term, if indeed ever. The practical impact, particularly of the former, presents the opponents of animal rights with a position that is very easy to attack and very difficult to defend. An illustration of this was the furor surrounding Ingrid Newkirk's statement that "a rat is a pig is a dog is a boy" (McCabe, 1985). Whether or not this was actually what Newkirk said[2], the fact that this extreme version of the species-egalitarian position was met, by many, with incredulity, is indicative of its utopian character.

The major theme of this book is that denying the comparison Newkirk allegedly sought to draw does not spell the death knell of the animal rights project. The preferred ideal theory developed in this book, for instance, recognizes the superior moral position of humans, and yet this does not mean sacrificing a rights-based ethic for animals. Equally importantly, it has been shown that even if we dispense, for now, with ideal theorizing, a nonideal theory of justice for animals can also be based on rights. The sentience position developed in this book recognizes that humans have interests that are not shared equally by most, if any, animals, and yet insists that in the case of those interests—in suffering—that animals do share equally with humans—it is not inappropriate to accord rights to them.

The value of the debate surrounding nonideal theory is that it helps to elucidate the oft-made observation in political theory that normative theorizing should not run too far ahead of what is likely to be politically and socially acceptable. This is particularly appropriate to animal rights. Throughout this book I have tried to make a distinction between the ethical correctness of arguments and their social and political efficacy. Discussing both of these dimensions is essential for a comprehensive *political* theory of animal protection. I am eager for animal advocates to avoid being what Swift and White (2008: 55) describe as "would-be philosopher kings, inpatient of the moral myopia of their fellow citizens, contemptuous of popular opinion and disappointed not to find themselves in the utopian polity outlined in Plato's Republic, a polity where an intellectual elite is trained from birth to rule over the ignorant masses."

This concern for social and political reality, however, should not be confused with a moral relativism. We can reject Miller's claim that there "can be no conclusive arguments in political theory" (1976: 343), but nevertheless retain some of his skepticism about normative theorizing undertaken without reference to social, political, and economic realities. It *is* being claimed in this book, then, that any realistic, and theoretically proficient, set of moral arguments must be aware of the likelihood of being acceptable. In this sense, as Wolff (2008: 188) remarks, the "task for the political philosopher is not to design the best possible world, but to design the best possible world *starting from here.*"

Given the need to think in terms of nonideal theory, this book has surveyed various contenders before settling on what I have described as the sentience position as the ideal nonideal theory of justice for animals. I have here followed the advice of Robeyns (2008: 348), who speculates that "we need to develop a new set of nonideal principles of justice, which are developed by adding layers of relevant facts from the nonideal world to the ideal theory, using the theoretical resources that are available in the ideal theory." This choice of the sentience position is, of course, contentious, criticizable both by those who think it is unrealistically optimistic *and* those who think it does not go far enough. Both objections are rejected. The sentience position is chosen with due regard to Rawls's useful criteria for a valid nonideal theory. In particular, the sentience position seeks to remove the most grievous injustice—animal suffering—which, it is argued, does not inhibit the movement toward the ideal position.

The adoption of the sentience position is contentious not least because it dispenses with the animal welfare ethic as the most appropriate nonideal theory of justice for animals. Animal welfare, though, has one key problem: it allows for the complete trading off of fundamental animal interests if by so doing a significant enough human benefit accrues. This means that animal suffering, when it is not deemed to be unnecessary, is rife. It is only by granting a right to animals not to have suffering inflicted on them by humans that this trade-off becomes morally illegitimate. Utilizing the discourse of rights is also politically advantageous. Here, Campbell's (2006: 3) assertion is worth repeating again: "There is little chance that any cause will be taken seriously in the contemporary world that cannot be expressed as a demand for the recognition or enforcement of rights of one sort or another."

To conclude, animals deserve justice, and can benefit enormously from it. What animals are due as a matter of justice reflects primarily their interest in not suffering, which is, all things being equal, equivalent to a human interest in not suffering. Given that this human interest is best served by the granting of a right, consistency demands that animals are also accorded such a right. Animals are due much more than this because they also have an interest in continued life. However, given the truism that "Any theory that asks people to be moral saints is doomed to be politically ineffective, and it would be naive to expect otherwise" (Donaldson and Kymlicka, 2011: 252), eradicating the suffering of animals is the goal to which animal advocates ought to direct their attention. As a matter of justice, too, this goal should be an obligation of the state.

Notes

CHAPTER 1

1. The exceptions are my own earlier work, particularly Garner (2005), as well as Cochrane (2010, 2012), Donaldson and Kymlicka (2011), and Nussbaum (2004, 2006).

2. Dobson (1998: 11) makes the same point in a different context when he writes that "my aim would be to encourage political theorists, and particularly, here, theorists of justice, to the view that their reflections on social justice will not be complete until they take the issues raised by environmental sustainability into account."

3. Since Rowlands originally wrote this in 1998, a fourth approach, based on virtue ethics, has appeared (see chapter 4 in this volume). In the second edition of his text, Rowlands (2009) does engage with virtue ethics, but still prefers an adaptation of Rawls as his chosen model of animal ethics.

CHAPTER 2

1. A direct duty to animals can be contrasted with an indirect duty. According to an indirect duty view, the protection of animals does not come about because they are regarded as having intrinsic value, but because (some) humans regard the protection of animals as being part of a good (human) life. Thus, whereas a direct moral object is "something *to* which moral consideration is paid" an indirect moral object is "something *about* or *concerning* which moral consideration is paid" (Morris, 1998: 191).

2. An alternative approach is to challenge Rawls's view that *all* animals do not have a sense of justice. If this can be established, then we can conceive of animals being, at least in a hypothetical sense, participants in drawing up the contractual agreement. Elliot (1984: 98–7) seeks to argue for this on the grounds that some animals, like some humans, pair for life, are faithful spouses and parents, and show loyalty and courage. The problem with this approach is that few species of animals seem to have these characteristics. Moreover, it is contentious, to say the least, that having them constitutes a sense of justice in the way that Rawls has in mind.

3. Rowlands takes this distinction from Kymlicka (1993). Hobbes was clear that the social contract could not include animals. "To make covenants with brute beasts," he wrote, "is impossible, because not understanding our speech, they understand not, nor accept of any translation of right, nor can translate any right to another; and without mutual acceptation, there is no covenant" (quoted in Fellenz, 2007: 107). A contemporary version of the Hobbesian contract is provided by David Gauthier. For him (1986: 4), morality "can be generated as a rational constraint from the non-moral premises of rational choice." This will be achieved, he argues (6), "without incorporating into the premises of our argument any of the moral conceptions that emerge in our conclusions." It follows, therefore, (268) that: "Animals, the unborn, the congenitally handicapped and defective, fall beyond the pale of a morality tied to mutuality." Narveson (1983) excludes animals on the same grounds. He writes: (58) "Contractarianism leaves animals out of it … They are, by and large, to be dealt with in terms of our self-interest, unconstrained by the terms of hypothetical agreements with them. Just exactly what our interest in them is may, of course, be matter for debate; but that those are the terms on which we may deal with them is, on this view of morality, overwhelmingly indicated."

4. That said, I am grateful for a reviewer's, surely correct, retort that if we do include animals as beneficiaries of principles of justice the chances of a contractor turning out to be human is very small, given the degree to which the number of animals dwarfs those of humans. As a result, I agree that the contractors are unlikely to accept the solution I suggested.

5. It has been pointed out to me, too, that exactly the same argument is utilized by defenders of bullfighting in Spain—particularly after its abolition in Catalonia—and other countries.

CHAPTER 3

1. There is another dimension to this debate that is relevant to the question of animals. Needs due to maltreatment are clearly relevant in the case of animals, and therefore if we take, for example, Thomas Pogge's line (2008), then it makes sense to say that we have obligations of justice to avoid maltreating them. But there are needs caused by neither maltreatment nor personal failure. For example, Pogge has been criticized for failing to account for our obligations to human victims—of, for example, disease, flood, or tsunami—to whom he thinks we have no duty to assist as a matter of justice because we have not caused them (Brooks, 2007). Since a great deal of animal suffering is caused by nature (rather than personal failure or maltreatment), the implication is that we do not owe duties of justice in such cases to assist those animals who suffer through no fault of human beings. One implication of this position is that it would involve us having radically different obligations to wild animals since they, as opposed to domesticated animals, are more likely to suffer from the dictates of nature.

CHAPTER 4

1. Utilizing environmental arguments would, of course, only justify prohibiting factory farming, and not necessarily animal agriculture in general. Moreover, invoking health grounds for desisting from eating meat does not necessarily translate into a justification for vegetarianism. As Hare (1997 236) argues, it is consistent with reducing meat intake and being more selective in the kind of meat eaten. He describes such an approach as constituting what he calls "demi-vegetarianism."

2. Satz (2009), for one, argues that, in actual fact, humans only protect animals when it is in their interests to do so. As I will argue in more detail in chapter 5, however, this is not quite correct. An indirect duty approach does not recognize that we have direct duties to animals. By contrast, the widely accepted animal welfare ethic does accept that animals have interests worthy of protection. The fact that these interests may be overridden, as they are to a greater or lesser extent, does not undermine the acceptance that we owe direct duties to animals. Moreover, according to the animal welfare ethic, the interests of animals do take priority when it is deemed that there is no significant benefit to be had by humans in overriding them. What counts as "significant," of course, will vary from time to time and from country to country.

3. It is useful at this point to clarify what is meant by intrinsic value. As O'Neil (2003) notes, intrinsic value is sometimes defined in terms of objective value, as opposed to the noninstrumental value definition that we have employed up to this point. That is, we can make a distinction between intrinsic and instrumental value, on the one hand, and objective and subjective value, on the other. In this latter sense, intrinsic value can be either objective or subjective. In the objective sense, animals have intrinsic value if they possess value independently of the valuation of the human valuers. In defense of this objective value version of according intrinsic value to animals, it is important to note that it is possible to distinguish between the fact that a moral statement about animals is "by definition a 'human-based-interest' statement" and the claim that "none of my statements about the world have any independence or informative content outside the fact of my humanity" (Vincent, 1998: 133). In other words, the fact that the valuer of the moral status of animals is human does not exclude the possibility that animals have intrinsic value—a value, that is, existing independently of the human valuer. The alternative to such an objectivist view of value is a subjectivist position that holds that the source of all value lies with those doing the valuing. By definition, adopting such a subjectivist position would mean that, since humans are doing the valuing, if they ceased to exist there would be nothing left of value in the world. However, as O'Neil (2003) also notes, the case for intrinsic value defined as noninstrumental value does not depend upon accepting the metaethical claim of objectivism. To insist that it does is to confuse the source and the object of value. As he points out: "That humans are the source of

value is not incompatible with their assigning value to a world in which they do not exist." In other words, the ethical claim that animals have noninstrumental value, that they should not be treated merely as a means to the satisfaction of human wants, is independent from the meta-ethical claim that the source of all value is human beings. The fact that we do not have to establish the viability of an objectivist case for value in order to justify the claim that animals have intrinsic value (in the noninstrumental sense) is important. It further strengthens the argument that animals do have intrinsic value, and therefore should not be treated in an instrumental manner.

CHAPTER 5

1. I add this caveat because, for some philosophers, cruelty and unnecessary suffering are synonymous. See, for example, Steinbock (1978: 250).
2. I am assuming in this book that animals can actually experience pain, and will not repeat the extremely strong evidence for it here. For a review of the evidence, see Palmer (2010: 11–15), and Rowlands (2002: 5–9).
3. Some environmental ethicists also seek to accord moral standing to nonsentient parts of nature, Baxter, (2005) and Taylor (1986) to name but two. I do not want to pursue this debate here. I am assuming that sentience is sufficient for moral standing. Whether or not it is necessary is another question. Two points are worth making. The first is that granting moral standing to those entities that are nonsentient does not, of course, effect the granting of moral standing to those animals who are. Secondly, few of those who want to accord moral standing to those entities that are not sentient would want to claim that their interests are as morally weighty as those who are sentient. In the words of Warwick Fox (1984: 199), "cows scream louder than carrots."
4. It is true that courts in Britain and the United States have sometimes questioned the moral legitimacy of killing healthy animals for trivial reasons (Yeates, 2010). I have also been told that in Austria it is now an offense to kill an animal for a trivial reason, even when it is undertaken painlessly. In this case, the law goes beyond what the animal welfare ethic prescribes.
5. As I will show later in this chapter, Rachels rejects both radical speciesism and mild speciesism. Other scholars have made similar distinctions. For instance, Midgley (1983: 13) distinguishes between the "absolute dismissal" and the "relative dismissal" of animal interests.
6. To get a more accurate sense of the morphology of personhood, Michael Tooley (2009: 133) lists seventeen properties it possesses.
7. One possible additional argument here from the defenders of the animal welfare ethic is that suffering is greater for those whose lives are of greater value. This claim is discussed in chapter 8.

CHAPTER 6

1. Of course, one might argue (as Frey, 1980 does) that animals do not possess interests. It is not my intention to discuss this issue here, so it is assumed that animals do possess interests. One argument supporting this assumption that can be mentioned is that if animals do not possess interests on the grounds of their cognitive state, then neither do at least some marginal humans. Given that we intuitively regard marginal humans as beings with interests, it would be inconsistent to regard animals as lacking them. For a discussion of this issue, see Cochrane (2012: 33–6).

2. DeGrazia puts forward a position that he argues is a cross between utilitarianism and rights. He describes the debate between the two as "much ado about little," (DeGrazia, 1999: 112) a view that I do not share.

3. My position differs from Cochrane's in two principal ways. In the first place, I offer a nonideal theory of animal rights (in the form of the sentience position), which, as I will show, is suboptimal in ethical terms. Second, as I will show in chapter 9, Cochrane uses the argument from marginal cases in a way that I regard as potentially inconsistent in order to justify according to animals a right to life. I also think that Cochrane underestimates the degree to which philosophers advocating animal rights have done so by utilizing an interest-based argument. Feinberg (1980) is one such account. In addition, Rachels should probably be regarded as an advocate of an interest-based theory of animal rights. Even Steve Sapontzis (1987), who adopts a species-egalitarian version of animal rights, invokes interests. He writes (74) that: "All and only beings with interests can have moral rights," and does consider calling his position "interest liberation." What Cochrane does, unlike Sapontzis, is to draw what I think are the correct conclusions from the adoption of an interest-based theory of animal rights.

4. We have already encountered attempts to apply a relational ethic in this book, in the context of contractarian theories of justice discussed in chapter 2, and the care ethic discussed in chapter 3. I will have cause to discuss it again in later chapters.

5. Donaldson and Kymlicka (2011: 180) complicate this simplistic dichotomy by arguing that the notion of sovereign communities of wild animals provides a "far richer moral notion than simply 'letting them be,'" on the grounds that it involves consideration of when it is right to intervene in wild animal communities, and, more specifically, the degree to which risks to wild animal communities ought to be minimized. Despite this, if the distinctions they make are to have any real meaning, the default position surely is that we should not intervene.

CHAPTER 7

1. It is not my intention to provide a comprehensive account of utilitarianism as it relates to animal ethics. There is, for instance, an extensive debate about the

degree to which the adoption of a vegetarian lifestyle results in fewer animals being killed, and what a utilitarian should do if it does not. I do not touch upon this debate here. For those who are interested in this debate, see Garrett, 2007 and Nobis, 2002, both of whom provide a useful summary of the literature, and Frey (1983: 206–14; 2004), who argues that vegetarianism is not the best option for those concerned about the well-being of farm animals, and Singer (1980: 335–7), who argues that it is.

2. In an article originally published in 1974, Singer (1989; 155) initially adopted this approach, but in a later work (1980) he recognized that critics such as Regan were right to point out that all of the consequences of an end to eating animals need to be considered, and not just the trivial one of taste.

3. Having said that, there is a utilitarian case to be made against animal experimentation. Somewhat ironically, it is Tom Regan who probably provides the best account. This can be found in the context of a debate with Carl Cohen (Cohen and Regan, 2001: 297–306). Although somewhat loath to provide such a defense since his rights-based theory renders human benefits from animal experimentation morally irrelevant, Regan engages in a utilitarian analysis to challenge what he sees as the factual errors in Cohen's defense of the benefits accruing from animal experimentation. These relate to an underestimation of the number of animals used, a downplaying of the number of higher mammals used, an inaccurate account of the care animals receive whilst they are being used, and, most importantly of all, an exaggeration of the human benefits of animal experimentation.

4. Singer (1999: 283) claims that "the text of *Animal Liberation* is not utilitarian." Rather, "it was specifically intended to appeal to readers who were concerned about equality, or justice, or fairness, irrespective of the precise nature of their commitment." This can be accepted, as can the pre-redistributive equality principle put forward by Singer. Indeed, as I will show in chapter 8, it forms the basis of my preferred version of animal rights. It is the case, however, that in subsequent publications Singer does lay his utilitarian cards on the table. For example, he states in an article published after the first edition of *Animal Liberation*: "I am a utilitarian. I am also a vegetarian. I am a vegetarian *because* I am a utilitarian" (1980: 325).

5. The fact that the capabilities approach is a version of a rights approach is confirmed when Nussbaum (2001: 1538) writes that "we still need to use the language of rights to emphasize that people have a justified claim to the capabilities on my list. But the language of rights needs articulation and clarification via the language of capabilities." This position is confirmed in her mature capabilities theory, where she argues (2006: 7) that it "is one species of a human rights approach."

6. This term is borrowed from Van De Veer, 1979b: 65–6.

7. The species-egalitarian version of animal rights claims that the use of nonhuman animals should be abolished because animals have (or should have) rights. I do recognize that abolitionism can also be justified on other grounds, too. For instance, it might be argued that the use of animals for human benefit should be

abolished because it is unnecessary, or that to do so will maximize happiness or preference satisfaction.

8. Even Regan, somewhat ironically, admits this. Thus, in a lifeboat case, where one individual has to be thrown overboard if all the others are to survive, Regan thinks that if a dog is one of the individuals it would be necessary morally to sacrifice him. This is on the grounds that "death for the dog... though a harm, is not comparable to the harm that death would be for any of the humans" (Regan, 1984: 324). As has been pointed out (see Jamieson, 1990: 358), this would seem to be inconsistent with Regan's principle of equal inherent value. Of course, it may be that Regan—unlike, it seems, thinkers such as Francione (2008), Dunayer (2004), and Cavalieri (2001), for instance—does not hold to a species-egalitarian position, in the sense that I have defined it. The problem with this interpretation, however, is that if it is accurate then Regan cannot logically draw the abolitionist conclusions he does. For if the rights of humans are, in most cases, stronger than those of nonhuman animals, it may be the case that the use of, and killing of, animals is justified under certain circumstances as morally permissible. This, of course, is exactly what Regan is arguing in the passage cited above.

9. Other uses of animals have been abolished, such as, in Britain, fur farming, hunting with hounds, and the testing of cosmetics on animals. In the first two, however, this is not equivalent to a ban on the killing of fur-bearing animals or the killing of foxes. In the latter, there is no ban on the import of cosmetic products that have been tested on animals in other countries.

10. Robeyns (2008) appears to approve of the "mythical" nature of ideal theory, arguing that it does not really matter if the principles it establishes are unlikely to ever exist in practice. Taking my lead from Rawls's definition, I argue that such a theory is either an inadequate ideal theory or not an ideal theory at all.

CHAPTER 8

1. Two general points are appropriate here. In the first place, it is correct to say that the label "sentience position" might also be sensibly applied to other approaches. For example, abolitionist animal rightists can also insist that their view is based on the claim that all sentient beings should have rights. As a matter of fact, as we have seen, this describes Francione's position but not Regan's mature position. I am using the label in a particular way, to accord a right not to suffer to sentient animals. Secondly, the formulation of the sentience position I have provided leaves a number of important questions unanswered. In particular, it does not enter into a discussion of whether we are obliged to act positively to prevent animals from suffering, as opposed to avoiding inflicting suffering on them ourselves. Should we, for instance, prevent animals from being harmed by other animals, or from suffering as a result of injury? Here, as I argued in chapter 6, I think we can profitably invoke a relational ethic. My main concern, as it has been throughout this

book, is to establish to what extent it is wrong to raise and kill animals for food and for experimental purposes, and for that purpose establishing a negative right of noninterference is sufficient.

2. It is being assumed here that animals can suffer, but, of course, the types and levels of suffering will depend upon the species involved. Taking this into account is consistent with an ethical position based on deriving moral conclusions from particular characteristics. It is recognized that these characteristics, and the moral principles deriving from them, can differ among and within species. In terms of humans, this is exactly what the argument from marginal cases does. Even amongst "normal" adult humans, we can make normative decisions based on levels of cognitive capacities. For instance, a right to a university education only applies to those with the intellectual capacity to benefit from it. Before anyone objects that this would lead to a perfectionist theory of justice, however, it is also being claimed here that all normal adult humans have a level of cognitive ability that far surpasses that of even the most intellectually able nonhuman animal. It is credible to claim that all such humans have an interest in life and liberty.

3. On the grounds that no rights are inviolable, we should consider whether it is ever appropriate to override an animal's right not to suffer if human lives are at stake. Of course, there might be circumstances when we would probably answer in the affirmative. It is important, however, to note how the sentience position contextualizes this decision. Because we have argued that an animal's interest in avoiding suffering is, all things being equal, equivalent to a human's interest in avoiding the same degree of suffering, then we need to ask whether it would be appropriate to sacrifice a human's right not to suffer as well as an animal's. At the very least, most people would want to think long and hard before accepting that such a right, in any particular circumstance, should be sacrificed.

4. Using the words "inferior" or "superior" in connection with moral status is misleading. The argument that animals have less of an interest than humans in life or liberty is not some kind of punishment meted out because animals are inferior. Rather, the aim of the exercise is to attach moral entitlements to those who can benefit from them. To put it simply, if one thinks, as I do not, that animals have no interest in continued life, and therefore cannot be harmed by death, there is not much to be gained by granting a moral entitlement such as a right to life.

5. Hon-Lam Li's analysis does not include the idea that rights can act as side constraints. The enhanced sentience position does not regard animals as having a right to life or liberty, and so trade-offs are less problematic. However, I argue that animals do have a right not to have suffering inflicted on them by humans, and therefore this cannot be traded off in the way that an animal's interest in continued life can be.

6. By contrast, those who hold the position that it is wrong to use animals, irrespective of what is done to them whilst they are being used, would presumably oppose the use of animals for their cells, however benign the procedure, and even though this might result in the end of the raising and killing of animals for food.

7. Palmer (2010: 129) makes the point that controversies surrounding the different methods of capital punishment illustrate just how hard it is to establish that there is such a thing as painless killing. Whilst accepting this point, I would want to maintain that it is possible to distinguish between pain, suffering, and death in a way that is morally significant.

8. It has been pointed out that the "five freedoms" may actually be contradictory. For example, complete behavioral freedom may conflict with freedom from injury and disease (Appleby, 1999: 38). For our purposes here, however, this is irrelevant.

9. As Haynes (2008: xii) points out, the Brambell Report "was taken as a mandate for animal scientists to undertake a study of animal welfare."

CHAPTER 9

1. It should be pointed out here that the term "marginal" human has fallen out of favor now, being widely regarded as offensive and derogatory. In addition, I am grateful to a reviewer who points out that the term "marginal cases" does tend to give the impression that they are not important. This reflects the fact, perhaps, that the term was introduced by Jan Narveson (1977), an opponent of its validity. As a result, alternative phrases, such as the "argument from species overlap," (Horta, 2010: 243; Wilson, 2005) have been suggested. I appreciate these points, but agree with Dombrowski (1997: 2) that the term "marginal" remains useful not least because it enables the reader to follow the extensive debate, where marginal is the usual label, and because it encompasses all of the humans we want to consider, including the congenitally mentally disabled, those who have acquired mental deficiencies, and infants.

2. Tooley (2009: 135) suggests a way, which he ultimately rejects, of distinguishing morally between the cases of using contraception and abortion. To do this he suggests distinguishing between "passive" and "active" potentialities, so "while an unfertilized human ovum together with a neighbouring spermatozoon are, in a sense, potentially a person, the potentiality is a passive one, since it requires outside intervention to start a process that will ultimately give rise to a person." By contrast, once the fetus is created, "an active potentiality for personhood" exists. One reason for rejecting this distinction, he suggests, is that in neither case is there a fully active potentiality since the fetus requires outside interference—in the form of the provision of a safe environment—if it is to survive.

3. The organs of anencephalic infants deteriorate soon after death and it is prudent to remove them prior to death if they are to be suitable for transplantation. The AMA's decision occurred in the context of a debate following a well-publicized case in Florida in 1992, where the parents of an anencephalic infant agreed to let her organs be used for transplants, but Florida law would not allow it (Rachels, 2009: 16).

CHAPTER 10

1. I am not here seeking to defend the normative claim that, because animals have not figured as moral equals in the traditions, values, and customs of any society, they *ought* not to do so now or in the future. All I am claiming is that, however ethically valid, the species-egalitarian version of animal rights is made more difficult, if not impossible, because of these prevailing traditions, values, and customs. One academic illustration of the difficulty of establishing concern for animals as one of our key moral preoccupations is provided by Michael Sandel's long, accessible, and much admired treatise on justice, in which the author extols the virtues of including moral questions within the ambit of justice. Significantly, he does not once mention the question of our treatment of animals (Sandel, 2009).

2. Newkirk is the founder and president of People for the Ethical Treatment of Animals, America's largest animal rights organization. Another version of Newkirk's comment has her as saying, "When it comes to feelings like hunger or thirst, pain, joy—a rat is a pig is a dog is a boy." (http://www.hbo.com/documentaries/i-am-an-animal-ingrid-newkirk-peta/interview/ingrid-newkirk.htmlhttp://www.hbo.com/documentaries/i-am-an-animal-ingrid-newkirk-peta/interview/ingrid-newkirk.html). This interpretation is fully in line with the sentience position I have advocated in this book. Interestingly, too, PETA is regularly attacked by abolitionists such as Francione (Francione and Garner, 2010: 30–8) for being an advocate of New Welfarism in the sense that it advocates an animal welfare means to an animal rights end.

Bibliography

Aaltola, E., 2005, "Animal Ethics and Interest Conflicts," *Ethics and the Environment*, 10, 1: 19–48.

Abbey, R., 2007, "Rawlsian Resources for Animal Ethics," *Ethics and the Environment*, 12, 1–22.

Anderson, E., 2004, "Animal Rights and the Values of Nonhuman Life," in C. Sunstein and M. Nussbaum (eds.) *Animal Rights: Current Debates and New Directions*, 277–98, New York: Oxford University Press.

Anstotz, C., 1993, "Profoundly Intellectually Disabled Humans and the Great Apes: A Comparison," in P. Cavalieri, and P. Singer (eds.) *The Great Ape Project: Equality Beyond Humanity*, London: Fourth Estate: 158–72.

Appleby, M., 1999, *What Should We Do About Animal Welfare?* Oxford: Blackwell.

Arneson, R., 1998, "The Priority of the Right Over the Good Rides Again," in P. Kelly, ed., *Impartiality, Neutrality and Justice. Re-reading Brian Barry's Justice as Impartiality*, Edinburgh: Edinburgh University Press, 60–86.

Attfield, R., 2003, *Environmental Ethics*, Cambridge: Polity.

Barry, B., 1989, *Theories of Justice*, Hemel Hempstead: Harvester-Wheatsheaf.

Barry, B., 1991, "Humanity and Justice in Global Perspective" in B. Barry, *Liberty and Justice: Essays in Political Theory 2*, Oxford: Oxford University Press, 182–210.

Barry, B., 1995, *Justice as Impartiality*, Oxford: Clarendon Press.

Barry, B., 1998, "Something in the Disputation not Unpleasant," in P. Kelly, ed., *Impartiality, Neutrality and Justice. Re-reading Brian Barry's Justice as Impartiality*, Edinburgh: Edinburgh University Press, 186–257.

Barry, B. 1999, "Sustainability and Intergenerational Justice" in A. Dobson, ed., *Fairness and Futurity: Essays on Environmental Sustainability and Social Justice*, Oxford: Oxford University Press, 93–117.

Barry, B., 2001, *Culture and Equality: An Egalitarian Critique of Multiculturalism*, Cambridge: Polity.

Baxter, B., 2000, "Ecological Justice and Justice as Impartiality," *Environmental Politics*, 9, 3, 43–64.

Baxter, B., 2005, *A Theory of Ecological Justice*, London: Routledge.

Becker, L., 1983, "The priority of Human Interests" in H. Miller and W. Williams, eds., *Ethics and Animals*, CliftonNJ: Humana Press: 225–42.

Becker, L., 2005, "Reciprocity, Justice and Disability," *Ethics*, 116, 1: 9–39.

Bell, L., 2001, "Abusing Children—Abusing Animals," *Journal of Social Work*, 1, 2: 223–34.

Bell, D., 2002, "How Can Political Liberals be Environmentalists," *Political Studies*, 50: 703–24.

Benson, J., 1978, "Duty and the Beast," *Philosophy*, 53, 206, 529–49.

Bentham, J., 1948, *An Introduction to the Principles of Morals and Legislation*. New York: Hafner Press.

Benton, T., 1993, *Natural Relations: Ecology, Social Justice and Animal Rights*. London: Verso.

Blum, L., 1988, "Gilligan and Kohlberg: Implications for Moral Theory," *Ethics*, 98, 3.

Brambell Report, 1965, Technical Advisory Committee on Intensive Husbandry Systems (Brambell Committee), MAFF 386/42.

Brody, B., 2001, "Defending Animal Research: An International Perspective," in Paul, E. and Paul, J., *Why Animal Experimentation Matters: The Use of Animals in Medical Research*, New Brunswick: Transaction Publishers: 131–47.

Brooks, T., 2007, "Punishing States that Cause Global Poverty," *William Mitchell Law Review* 33, 2: 519–32.

Bryant, T., 2007, "Similarity or Difference as a basis for Justice: Must Animals Be Like Humans to Be Legally Protected From Humans," *Law and Contemporary Problems*, 70: 207: 207–22.

Bubeck, D., 1998, "Care, Justice and the Good," in P. Kelly, ed., *Impartiality, Neutrality and Justice: Re-Reading Brian Barry's Justice as Impartiality*, Edinburgh: Edinburgh University Press, 154–75.

Buchanan, A., 1990, "Justice as Reciprocity Versus Subject-Centred Justice," *Philosophy and Public Affairs*, 19, 3, 227–52.

Callahan, D., 2006, "Terminating Life-Saving Treatment of the Demented," in J. Harris (ed.) *Bioethics*, Oxford: Oxford University Press: 93–108.

Campbell, T., 1974, "Humanity Before Justice" in *British Journal of Political Science*, 4, 1: 1–16.

Campbell, T., 1988, *Justice*, Basingstoke: Macmillan.

Campbell, T., 2006, *Rights: A Critical Introduction*, London: Routledge.

Carens, J., 2000, *Culture, Citizenship and Community: A Contextual Exploration of Justice and Evenhandedness*, Oxford: Oxford University Press.

Carruthers, P., 1992, *The Animals Issue*, Cambridge: Cambridge University Press.

Cavalieri, P., 2001, *The Animal Question: Why Nonhuman Animals Deserve Rights*, Oxford: Oxford University Press.

Cavalieri, P. and Singer, P. (eds), 1993, *The Great Ape Project: Equality Beyond Humanity*. London: Fourth Estate.

Cochrane, A., 2007, "Animal Rights and Animal Experiments: An Interest-Based Approach," *Res Publica*, 13, 293–318.

Cochrane, A., 2009, "Do Animals Have an Interest in Liberty?" *Political Studies*, 57, 660–79.

Cochrane, A., 2010, *An Introduction to Animals and Political Theory*, Basingstoke: Palgrave Macmillan.

Cochrane, A., 2012, *Animal Rights Without Liberation*, New York: Columbia University Press.

Cochrane, A., forthcoming, "Cosmozoopolis: The Case Against Group-Differentiated Animal Rights," *Law, Ethics and Philosophy*.

Coeckelbergh, M., 2009, "Distributive Justice and Co-operation in a World of Humans and Non-humans: A Contractarian Argument for Drawing Non-humans into the Sphere of Justice," *Res Publica*, 15, 67–84.

Cohen, A., 2007, "Contractarianism, Other-regarding Attitudes and the Moral Standing of Non-human Animals," *Journal of Applied Philosophy*, 24, 2, 188–201.

Cohen, C., 1986, "The Case for the Use of Animals in Biomedical Research," *New England Journal of Medicine*, 315: 865–870.

Cohen C. and Regan, T., 2001, *The Animal Rights Debate*, New York: Rowman & Littlefield.

Cooper, D., 1995, "Other Species and Moral Reason" in D. Cooper and J. Palmer, eds., *Just Environments: Intergenerational, International and Interspecies Issues*, London: Routledge, 137–48.

Cripps, E., 2010, "Saving the Polar Bear, Saving the World: Can the Capabilities Approach do Justice to Humans, Animals and Ecosystems," *Res Publica*, 16, 1: 1–22.

Cushing, S., 2003, "Against 'Humanism': Speciesism, Personhood and Preference," *Journal of Social Philosophy*, 34, 4: 556–71.

DeGrazia, D., 1996, *Taking Animals Seriously: Mental Life and Moral Status*, Cambridge: Cambridge University Press.

DeGrazia, D., 1999, "Animal Ethics Around the Turn of the Twenty-First Century," *Journal of Agricultural and Environmental Ethics*, 11: 111–29.

DeGrazia, D., 2002, *Animal Rights: A Very Short Introduction*, Oxford: Oxford University Press.

DeGrazia, D., 2006, "On the Question of Personhood Beyond Homo Sapiens," in Singer, P. (ed.) 2006, *In Defense of Animals: The Second Wave*, Oxford: Blackwell, 40–53.

Devine, P., 1978, "The Moral Basis of Vegetarianism," *Philosophy*, 53: 481–505.

Dobson, A., 1998, *Justice and the Environment*, Oxford: Oxford University Press.

Dombrowski, D., 1997, *Babies and Beasts: The Argument from Marginal Cases*, Chicago: University of Illinois Press.

Donaldson, S. and Kymlicka, W., 2011, *Zoopolis: A Political Theory of Animal Rights*, New York: Oxford University Press.

Donovan J. and Adams, C. (eds.) 2007, *The Feminist Care Tradition in Animal Ethics*, New York: Columbia University Press.

Donovan, J., 2007, "Attention to Suffering: Sympathy as a Basis for Ethical Treatment of Animals," in Donovan J. and Adams, C., eds., 2007, *The Feminist Care Tradition in Animal Ethics*, New York: Columbia University Press, 174–97.

Dunayer, J., 2004, *Speciesism*, (Derwood, Md: Ryce Publishing).

Dunn, J., 1990, "Reconceiving the Content and Character of Modern Political Community," in J. Dunn, *Interpreting Political Responsibility*, Cambridge: Polity Press: 193–215.

Dworkin, R., 1977, *Taking Rights Seriously*, London: Duckworth.

E. H. Kluge, 2009, "Severely Disabled Newborns" in H. Kuhse and P. Singer (eds.) *A Companion to Bioethics* (second edition) Oxford: Wiley-Blackwell: 274–85.

Elliot, R., 1984, "Rawlsian Justice and non-Human Animals," *Journal of Applied Philosophy*, 1: 95–106.

Engster, D., 2007, *The Heart of Justice: Care Ethics and Political Theory*, Oxford: Oxford University Press.

Farrelly, C., 2007, "Justice in Ideal Theory: A Refutation," *Political Studies*, 55: 844–64.

Farrelly, C., 2007a, *Justice, Democracy and Reasonable Agreement*, Basingstoke: Palgrave Macmillan.

FAWC (Farm Animal Welfare Council), 1985, *Report on the Welfare of Livestock When Slaughtered by Religious Methods*, London: HMSO.

Feder Kittay, E., 2005, "At the Margins of Moral Personhood," *Ethics*, 116, 1: 100–31.

Feinberg, J., 1980, "The Rights of Animals and Unborn Generations" in J. Feinberg, *Rights, Justice and the Bounds of Liberty: Essays in Social Philosophy*, Princeton, NJ: Princeton University Press: 159–184.

Feinberg, J., 1980a, "Human Duties and Animal Rights" in J. Feinberg, *Rights, Justice and the Bounds of Liberty: Essays in Social Philosophy*, Princeton, NJ: Princeton University Press: 185–206.

Fellenz, M., 2007, *The Moral Menagerie: Philosophy and Animal Rights*, Chicago: University of Illinois Press.

Filice, C., 2006, "Rawls and Non-rational Beneficiaries," *Between the Species*, Issue VI, http://digitalcommons.calpoly.edu/cgi/viewcontent.cgi?article=1033&context=bts.http://digitalcommons.calpoly.edu/cgi/viewcontent.cgi?article=1033&context=bts.

Flew, A., 1985, *Thinking about Social Thinking: The Philosophy of the Social Sciences*, Oxford: Blackwell.

Foot, P., 1978, *Virtues and Vices and Other Essays in Moral Philosophy*, Oxford: Basil Blackwell.

Fox, W., 1984, "Deep Ecology: A New Philosophy of our Times," *The Ecologist*, 14, 5: 199–200.

Francione, G., 1995, *Animals, Property and the Law*. Philadelphia: Temple University Press.

Francione, G., 1996, *Rain Without Thunder: The Ideology of the Animal Rights Movement*, Philadelphia: Temple University Press.

Francione, G., 2000, *Introduction to Animal Rights: Your Child or the Dog*, Philadelphia: Temple University Press.

Francione, G., 2008, *Animals as Persons*, New York: Columbia University Press.

Francione, G. and Garner, R., 2010, *The Animal Rights Debate: Abolition or Regulation*, New York: Columbia University Press.

Franklin, J., 2005, *Animal Rights and Moral Philosophy*, New York: Columbia University Press.

Fraser, A. and Broom, D., 1990, *Farm Animal Behaviour and Welfare*, Wallingford: Cabi Publishing.

Fraser, D. and Weary, D., 2004, "Quality of Life for Farm Animals: Linking Science, Ethics and Animal Welfare" in J. Benson and B. Rollin (eds.) *The Well-Being of Farm Animals: Challenges and Solutions*, Oxford: Blackwell: 39–60.

Frey, R., 1983, *Rights, Killing and Suffering*, Oxford: Clarendon Press.

Frey, R. G., 2003, "Animals," in H. Lafollette, *The Oxford Handbook of Practical Ethics*, Oxford: Oxford University Press: 161–87.

Frey, R., 2006, "Morals and Medicine" in H. Kuhse and P. Singer (eds.) *Bioethics: An Anthology*, Oxford: Blackwell: 579–83.

Frey, R., 1987, "Autonomy and the Value of Animal Life," *Monist*, 70: 50–63.

Friedman, M., 1987, "Beyond Caring: The De-moralization of Gender," *Canadian Journal of Philosophy*, 13: 87–110.

Galston, W., 1980, *Justice and the Human Good*, Chicago: University of Chicago Press.

Garner, R., 1998, *Political Animals: Animal Protection Politics in Britain and the United States*, Basingstoke: Macmillan.

Garner, R., 2003, "Animals, Politics and Justice: Rawlsian Liberalism and the Plight of Non-humans," *Environmental Politics*, 12, 2: 3–22.

Garner, R., 2005, *Animal Ethics*, Cambridge: Polity Press.

Garner, R., 2005a, *The Political Theory of Animal Rights*, Manchester: Manchester University Press.

Garner, R., 2011, "In Defence of Sentience: A Critique of Cochrane's Liberty Thesis," *Political Studies*, 59, 1: 175–87.

Garrett, J., 2007, "Utilitarianism, Vegetarianism, and Human Health: A Response to the Causal Impotence Objection," *Journal of Applied Philosophy*, 24, 3: 223–37.

Gauthier, D., 1986, *Morals by Agreement*, Oxford: Clarendon Press.

Gilligan, C., 1983, *In a Different Voice: Psychological Theory and Women's Development*, Cambridge, Mass: Harvard University Press.

Goodpaster, K., 1978, "On Being Morally Considerable," *Journal of Philosophy*, 75: 308–25.

Groce, N. and Marks, J., 2001, "The Great Ape Project and Disability Rights: Ominous Undercurrents of Eugenics in Action," *American Anthropologist*, 102, 4: 818–22.

Gruzalski, B., 1997, "Why It's Wrong to Eat Animals Raised and Slaughtered for Food," in D. Jamieson (ed.) *Singer and His Critics*, Oxford: Blackwell: 124–37.

Gunnarsson, L., 2008, "The Great Apes and the Severely Disabled: Moral Status and Thick Evaluative Concepts," *Ethical Theory and Moral Practice*, 11: 305–26.

Hare, R. M., 1981, *Moral Thinking*, Oxford: Clarendon Press.

Hare, R. M., 1999, "Why I Am Only a Demi-vegetarian," in D. Jamieson (ed.) *Singer and His Critics*, Oxford: Blackwell: 233–46.

Hart, H. L. A., 1967, "Are there any Natural Rights?" in A. Quinton (ed.) *Political Philosophy*, Oxford: Oxford University Press: 53–66.

Haynes, R., 2008, *Animal Welfare: Competing Conceptions and Their Ethical Implications*, Springer Science.

Holland, S., 2003, *Bioethics: A Philosophical Introduction*, Cambridge: Polity Press.

Hills, A., 2005, *Do Animals Have Rights?* Cambridge: Icon Books.

Hooker, B., 1996, "Does Moral Virtue Constitute a Benefit to the Agent?" in R. Crisp, ed., *How Should One Live? Essays on the Virtues*, Oxford: Clarendon Press: 141–55.

Horta, O., 2010, "What Is Speciesism," *Journal of Agricultural and Environmental Ethics*, 23: 243–266.

Hursthouse, R., 1999, *On Virtue Ethics*, Oxford: Oxford University Press.

Hursthouse, R., 2000, "Ethics, Humans and Other Animals,"London: Routledge.

Hursthouse, R., 2007, "Environmental Virtue Ethics," in R. Walker and P. Ivanhoe, eds., 2007, *Working Virtue: Virtue Ethics and Contemporary Moral Problems*, Oxford: Clarendon Press: 155–71.

Ilea, R., 2008, "Nussbaum's Capabilities Approach and Nonhuman Animals: Theory and Public Policy," *Journal of Social Philosophy*, 39, 4: 547–63.

Jamieson, D., 1990, "Rights, Justice and Duties to Provide Assistance: A Critique of Regan's Theory of Rights," *Ethics*, 100, 2, 349–62.

Jamieson, D. (ed.) 1999, *Singer and His Critics*, Oxford: Blackwell.

Kant. I., 1970, "On the Common Saying: 'This May Be True in Theory, but It Does Not Apply in Practice'" in H. Reiss, ed., *Kant: Political Writings*, Cambridge: Cambridge University Press, 61–92.

Kelly, P., 1998, "Taking Utilitarianism Seriously," in P. Kelly (ed.) *Impartiality, Neutrality and Justice. Re-reading Brian Barry's Justice as Impartiality*, Edinburgh: Edinburgh University Press, 44–59.

Koller, P., 2007, "Law, Morality and Virtue" in R. Walker and P. Ivanhoe, eds., *Working Virtue: Virtue Ethics and Contemporary Moral Problems*, Oxford: Clarendon Press: 191–205.

Kramer, M., 1998, "Rights Without Trimmings" in M. Kramer, N. Simmonds and H. Steiner (eds.), *A Debate Over Rights: Philosophical Enquires*, Oxford: Clarendon Press: 7–111.

Kuper, A., 2002, "More than Charity: Cosmopolitan Alternatives to the 'Singer Solution,'" *Ethics and International Affairs*, 16, 1: 107–20.

Kuhse, H. and Singer, P., (2006) "Killing and Letting Die", in J. Harris (ed.) *Bioethics*, Oxford: Oxford University Press: 42–61.

Kymlicka, W., 1993, "The Social Contract Tradition" in P. Singer, ed., *A Companion to Ethics*, Blackwell: Oxford: 186–96.

Kymlicka, W., 1995, *Multicultural Citizenship*, Oxford: Clarendon Press.

Langlois, A., 2008, "Charity and Justice in Global Policy Relief," *Australian Journal of Political Science*, 43, 4: 685–98.

Lekan, T., 2004, "Integrating Justice and Care in Animal Ethics," in *Journal of Applied Philosophy*, 21, 2: 183–95.

Levy, N., 2004, "Cohen and Kinds: A Response to Nathan Nobis," *Journal of Appiled Philosophy*, 21, 2: 213–17.

Li, Hon-Lam, 2002, "Animal Research, Non-vegetarianism, and the Moral Status of Animals: Understanding the Impasse of the Animal Rights Problem," *Journal of Medicine and Philosophy*, 27, 5: 589–615.

Li, Hon-Lam, 2007, "Towards Quasi-Vegetarianism" in Hon-Lan Li and A. Yeung (eds.) *New Essays in Applied Ethics: Animal Rights, Personhood and the Ethics of Killing*, Basingstoke: Palgrave Macmillan: 64–90.

Luna, F. and Macklin, R., 2009, "Research Involving Human Beings" in H. Kuhse and P. Singer (eds.) *A Companion to Bioethics* (second edition) Oxford: Wiley-Blackwell: 457–68.

Luke B., 2007, "Justice, Caring, and Animal Liberation" in J. Donovan and C. Adams, eds., 2007, *The Feminist Care Tradition in Animal Ethics*, New York: Columbia University Press, 125–52

Lyons, D., forthcoming, *The Politics of Animal Experimentation*, Basingstoke: Palgrave Macmillan.

Machan, T., 2007. "Rights, Liberation and Interests: Is there a Sound Case for Animal Rights or Liberation?" in Hon-Lan Li and A. Yeung (eds.) *New Essays in Applied Ethics: Animal Rights, Personhood and the Ethics of Killing*, Basingstoke: Palgrave Macmillan: 42–63.

MacIntyre, A., 1981, *After Virtue*, London: Duckworth.

Macneill, P., 1993, *The Ethics and Politics of Human Experimentation*, Cambridge: Cambridge University Press.

McNeill, P., 2009, "Regulating Experimentation in Research and Medical Practice" in H. Kuhse and P. Singer (eds.) *A Companion to Bioethics* (second edition) Oxford: Wiley-Blackwell: 469–86.

Mason, A., 1996, "Justice, Contestability and Conceptions of the Good," *Utilitas*, 8, 3: 295–305.

Matheny, G., 2002, "Expected Utility,Contributory Causation, and Vegetarianism," *Journal of Applied Philosophy*, 19, 3: 293–97.

Mason, J. and Singer, P., 1990, *Animal Factories*. New York: Harmony Books.

McCabe, K., 1985, "Who Will Live, Who Will Die" *The Washingtonian*, 112–57.

McCloskey, H., 1979, "Moral Rights and Animals," *Inquiry*, 22: 23–54.

McCloskey, H., 1987, "The Moral Case for Experimentation on Animals," *Monist*, 70, 1: 64–82.

McMahan, J., 1996, "Cognitive Disability, Misfortune and Justice," *Philosophy and Public Affairs*, 25, 1: 3–35.

McMahan, J., 2002, *The Ethics of Killing: Problems at the Margins of Life*, Oxford: Oxford University Press.

Mench, J., 1998, "Thirty Years after Brambell," *Journal of Applied Animal Welfare Science*, 1, 2: 91–102.

Midgley, M., 1983, *Animals and Why They Matter*. Harmondsworth: Penguin.

Mill, J.S., 2002, *Utilitarianism*, Cambridge, Mass.: Hackett Publishing Company.

Miller, D., 1976, *Social Justice*, Clarendon Press: Oxford.

Miller, D., 1999, *Principles of Social Justice*, Cambridge, Mass.: Harvard University Press.

Miller, D., 2008, "Political Philosophy for Earthlings," in D. Leopold and M. Stears, eds., *Political Theory: Methods and Approaches*, Oxford: Oxford University Press: 29–48.

Moller Okin, S., 1989, "Reason and Feeling in Thinking about Justice," *Ethics*, 99, 2: 229–49.

Morris, C., 1996, "A Contractarian Account of Moral Justification" in W. Sinnott-Armstrong and M. Timmons, eds., *Moral Knowledge? New Readings in Moral Epistemology*, Oxford: Oxford University Press, 215–42.

Morris, C., 1998, "Justice, Reasons and Moral Standing," in J. Coleman and C. Morris, eds., *Rational Commitment and Social Justice*, Cambridge: Cambridge University Press, 186–207.

Morris, C., 2008, "The Trouble with Justice," in P. Bloomfield, ed., *Morality and Self Interest*, Oxford: Oxford University Press, 15–30.

Murphy, L., 2000, *Moral Demands in Non-ideal Theory*, Oxford: Oxford University Press.

Nagel, T., 1989, "What Makes a Political Theory Utopian?" *Social Research*, 56, 4: 903–15.

Narveson, J., 1977, 'Animal Rights', *Canadian Journal of Philosophy*, 7, 161–78.

Narveson, J., 1983,"Animal Rights Revisited" in H. Miller and W. Williams, eds., *Ethics and Animals*, Clifton, NJ: Humana Press, 45–59.

Nobis, N., 2002, "Vegetarianism and Virtue: Does Consequentialism Demand Too Little?" *Social Theory and Practice*, 28, 1: 135–56.

Nobis, N., 2004, "Carl Cohen's 'Kind' Arguments for Animal Rights and Against Human Rights," *Journal of Applied Philosophy*, 21, 1: 43–59.

Noddings, N., 1984, *Caring: A Feminine Approach to Ethics and Moral Education*, Berkeley: University of California Press.

Nozick, R., 1974, *Anarchy, State and Utopia*. Oxford: Basil Blackwell.

Nussbaum, M., 2001, "Animal Rights: The Needs for a Theoretical Basis," *Harvard Law Review*, 114, 5: 1506–549.

Nussbaum, M., 2004, "Beyond Compassion and Humanity: Justice for Nonhuman Animals" in C. Sunstein and M. Nussbaum (eds.) *Animal Rights: Current Debates and New Directions*, Oxford: Oxford University Press: 299–320.

Nussbaum, M, 2006, *Frontiers of Justice: Disability, Nationality, Species Membership*, Cambridge, Mass.: Harvard University Press.

O'Neil, O., 1997, "Environmental Values, Anthropocentrism and Speciesism," *Environmental Values*, 6: 127–42.

O'Neil, J., 2003, "Varieties of Intrinsic Value," in A. Light and Holmes Rolston III, *Environmental Ethics: An Anthology*, Oxford: Blackwell: 131–42.

O'Neill, O., 2001, "Agents of Justice" in T. Pogge, ed., *Global Justice*, Oxford: Blackwell, 2001: 188–203.

O'Sullivan, S., 2007, "Advocating for animals equally from within a liberal paradigm," *Environmental Politics*, 16, 1: 1–14.

Palmer, C., 2003, "Placing Animals in Urban Environmental Ethics," *Journal of Social Philosophy*, 34, 1: 64–78.

Palmer, C., 2010, *Animal Ethics in Context*, New York: Columbia University Press.

Passmore, J., 1979, "Civil Justice and its Rivals" in E. Kamenka and A. Erh-Soon Tay (eds.) *Justice*, London: Edward Arnold: 25–49.

Phillips, C., 2009, *The Welfare of Animals: The Silent Majority*, Springer Scientific.

Phillips, D., 1964–5, "Does It Pay to Be Good?", *Proceedings of the Aristotelian Society*, LXV: 45–60.

Pickering-Francis, L. and Norman, R., 1978, "Some Animals Are More Equal than Others," *Philosophy*, 55, 206: 507–27.

Pifer, L. and Shimizu, K., 1994, "Public Attitudes Towards Animal Research: Some International Comparisons," *Society and Animals*, 2: 95–113.

Piper, H., 2003, "The Linkage of Animal Abuse with Interpersonal Violence. A Sheep in Wolf's Clothing," *Journal of Social Work*, 3, 2: 161–77.

Pluhar, E., 1988, "Is There a Morally Relevant Difference between Human and Animal Nonpersons?" *Journal of Agricultural Ethics*, 1: 59–68.

Pluhar, E., 1995, *Beyond Prejudice: The Moral Significance of Human and Nonhuman Animals*. Durham: Duke University Press.

Pluhar, E., 2010, "Meat and Morality: Alternatives to Factory Farming," *Journal of Agricultural and Environmental Ethics*, 23: 455–68.

Pogge, T., 2008, *World Poverty and Human Rights: Cosmopolitan Responsibilities and Reforms*, Second edition, Cambridge: Polity Press.

Prichard, H., 1949, "Does Moral Philosophy Rest on a Mistake?", in H. Prichard, ed., *Moral Obligation*, Oxford: Clarendon Press: 1–17.

Rachels, J., 1990, *Created from Animals: The Moral Implications of Darwinism*, Oxford: Oxford University Press.

Rachels, J., 2004, "The Basic Argument for Vegetarianism," in Sapontzis, S. (ed) *Food for Thought: The Debate over Eating Meat*, New York: Prometheus Books: 70–80.

Rachels, J., 2009, "Ethical Theory and Bioethics" in H. Kuhse and P. Singer (eds.), *A Companion to Bioethics* (second edition), Oxford: Wiley-Blackwell: 15–23.

Raphael, D., 2001, *Concepts of Justice*, Clarendon Press: Oxford.

Rawls, J. (1963) "The Sense of Justice," *The Philosophical Review*, Vol. 122: 281–305.

Rawls, J., 1971, *A Theory of Justice*, Oxford: Oxford University Press, 1972.

Rawls, J., 1993, *Political Liberalism*, New York: Columbia University Press.

Rawls, J., 1999, *The Law of People's*, Cambridge, Mass.: Harvard University Press.

Rawls, J., 2001, *Justice as Fairness: A Restatement*, Cambridge, Mass.: Belknap Press.

Raz, J., 1986, *The Morality of Freedom*, Oxford: Clarendon Press.

Regan, T., 1979, "Exploring the Idea of Animal Rights" in D. Paterson and R. Ryder (eds.), *Animal Rights: A Symposium*, Fontwell, Sussex: Centaur Press: 73–86.

Regan, T., 1980a, "On the Right Not to Be Made to Suffer Gratuitously," *Canadian Journal of Philosophy*, X, 3: 473–78.

Regan, T., 1980b, "Utilitarianism, Vegetarianism and Animal Rights," *Philosophy and Public Affairs*, 9, 4: 305–24.

Regan, T., 1984, *The Case for Animal Rights*, London: Routledge.

Regan, T., 1985, "The Case for Animal Rights" in Peter Singer (ed.) *Taking Animals Seriously*, Oxford: Basil Blackwell.

Regan, T., 1987, *The Struggle for Animal Rights*, Clark'sSummit, PA: International Society for Animal Rights.

Regan, T., 1991, *The Thee Generation*, Philadelphia: Temple University Press.

Richards, D., 1971, *A Theory of Reasons for Action*, Oxford: Clarendon Press.

Ritvo, H., 1987, *The Animal Estate*, Cambridge, Mass.: Harvard University Press.

Robeyns, I., 2008, "Ideal theory in Theory and Practice," *Social Theory and Practice*, 34, 3: 341–62.

Rollin, B., 2005, "Reasonable Partiality and Animal Ethics," *Ethical Theory and Moral Practice*, 8: 105–21.

Rollin, B., 2006, *Science and Ethics*, Cambridge: Cambridge University Press.

Rollin, B., 2009, "The Moral Status of Animals and their use as Experimental Subjects" in H. Kuhse and P. Singer (eds.) *A Companion to Bioethics* (second edition) Oxford: Wiley-Blackwell: 495–509.

Rollin, B., 2011, *Putting the Horse Before Descartes: My Life's Work on Behalf of Animals*, Philadelphia: Temple University Press.

Rose-Ackerman, S., 1982, "Mental Retardation and Society: The Ethics and Politics of Normalization," *Ethics*, 93, 1: 81–101.

Rowlands, M., 1997, "Contractarianism and Animal Rights," *Journal of Applied Philosophy*, 14, 3: 235–247.

Rowlands, M., 1998, *Animal Rights: A Philosophical Defence*, Basingstoke: Macmillan.

Rowlands, M., 2002, *Animals Like Us*, London: Verson.

Rowlands, M., 2009, *Animal Rights: Moral Theory and Practice*, Basingstoke: Palgrave, second edition.

Sandel, M., 1998, *Liberalism and the Limits of Justice*, Cambridge: Cambridge University Press.

Sandel, M., 2009, *Justice: What's the Right Thing to Do?* Allen Lane: London.

Sandoe, P. and Christiansen, S., 2008, *Ethics of Animal Use*, Oxford: Blackwell.

Sapontzis, S., 1987, *Morals, Reason, and Animals*. Philadelphia: Temple University Press.

Satz, A., 2009, "Animals as Vulnerable Subjects: Beyond Interest-Convergence, Hierarchy and Property," *Animal Law*, 16, 2: 1–50.

Sayre-McCord, G., 1989, "Deception and Reasons to be Moral," *American Philosophical Quarterly*, 26, 2: 113–22.

Scanlon, T., 1982, "Contractualism and Utilitarianism" in A. Sen and B. Williams, eds.,*Utilitarianism and Beyond,* Cambridge: Cambridge University Press, 103–28.

Scanlon, T., 1988, "Levels of Moral Thinking" in D. Seanor and N. Fotion, eds., *Hare and Critics*, Oxford: Clarendon Press, 129–46.

Scanlon, T., 1998, *What We Owe to Each Other*, Cambridge, Mass.: Harvard University Press.

Schinkel, A., 2008, "Martha Nussbaum on Animal Rights," *Ethics and the Environment*, 13, 1: 41–69.

Scruton, R., 1996, *Animal Rights and Wrongs*. London: Demos.

Sen, A., 1993, "Capability and Well-Being" in M. Nussbaum and A. Sen (eds.) *The Quality of Life*, Oxford: Clarendon Press: 30–53.

Sen, A., 2009, *The Idea of Justice*, London: Allen Lane.

Sher, G., 1997, *Approximate Justice: Studies in Non-Ideal Theory*, Lanham, Md.: Rowman and Littlefield.

Shriver, A., 2009, "Knocking out Pain in Livestock: Can Technology Succeed Where Morality has Stalled?" *Neuroethics*, 2: 115–24.

Shue, H., 1995, "Ethics, the environment and the changing international order," *International Affairs*, 71, 3: 453–61.

Simmons, J., 2010, "Ideal and Nonideal Theory," *Philosophy and Public Affairs*, 38, 1: 5–36.

Singer, P., 1972, "Famine, Affluence and Morality," *Philosophy and Public Affairs*, 1, 3: 229–43.

Singer, P., 1980, "Utilitarianism and Vegetarianism," *Philosophy and Public Affairs*, 9, 4, 1980: 325–37.

Singer, P., 1983, *Hegel*, Oxford: Oxford University Press.

Singer, P., 1989, "All Animals Are Equal," in T. Regan and P. Singer (eds.) *Animal Rights and Human Obligations*, second edition, Englewood Cliffs, NJ: Prentice Hall: 148–62.

Singer, P., 1990, *Animal Liberation*, second edition, London: Cape.

Singer, P., 1993, *Practical Ethics*, second edition, Cambridge: Cambridge University Press.

Singer, P., 1999, "A Response" in D. Jamieson (ed.) *Singer and His Critics*, Oxford: Blackwell: 269–335.

Singer, P. (ed.), 2006, *In Defense of Animals: The Second Wave*, Oxford: Blackwell.

Slote, M., 2001, *Morals From Motives*, Oxford: Oxford University Press.

Slote, M., 2007, *The Ethics of Care and Empathy*, London: Routledge.

Spedding, C., 2000, *Animal Welfare*, London: Earthscan.

Spiegel, M., 1988, *The Dreaded Comparison: Humans and Animal Slavery*, New York: Mirror Books.

Steinbock, B., 1978, "Speciesism and the Idea of Equality," *Philosophy*, 53: 247–56.

Steiner, G., 2008, *Animals and the Moral Community: Mental Life, Moral Status, and Kinship*, New York: Columbia University Press.

Steiner, H., 1998, "Working Rights" in M. Kramer, N. Simmonds and H. Steiner (eds.), *A Debate Over Rights: Philosophical Enquires*, Oxford: Clarendon Press: 233–301.

Stemplowska, Z., 2008, "Worth the Paper It's Written On," *Journal of Political Ideologies*, 13, 3: 228–33.

Swanton, C., 1980, "The Concept of Interests," *Political Theory*, 8, 1: 83–101.

Swanton, C., 2003, *Virtue Ethics: A Pluralistic View*, Oxford: Oxford University Press.

Swift, A. and White S., 2008, "Political Theory, Social Science and Real Politics," in D. Leopold and M. Stears, eds., *Political Theory: Methods and Approaches*, Oxford: Oxford University Press: 49–69.

Sztybel, D., 2000, "Response to Everlyn Pluhar's 'Non-Obligatory Anthropocentrism,'" *Journal of Agricultural and Environmental Ethics*, 13: 337–40.

Tannenbaum, J., 1995, "Animals and the Law: Property, Cruelty, Rights," *Social Research*, 539: 125–93.

Taylor, A., 2009, *Animal and Ethics: An Overview of the Philosophical Debate*, third edition, Ontario: Broadview Press.

Taylor, C., 1985, "The Nature and Scope of Distributive Justice" in C. Taylor, *Philosophy and the Human Sciences: Philosophical Papers 2*, Cambridge: Cambridge University Press, 289–317.

Taylor, P., 1986, *Respect for Nature: A Theory of Environmental Ethics*, Princeton: Princeton University Press.

Tooley, M., 2009, "Personhood," in H. Kuhse and P. Singer (eds.) *A Companion to Bioethics* (second edition) Oxford: Wiley-Blackwell: 129–39.

Tronto, J., 1987, "Beyond Gender Differences to a Theory of Care," *Signs*, 12, 4.

Vallentyne, P., (ed.) 1991, *Contractarianism and Rational Choice*. Cambridge: Cambridge University Press.

Van De Veer, D., 1979a, "Of Beasts, Persons and the Original Position," *Monist*, 62, 3: 368–77.

Van De Veer, D., 1979b, "Interspecific Justice," *Inquiry*, 22: 55–79.

Vaughn, L., 2010, *Bioethics: Principles, Issues and Cases*, Oxford: Oxford University Press.

Vincent, A., 1998, "Is Environmental Justice a Misnomer?" in D. Boucher and P. Kelly, eds., *Social Justice from Hume to Walzer*, London: Routledge, 1998, 120–40.

Vincent, A., 2004, *The Nature of Political Theory*, Oxford: Oxford University Press.

Waldron, J., 1989, "Rights in Conflict," *Ethics*, 99, 3: 503–19.

Walker, R. and Ivanhoe, P., eds., 2007, *Working Virtue: Virtue Ethics and Contemporary Moral Problems*, Oxford: Clarendon Press.

Warren, M., 1986, "Difficulties with the Strong Animal Rights Position," *Between the Species*, 2: 163–73.

Wenar, L., 2005, "The Nature of Rights," *Philosophy and Public Affairs*, 33, 2: 223–53.

Wenz, P., 1988, *Environmental Justice*, Albany, State University of New York Press.

Williams, M., 1980, "Rights, Interests and Moral Equality," *Environmental Ethics*, 2: 159–61.

Wilson, S., 2005, "The Species Norm Account of Moral Status," *Between the Species*, http://works.bepress.com/scott_wilson/1http://works.bepress.com/scott_wilson/1..

Wissenburg, M., 2011, "The Lion and the Lamb: Ecological Implications of Martha Nussbaum's Animal Ethics" *Environmental Politics* 20, 3: 391–409.

Wolff, J., 1996, *An Introduction to Political Philosophy*, Oxford: Oxford University Press.

Wolff, J., 2008, "Social Justice" in C. McKinnon (ed.) *Issues in Political Theory*, Oxford: Oxford University Press: 172–93.

World Medical Association, 1964, *Declaration of Helsinki*. Adopted by the 18th World Medicine Association General Assembly, Helsinki.

Yeates, J., 2010, "Death Is a Welfare Issue," *Journal of Agricultural and Environmental Ethics*, 23: 229–41.

Young, I., 1990, *Justice and the Politics of Difference*, Princeton, NJ: Princeton University Press.

Ypi, L., 2010, "On the Confusion between Ideal and Non-ideal Theory in Recent Debates on Global Justice," *Political Studies* 58 (3) 536–55.

Index

Friedman, Marilyn, 54
future generations, 28
　See also Barry, Brian

Galston, William, 4, 77, 79
Gandhi, Mahatma, 73
Gauthier, David, 37, 170n
Gilligan, Carol, 54
Goodpaster, Kenneth, 78

Hare, R.M., 72, 73, 108, 171
Hart, H.L.A., 95
Haynes, Richard, 78, 80, 177n
Hills, Alison, 46
Hobbes, Thomas, 37, 170n
Hooker, Brad, 72
Horta, Oscar, 150
human experimentation, 146, 154–157
hunting, 26, 40, 70, 175n
Hursthouse, Rosalind, 67, 69–70,
　71, 72

ideal theory,
　definition of, 1, 2, 3, 10, 11–13
　enhanced sentience position and,
　　134–135, 165, 166
　indirect duty position and, 74
　species-egalitarian theory of animal
　　rights and, 2–3, 14–16, 87, 119–121,
　　147, 164, 165, 166
　See also animal welfare; Rawls, John
indirect duty position, 8–9, 18, 45, 59, 60,
　61–75, 76, 150, 163, 169n, 171n
　See also ideal theory; nonideal theory

Jamieson, Dale, 107

Kant, Immanuel, 11, 33, 35, 46, 64, 83
Kelly, Paul, 38
Koller, Peter, 69
Kuper, Andrew, 51
Kymlicka, Will, 5, 30, 62, 101–103, 104,
　119, 121, 170n, 173n

laboratory animals, *see* animal
　experimentation
Langlois, Anthony, 51
Lekan, Todd, 54
Levy, Neil, 146
Li, Hon-Lam, 133–134, 176n
Locke, John, 64
Luke, Brian, 58

MacIntyre, Alasdair, 41, 165
McCloskey, H.J., 79, 87, 93–94,
　95, 96
McMahan, Jeffrey, 86, 87, 129, 131–132,
　147, 150, 160
McNeill, Paul, 155
Mench, Joy, 80
Midgley, Mary, 100, 150, 172n
Mill, John Stuart, 47, 48, 130
Miller, David, 4, 11, 13, 21, 22, 166
Morris, Christopher, 40, 48,
　61–62, 74

Nagel, Thomas, 119
Narveson, Jan, 170n, 177n
New Welfarism, 10, 88, 90, 178n
Newkirk, Ingrid, 166, 178n
Noddings, Nel, 55, 56
nonideal theory,
　animal welfare and, 88–92
　argument from marginal cases and, 152
　care ethic and, 57–59
　definition of, 10, 16, 11–13, 16–17
　human-animal relationships and, 121
　indirect duty position and, 74
　sentience position and, 3, 134–141, 162,
　　166, 167, 173n
　See also animal experimentation,
　　Rawls, John;
Nozick, Robert, 26, 78, 94
Nussbaum, Martha, 4, 15, 22, 39, 47–48,
　93, 104, 110–116, 121, 157, 174n
　See also species-egalitarian version of
　　animal rights